Failed Frontiersmen

Cultural Frames, Framing Culture

Robert Newman, *Editor*

Failed Frontiersmen

White Men and Myth in the Post-Sixties American Historical Romance

JAMES J. DONAHUE

University of Virginia Press
CHARLOTTESVILLE AND LONDON

University of Virginia Press

Printed in the United States of America on acid-free paper
First published 2015
9 8 7 6 5 4 3 2 1

LIBRARY OF CONGRESS CATALOGING-IN-PUBLICATION DATA

Donahue, James J.

Failed frontiersmen : white men and myth in the post-sixties American historical romance / James J. Donahue.

pages cm. (Cultural frames, framing culture)

Includes bibliographical references and index.

ISBN 978-0-8139-3682-6 (cloth : acid-free paper)

ISBN 978-0-8139-3683-3 (pbk. : acid-free paper)

ISBN 978-0-8139-3684-0 (e-book)

1. American fiction—20th century—History and criticism. 2. American fiction—21st century—History and criticism. 3. Frontier and pioneer life in literature. 4. Men in literature. 5. Racism in literature. 6. Sexism in literature. I. Title.

PS374.F73D66 2015
813'.509355—dc23

2014024535

THE AMERICAN LITERATURES INITIATIVE

A book in the American Literatures Initiative (ALI), a collaborative publishing project of NYU Press, Fordham University Press, Rutgers University Press, Temple University Press, and the University of Virginia Press. The Initiative is supported by The Andrew W. Mellon Foundation. For more information, please visit www.americanliteratures.org.

Contents

Acknowledgments

Despite there being only one name on the cover and title page, I cannot claim full credit for the genesis and development of this book. At every stage of the process, I benefitted from the assistance of the finest scholars, mentors, and friends that anyone could ask for. What follows is but a quick accounting of the most important influences on this book.

First, I would like to thank everyone at the University of Connecticut who helped guide me in the earliest stages of this project. Wayne Franklin, Jerry Phillips, and Robert Tilton encouraged me when I needed encouragement, and kicked me in the ass when I needed that, too. Michael Meyer and Thomas Recchio provided insight on the subject matter and helped me to see the whole project when I was immersed in the details and minutiae. Additionally, many colleagues listened to me work out ideas, read early drafts, and helped keep me sane after my many long days in the library; I will forever be grateful to Laurie and Matthew J. C. Cella, Rebecca Devers, Joshua Eyler, Mary-Elizabeth Lough, Frank Napolitano, and Wendy and Andrew Pfrenger, for reasons they all know well.

Many of my colleagues at SUNY Potsdam have been instrumental in helping me continue this project. Most importantly, they showed me how this project connects with the larger field in ways I had not considered. Further, they guided me in making connections between my research and my teaching, in ways benefitting both efforts. For their guidance, their mentorship, and especially for much-needed stress relief, I offer my gratitude to Trevor J. Blank, Christine Doran, Stephanie Hedge, Christina Knopf, Rebecca Lehmann, Joanna Luloff, Derek C. Maus, Donald

McNutt, Sue Novak, Liberty Stanavage, and John Youngblood. Further, my heartfelt thanks to all the students in my various sections of Historical Fiction for their engagement with and excitement about the material.

Additionally, numerous friends, colleagues, and professors at other institutions have assisted me in various ways, far too numerous to name here. However, I would like to thank Kathleen Coyne Kelly (Northeastern University) and Robert Stanton (Boston College), without whose guidance and continued support I would never have pursued a life in academia. I would also like to make special note of two online discussion groups to which I belong, whose members have been as helpful as anyone during the many years I have spent working on this project. First, a special thanks to the "Theory Crew" for their years of support, as well as their continued recommendations for reading that have reshaped my thinking in productive ways: Kara Andersen, Michelle Brown Boucher, Jane Dryden, Max Goldman, Rebecca Futo Kennedy, Jonathan Newman, Valéria Souza, Alana Vincent, and Erica Owens Yeager, I am forever in your debt. I would also like to thank the PNSI Accountability Group for helping to keep me on task as I completed the final work on this book: Leah Anderst, Jennifer Ho, Shaun Morgan, and Janine Utell, your support and encouragement were always both timely and inspiring.

This book you are holding would not exist without all the hard work done by the University of Virginia Press. Susan A. Murray, Tim Roberts, the anonymous readers, editorial board, and support staff cannot be thanked enough for their contributions to the style and substance of this book. But most important, I consider myself lucky to have worked with Cathie Brettschneider, without whose editorial guidance and insights I never would have completed this project. I am honored to have my book included in the American Literatures Initiative series.

Any success this book achieves should be attributed to those named above. Any faults, failures, and oversights are my burden to bear.

Finally, I would like to thank my parents, Margaret and James Donahue, without whom nothing would have been possible. Their unwavering support for my endeavors at every stage of my academic career can be felt on the pages of this book.

Introduction: The American Historical Frontier Romance as Vehicle for Cultural Critique

Great literature is at once the apprentice and the master of myth. Its sources are mythic, for its statements refer to the ultimate questions of human consciousness and human existence, and it employs metaphors appropriate to the experience of the writer and his audience, his culture, and his people.

—RICHARD SLOTKIN, *REGENERATION THROUGH VIOLENCE*

Americans have always loved stories set on the frontier. The exploits of rugged frontiersmen like Natty Bumppo, Daniel Boone, Buffalo Bill, and others have long entertained readers of dime novels and literary fiction, as well as viewers of popular television shows and movies. Such figures and their romanticized adventures form the backbone of the mythology of the American frontier that, since America's earliest days, has formed the bedrock upon which American cultural values have been built. In the 1960s, however, many writers took this mythology to task, calling into question the textual means by which that mythology had been transmitted, and exposing the mythology for its inherent racism and sexism.

Directly (and indirectly) responding to many of the social movements that challenged the status quo of American society, E. L. Doctorow, John Barth, Thomas Pynchon, Ishmael Reed, Gerald Vizenor, and Cormac McCarthy collectively work to revise America's national mythology for a generation that witnessed the failure of many of that mythology's central ideals and core presuppositions. They do so by focusing their attention on the figure of the frontiersman, the rugged American hero whose taming of the wilderness (and the savages who stand in his way) has long stood as the model of American masculinity. This frontiersman is exposed as a failure and denounced as a fitting figure for the embodiment of American cultural values. For some, the white frontiersman is recast as a failure, a bumbling figure incapable of living up to the terms of the mythology; for others, the successful frontiersman is characterized as the ethnic other, exposing the whitewashing of the actual frontier in favor of a racist ideology. But throughout, the mythology of the

American frontier is shown to be a poor model that, ultimately, fails to accurately convey America's complex cultural identity.

In short, the revival of the historical romance in postwar American fiction is centrally concerned with revising the mythology of the American frontier, inaugurating a new stage in the development of the American national myth. In his landmark study *Regeneration through Violence*, Richard Slotkin identifies three stages in the development of the American frontier mythology: the first, the "primary," is the mythopoeic mode engaged by both mythmaker and audience. The second, the "romantic," is the metaphoric phase characterized by the elaboration of the primary myths. Finally there is the "consummatory," where the artist operates as a prophet whose role is to inspire in his audience new visions. I would like to propose a fourth stage, the "reevaluatory," where the myth is challenged and its accepted truths reexamined in light of more recent cultural developments. In contrast to the consummatory phase, the reevaluation of myth is less a prophetic projection into the future than a critically sustained challenge of the past and those narratives about the past that have become paradigmatic.

In particular, mythology that finds its roots in the adventures of Daniel Boone—and the national values that have grown from the various retellings of stories about him and others like him—has long dominated discussions of American cultural values. Such values include the belief that through the adoption of a spirit of "rugged individualism" the hard work of taming the wild landscape—and the savages who inhabit those lands—will lead to political freedom, cultural advancement, and economic prosperity. Just as importantly, as I will demonstrate, these values are very often attached to a masculine identity, and embodied in male figures of power and authority.[1] For as R. W. Connell reminds us, "Exemplars of masculinity, whether legendary or real—from Paul Bunyan in Canada via Davy Crockett in the United States to Lawrence 'of Arabia' in England—have very often been men of the frontier."[2] In fact, one could argue that it is the frontiersman (and his various manifestations over time as an explorer of land, sea, air, and—in science fiction—outer space) that has provided the standard against which America defines masculinity.[3] This definition of masculinity, based on the mythology the authors of the present study seek to problematize, comes to be the vehicle for how we understand our nation and its history.

As Kaja Silverman noted in her study *Male Subjectivity at the Margins*, "If ideology is central to the maintenance of classic masculinity, the affirmation of classic masculinity is equally central to the maintenance of our governing 'reality.'"[4] Further, as Daniel Worden has argued in *Masculine Style: The American West and Literary Modernism*, "the American west offers an ideal setting for the exploration of masculine performativity in late-nineteenth- and twentieth-century culture."[5] However, where Worden demonstrates that modernist fiction explores "the emergences of new possibilities for subjectivity, embodiment, and action as they emerge in the aftermath of the 'closing of the frontier' through the 'containment culture' of the Cold War,"[6] I will demonstrate how the authors in this study demonstrate how traditional masculinity—what is now often called "hegemonic masculinity"—is a flawed construction upon which the national mythology was built.[7] As I hope to demonstrate throughout the following chapters, the authors included in this study critique the mythology of the American frontier in large part precisely because that mythology has long dominated how we define American cultural values; or, to adapt Silverman, the mythology has created our reality. And in the wake of the various protest movements from the 1960s—including but not limited to the movement against the war in Vietnam, the civil rights movement, and the American Indian Movement[8]—the writers responding to America's founding mythology show how it has failed our nation by providing a reading of our reality that did not conform with lived experience.

As Richard Slotkin explains in *Gunfighter Nation: The Myth of the Frontier in Twentieth-Century America*, the third volume of his study of the development of American frontier mythology, the myth of the American frontier has become central to America's efforts at self-definition:

> The myth of the frontier is our oldest and most characteristic myth, expressed in a body of literature, folklore, ritual, historiography, and polemics produced over a period of three centuries. According to this myth-historiography, the conquest of the wilderness and the subjugation or displacement of the Native Americans who originally inhabited it have been the means to our achievement of a national identity, a democratic polity, an ever-expanding economy, and a phenomenally dynamic and "progressive" civilization. The original ideological task of the Myth was to explain and justify the establishment of the American colonies; but as the colonies expanded and developed the Myth was called on to account for our rapid economic growth, our emergence as a powerful nation-state, and our distinctively American approach to the socially and culturally disruptive process of modernization.[9]

In its original formulation as a justification for both European entry into the New World as well as the nation's physical, economic, and military expansion, the American frontier mythology has long been employed to characterize a positive understanding of America's development. This understanding is also reflected in the ways that "the West" was characterized as the reward for those hardworking American men who braved the savage wilderness and hostile natives, as evidenced in the titles of such works as Theodore Roosevelt's four-volume history *The Winning of the West* (1889–96) and the popular western movie *How the West Was Won* (1963).[10] However, as Slotkin hints with his use of scare quotation marks for "progressive," this mythology has been challenged and reevaluated by historical romancers writing in the latter half of the twentieth century.

In addition to their critique of masculinity as it has been defined by the American frontier mythology, the authors included in this study also demonstrate the racist underpinnings of this mythology. When Slotkin (and others) refer to "civilization," they of course mean "white society"; its opposite term, "savagery," always refers to the ethnic other (often Native Americans and African Americans). Examples of popular and influential narratives that embrace and disseminate the values of the mythology of the American frontier are numerous, and (almost) always recount the exploits of white men who have tested themselves against the "savage" other; from the various biographies of Daniel Boone and other frontiersmen to many contemporary films, the American frontier is populated almost entirely by white men protecting their families from darker-skinned savages. And as Harlon Dalton has suggested, the "rugged individualism" that Boone embodies is itself part of the backbone of racism in America: "For a significant chunk [of white people], the inability to 'get' race, and to understand why it figures so prominently in the lives of most people of color, stems from a deep affiliation—the curse of rugged individualism."[11] By exploring issues of race (largely) through white protagonists, the authors I discuss here also provide a critique of the "positive investment of whiteness" that George Lipsitz notes "has always been influenced by its origins in the racialized history of the United States," a "legacy of slavery and segregation, of 'Indian' extermination and immigrant restriction, of conquest and colonialism" that was born on the frontier and disseminated through the national mythology.[12]

Writing in the wake of the various protest movements noted above—movements that directly engaged America's problematic history with race relations and the results (political, social, economic) of that history in contemporary America—the authors examined in this study exposed the inherent racism of this mythology and invented alternative visions of the past that provide a more accurate understanding of the historical moment(s) (by including people of color) as well as a more accurate reflection of the progressive social values that such a mythology should embody. That is, if it is the progressive mythology it claims on its face to be, the national mythology should embody more than simply economic advancement achieved at the expense of Native American sovereignty and African American self-determination.

My primary objective in this study is to develop a new reading of a few selected texts, all of which participate in the reevaluation of the American frontier mythology by challenging such progressive claims in light of the social and political upheavals in the second half of the twentieth century. These works, all of which address the white-male-dominated frontier mythology, represent a concerted effort in the postwar era by male authors to critically reexamine America's founding mythology. However, rather than merely challenging this mythology on the grounds that it is sexist and racist (which it most certainly is), these authors challenge the mythology on the grounds that, even taken at face value, it operates on flawed premises. Built on the very shaky foundation of inherently unreliable textual evidence, the frontier mythology fails a contemporary audience precisely because it cannot accommodate America's inherently complex cultural existence. In other words, the mythology of the American frontier fails contemporary America for two reasons: first, the mythology is both sexist and racist, and has worked to prop up a very narrow and limiting example of American cultural values: the (white, male) frontiersman;[13] second, and just as important, even on its face this mythology has failed the nation by ignoring America's complex cultural history. In the chapters that follow, I hope to demonstrate this duality by showing how the failed frontiersmen that are central to each work can be considered failures when set against the mythic figure of the frontiersman, as well as by exploring how these works rewrite the mythology of the American frontier by injecting into it the progressive social and cultural values embodied by the protest movements of the 1960s.

It is for this reason I have explicitly selected works of Historical Romance, the narrative tradition that developed in America from the works of James Fenimore Cooper and Nathaniel Hawthorne. The works I have selected continue the development of a discursive tradition in American letters primarily concerned with exploring America's founding mythology and engaging in sociopolitical critique, objectives that have been tied together from the very start. Dating back to such classic American masterpieces as the Leatherstocking Tales and *The Scarlet Letter*, the American Historical Romance has always had a dual focus: on the one hand, it creatively imagines the historical past, providing backstory by which we can understand our own cultural history; on the other hand, it injects the values of contemporary America onto the past. (In the first case, Cooper attempted to incorporate his version of Native American values into the mythology of the American frontier through the character of Natty Bumppo, a white man who embodied the lessons of the Delaware tribes and served as a foil to various aspects of white culture;[14] in the second case, Hawthorne attempted to incorporate a more progressive understanding of the role of women in society, and the strength Hester Prynne possesses, especially when contrasted to Dimmesdale and Chillingworth.)

The romance, as opposed to the novel, is not bound to historical fidelity, or even the normal operations of the world in which we live. If the novel is the vehicle for realism, the romance is the vehicle for imagination, for the world not as it is but as it could be (or, in the case of the Historical Romance,[15] as it could have been; more on this below). As it has long been the romance that has served as the vehicle for American cultural values by engaging the mythology of the American frontier and disseminating the values of that mythology to the reading public, it is only fitting that contemporary authors have participated in the tradition of the romance and penned works that critique that very mythology. Perry Miller, in his influential essay "The Romance and the Novel," claims of romancers as a whole that "all of them were basically concerned with . . . the continent, the heritage of America, the wilderness," devoting "themselves heart and soul to portraying the uniqueness, the glory, the ordeal of America."[16] Publishing texts in and after 1960, such writers as E. L. Doctorow, John Barth, Thomas Pynchon, Ishmael Reed, Gerald Vizenor, and Cormac McCarthy critique the American frontier myth through their participation in the romance tradition as it has evolved in American literature, as well as their various challenges to received authority during a period of significant social and political change.

A second, but no less significant objective of this study is a recognition that "the frontier" did not exist in any one time or place. Rather, as Euro-American expansion moved west across the American landscape over time, so too did the frontier. The "frontier chronotope" (to borrow from the narrative theorist Mikhail Bakhtin)[17] is a specific time/space matrix. It is for this reason that one can write of the "American frontier" in Maryland of the late 1600s as well as in the nineteenth-century Dakota Territory. Though itself fluid in its movement, the frontier always refers to some specific time/space—or chronotopic—reality. In other words, the historical romancers responding to the social pressures of the 1960s are not merely dressing up contemporary concerns in frontier costume, but are concerned with what Georg Lukács calls the "here and now" of the historical moment, with each writer selecting a different historical moment (and, as such, a different physical space).[18] Though Lukács was not working with Bakhtinian poetics, "here and now" is a close approximation of "chronotope," and reflects their similar concerns with regard to the narrative fidelity to the time and place of the setting. For Lukács, the genius of Sir Walter Scott (as well as many of his inheritors, such as James Fenimore Cooper and, as such, the American Historical Romance tradition) is based on "the creation of a real historical novel, i.e. one that brings the past close to us and allows us to experience its real and true being."[19] Lukács later clarifies this vague praise by commenting on Scott's "perfect artistic expression [of] the basic progressive tendency of the period, i.e. the historical defense of progress."[20] Similar to, and developing from Scott via Cooper, E. L. Doctorow, John Barth, and Thomas Pynchon bring the various frontier pasts close to their readers, demonstrating that our present moment is a direct result of the progress—or lack thereof—of cultural forces.

Ishmael Reed and Gerald Vizenor take this critique one step further, working to deconstruct the stability of the chronotopic situation of the American frontier. Both authors attempt to collapse the rigid space/time construction of the American frontier in order to demonstrate that the cultural problems America faces in the late twentieth century are the same as those faced on the American frontier; for all intents and purposes, we are still on the frontier, because we are still engaged with the same problems, which are not limited to any one geographical space. It is for this reason that Reed and Vizenor can construct frontier spaces not definitively located on a map, and peopled with characters from various periods of time. Unlike their contemporaries, Reed and Vizenor are engaged in modes of narrative that draw from African (by way of Haiti) and Anishinaabe traditions, respectively.

Where Doctorow, Barth, and Pynchon highlight the problems inherent in the documents used to transmit the frontier mythology while first alluding to and then openly critiquing the mythology's racist dimensions, Reed and Vizenor critique the conventions of western narrative that have been used to transmit and authorize this mythology as a means of writing the ethnic other out of the cultural imagination and mythological inheritance. Similarly, Reed and Vizenor explicitly explore the construction of the racialized male body on the frontier, highlighting the interconnections between race and gender with respect to the construction of stereotypes. As Michael T. Wilson has argued about Cooper and his contemporaries: "American novelists of the nineteenth century inclined to use the Indian as a literary motif found themselves in a quandary regarding two of the primary cultural projects of the day, the emphasis placed on civilized masculine self-control verses the 'need' to expand the western frontier and eliminate the Indian presence there."[21] The failure, then, of this mythology becomes all the more serious because it is not connected with one specific time and place in American history, but rather has characterized America's relationship to the fluid and ever-moving frontier space.

In their various reevaluations of the mythology of the American frontier, all of the writers included in this study explore the notion of "colorlined space" as it has been formulated by Anthony Paul Farley. Likely intentionally leading readers to think of color-*blind* space, or space that would be devoid of the complications of America's racial history, color*lined* space is the very opposite, space that insists on race as a defining feature of its cultural history. In his discussion of *The Great Gatsby* (itself a novel that explores racialized notions of privilege), Farley defines "colorlined space" as follows: "It is the space of longing and the space of refusal. It is the space that begets the elite and, necessarily, those others whose exclusion renders elitism possible. It is a way of seducing us into the space of white-over-black. That space, that colorline, is a space of longing and refusal."[22] This "colorline" sounds (unsurprisingly) like a frontier, an often-arbitrary line that exists in order to delineate the civilized (read, white) from the savage (read, ethnic other). It is the kind of line that, over time, becomes an established, official border (as we will see with the works of Gerald Vizenor and Cormac McCarthy), thus writing elitism and racial politics directly onto the map. Further, as Farley notes, "the colorline serves as the medium of communication between whiteness and itself";[23] that is to say, it is the frontier that serves as the means by which whiteness comes to understand itself and promote itself against the racial other. And as we will see in the various works included in this study, a colorline exists wherever we find the enactment of racial politics played out on the American landscape, regardless of the specific historical moment. The colorline, much like the chronotope, is fluid.[24]

This fluidity, this movement of the frontier chronotopes is given structure by the development of the mythology of the American frontier as it has been adapted and disseminated by generations of frontier romancers. Representative of the major concerns of their age, post-1960s American Historical Frontier Romances participate in a larger critique of inherited American mythology that is characteristic of the period of dissent and reform. The traditional mythology—widely employed in both print and film—had portrayed America as a land not only open to, but in seeming need of cultivation and civilization by Europeans and their descendants. Those who, like Daniel Boone, successfully tamed the savage land and its native inhabitants were portrayed as bold, adventurous heroes whose exploits became the stuff of legend; further, upon the shoulders of such heroes rested both the moral and physical authority predicating further western development.

Authority, particularly authority established by physical violence, is also at the core of the development of white American masculinity, and the myth of the American frontier is central to our modern understanding of masculinity and definitions of manhood. As Connell notes, "It is a striking fact that even before this frontier closed, with military defeat of the native peoples and the spread of white settlement across the continent, frontiersmen were being promoted as exemplars of masculinity."[25] The various white male figures we will encounter in the following chapters—the pioneer, the settler, the explorer, the cowboy—are all examples of the "male body" that Todd W. Reeser claims "functions as a kind of tabula rasa or inscriptive surface for masculinity and for culture, and discourse is inscribed on that matter, asserting its power through inscription and reinscription."[26] Further, the nonwhite male figures of frontier authority we will encounter will demonstrate that it need not be a white body that comes to represent power and authority, nor must such bodies be traditionally masculine (though they will all be male).

A quick survey of classic nineteenth-century Historical Romances of the frontier shows the prominence of this inheritance. In his Leatherstocking series, James Fenimore Cooper employed the figure of Natty Bumppo as his mythological frontier hero. A skilled hunter and woodsman, Bumppo was as seemingly incapable of moral error as he was of failure in his duties as hunter (or trapper, as in the case of *The Prairie*). In *The Pioneers*, Natty delivers a sermon against the wasteful killing of the pigeons, while demonstrating his superior shooting skills by taking down a small bird and competing in a turkey shoot on behalf of Elizabeth Templeton (who, as a woman, was not expected to possess survival skills suited to the frontier). In *The Deerslayer*, Bumppo serves as a corrective to Hurry Harry's brutish approach to both hunting and Indian killing; Bumppo may hunt and kill Indians, but he does so out of necessity and with a measure of proper respect for the slain.[27] In *The Yemassee*, William Gilmore Simms similarly employs the character of Gabriel Harrison as a masculine frontier hero. Harrison, like Bumppo, is the embodiment of both frontier knowledge and moral authority; unlike Bumppo, however, he is revealed to be Charles Craven, governor and lord palatine of South Carolina, and is thus invested with a measure of political authority foreign to Bumppo. For both Cooper and Simms, political authority should be wedded to moral authority; those white men who embody the pioneering spirit and have tested themselves against Native American "savagery" are best suited for leadership on the frontier.

Although I recognize that Cooper and Simms are but two romancers working within a much larger tradition (including such writers as Robert Montgomery Byrd, Lydia Maria Child, and Catharine Maria Sedgwick, to name but a few paradigmatic examples), Cooper and Simms were among the most popular frontier romancers of their time. Both writers characteristically engaged the American frontier mythology in order to perpetuate the advancement of a masculine-defined Euro-American culture, and established the frontier as a space upon which virtuous heroism and moral authority are continually defined. Both authors also established the character of the frontier hero that serves as the model for the frontiersmen depicted in the novels discussed in the following chapters. But perhaps most importantly for the present study, both writers employed their frontier Historical Romances as evaluations of their own immediate social and political environments.[28]

The Romance as Social and Political Critique

Despite the persistence of the prose romance as a meaningful (and not to mention popular) form of literary expression, literary artists, theorists, and historians have been compelled to reassert its existence, saving it from being lumped together under the broad umbrella term "fiction." Writing in the 1950s (and thus just before the romancers studied herein), Northrop Frye noted that the "prose romance, then, is an independent form of fiction to be distinguished from the novel and extracted from the miscellaneous heap of prose works now covered by that term."[29] He further expressed concern that such writers as William Morris might "be left on the side lines of prose fiction merely because the critic has not learned to take the romance form seriously."[30] Frye defines the "essential difference between novel and romance" in terms of character: "The romancer does not attempt to create 'real people' so much as stylized figures which expand into psychological archetypes."[31] This does not, of course, preclude the use of stylized historical figures, as many nineteenth- and twentieth-century romances (especially Historical Romances) have demonstrated. Rather, this means that the romance employs the figure of the "hero . . . whose actions are marvellous [*sic*] but who is himself identified as a human being."[32]

The romance, in other words, recounted the events of larger-than-life figures. This working definition of the romance has remained largely unchanged since Clara Reeve defined the romance in 1785 as "an heroic fable, which treats of fabulous persons and things.—The novel is a picture of real life and manners and of the times in which it is written. The Romance in lofty and elevated language, describes what has never happened nor is likely to happen.—The novel gives a familiar relation of such things as pass every day before our eyes."[33] As the form of prose expression devoted to heroic actions as opposed to the common events of daily life, the romance is a fit vehicle for the transmission and continuation of America's frontier mythology. Further, the romance need not concern itself with facts; specifically, the romancer is at liberty to describe "what has never happened," to take artistic liberty at the expense of truth. However, I would argue that the romance in America—and particularly those romances written in the latter half of the twentieth century—conflated this very sharp distinction. American romancers as early as Hawthorne have been unable to clearly mark the boundaries between "what has never happened" and "things that pass every day before our eyes." Further, our ability to know "what has never happened" is entirely built upon our understanding of history, which Doctorow and Barth demonstrate is transmitted by very unreliable textual means.

And while the romancer is not dealing with factual history, neither is he dealing with historical persons, even when such figures appear as characters. As Frye reminds us, the romancer is not creating "real people," but rather "stylized figures." Pynchon's Mason, Dixon, and even George Washington are thus no less stylized than Doctorow's stock western characters. Just as the Bad Man from Bodie can represent the inevitability of violent destruction on the American frontier, so too can Washington represent the inevitability of social destruction through the exertion of political and economic control. The one is no more stylized than the other for being absent from the historical record. Frye also notes that it is largely through such characters that the romance is "a more revolutionary form than the novel."[34] Although Frye is focused on form in his essay, we should not ignore the ways the romance has also been employed for social and political revolution; in this regard (as in so many), the form is the function.

The most explicit case for the romance as a vehicle for social and political revolution has perhaps been made by Peter J. Bellis in *Writing Revolution: Aesthetics and Politics in Hawthorne, Whitman, and Thoreau*. For Bellis, Hawthorne's romances are constantly in mediation "between the political and the aesthetic on which the romance depends."[35] This mediation, which Hawthorne had imagined as "neutral territory," is for Bellis remarkably political, whereby "the romance becomes a place of dissolving boundaries and oppositions—between actual and imaginary, natural and supernatural, past and present. *It takes the form of counterhistories, oppositional possibilities that haunt and trouble the present.*"[36] Although Bellis retains Hawthorne's neutral territory, he alters it to reflect the "oppositional possibilities" between which the romance mediates. Such possibilities, for Bellis, include the "counterhistories" that all Historical Romancers present. Each of the romances discussed in the chapters that follow will present—to varying degrees—such "counterhistories," alternative narratives that force the reader to reconsider how the past "haunts the present," as well as how present circumstances force a rereading of the past.

For the purposes of political expression, white male authors in the nineteenth century often turned to the romance. In fact, as one can see from a quick survey of major romances of that period, politics has been a central concern of the genre. James Fenimore Cooper's first romance, *The Spy* (interestingly subtitled *A Tale of Neutral Ground*), is set in Revolutionary America. His most famous romances—the Leatherstocking series—are set in significant times in America's political development, addressing such issues as land rights, the conversion to paper money, wars with the French, Manifest Destiny, and America's troubled history with Native Americans. Further, in his 1843 romance of the American Revolution, *Wyandotté, or The Hutted Knoll*, Cooper engaged with the complex motivations of the frontiersmen with respect to American independence, noting in his preface to the work that "one of the misfortunes of a nation, is to hear little besides its own praises."[37] Though not widely reviewed, the romance was negatively reviewed in both the *Southern Literary Messenger* and the *Ladies' Home Journal*. Both journals objected to the book on political grounds, with the latter noting its "spiteful anti-Americanism."[38] In other words, soon after establishing the American Historical Frontier Romance as a discursive tradition with which he would develop the mythology of the American frontier, Cooper then worked to reevaluate that very mythology, using his fiction to represent pressing political tensions. Such work is precisely what Cooper's inheritors in the latter half of the twentieth century were engaged in.

Nor was Cooper alone. Among the many subjects addressed in Herman Melville's early romances of the sea are colonization and the possibility of interracial love, both subjects with complicated political developments. And his own romance of the Revolution, *Israel Potter*, is not merely a vehicle of praise for the Founding Fathers. Even the works of an aesthete like Edgar Allan Poe have political implications, such as the critiques of aristocracy and the increasing distance between wealth and learning, on the one hand, and the political life of the community on the other in "The Fall of the House of Usher." And, closing the nineteenth century in his darkly satiric *A Connecticut Yankee in King Arthur's Court*, Mark Twain addresses the rise of commercialism in America as well as the negative effects of its booming technological development. Clearly, the romance in America has always been intimately if not openly concerned with both the formative as well as immediate concerns of American social and political history. This has been especially true in the case of the Historical Romance, given the necessity of selecting a time and place—in other words, a specific political environment—worthy of aesthetic description and social investigation.

Despite the serious national and international ramifications of the major sociopolitical contests that were waged in nineteenth-century America, one could argue that the twentieth century has been America's most politically charged century. The twentieth century witnessed two major world wars, as well as dozens of lesser military engagements, including but not limited to significant military action in Vietnam. Race relations were certainly strained throughout American history. However, in the 1950s and 1960s, violent racial tensions reached a level of national awareness and social protest arguably unlike anything that had previously been witnessed in American culture, and the aftershocks of the civil rights movement are still felt in many communities. Similarly, the American Indian Movement helped to give voice to people who for hundreds of years had endured social, political, economic, and military oppression.

Additionally, responses to war and the changing definition of the soldier as a figure used to define masculinity—in 1962 the first Women's

Army Corps (WAC) officer was assigned to Vietnam, and in 1967 President Johnson removed promotion restrictions for women officers—were only a small part of various second-wave feminist movements that forced America to reconsider traditional gender roles and the various social practices enforcing them (including, but not limited to, our national mythology and the body of work that supported such traditional social roles). Further, Sally Robinson has noted that in recent years "white masculine manhood finds itself at the mercy of the Third World, as it was in Vietnam."[39] Tying together issues of race and gender, Robinson is one of many scholars who note what is commonly called the "crisis" of white masculinity, as the white systems of power (as well as individual white people) are forced to reevaluate their cultural inheritance by reexamining the mythology that they have inherited. Though I will not go so far as to acknowledge this as a "crisis," I will suggest that this is part of the work of the reevaluation of the frontier mythology in which the writers in this study directly engage.

The increased availability of various forms of language-based media—both in print (books, magazines, newspapers) and now the Internet—have arguably made the average American more aware of the various sociopolitical conversations taking place at both the national and international levels. I would argue that all of these factors have made it more difficult for the literary artist in America to avoid engaging the political. In fact, many politically engaged writers in the twentieth century have returned to the Historical Romance in order to more fully participate in the ever-increasing political conversations in contemporary America. And by returning to the romance, such writers have similarly returned to the American frontier in their works to demonstrate that the sociopolitical conversations in the twentieth century have their roots in America's founding mythology. Just as the romance has been rediscovered by American authors as a powerful means of wrestling with important social and political tensions, the frontier mythology has been rediscovered by American authors as the source of many of those tensions. American romancers of the latter half of the twentieth century wrote during a highly politically charged time of social revolution and political protest. The 1960s and 1970s saw a powerful antiwar movement working against America's involvement in Vietnam, as well as major social revolutions with respect to race and class. I argue that the following writers, all of whom write within this highly contentious political atmosphere, embrace the Historical Romance for its ability to provide the "counterhistories" and "oppositional possibilities" that they believe

America needs in its time of political crisis. Or, as Mikhail Bakhtin has argued for fiction generally in "Epic and Novel": "Reality as we have it in the novel is only one of many possible realities; it is not inevitable, not arbitrary, it bears within itself other possibilities."[40]

The American Romance Controversy and the Situation of Twentieth-Century American Romances

In his influential study *The American Novel and Its Tradition*, Richard Chase distinguishes American from English fiction based on a split between realism and romance. He takes as "fact" that "since the earliest days the American novel, in its most original and characteristic form, has worked out its destiny and defined itself by incorporating an element of romance."[41] This view was not directly challenged until Nina Baym's charge thirty years later that the Romance Theory—and those who supported its claims—was attempting to subvert the importance of women in the development of American fiction. The Romance Theory, she argued, was both a chauvinistic and nationalistic tool, designed to help New Critics promote a cultural agenda that supported conservative politics, noting that "the term romance turns out to have been used so broadly and so inconsistently in the era that in any given instance of trying to fix its meaning the critic or writer was evidently indulging in a creative rather than a descriptive activity."[42] One might also argue that the Romance Theory was a tool that supported (perhaps even only indirectly) the exclusion of nonwhite authors from the American literary canon.

Useful as Baym's work was to help recover and reevaluate important texts in nineteenth-century American literature that did not fall into Chase's paradigm, Baym's (and others') critiques of the motivation of Chase and his followers ultimately failed to discredit the original premise of Chase's Romance Theory, in which he argued that the "most characteristic American fiction has been shaped by the contradictions and not by the unities and harmonies of our culture," and that the romance was the major form of fiction devoted to uncovering such contradictions in American culture.[43] As has been demonstrated by Thompson and Link in their *Neutral Ground: New Traditionalism and the American Romance Controversy*, Baym—as well as others who argued virulently throughout the 1980s and 1990s that the Chase thesis is a misrepresentation of nineteenth- and twentieth-century views on the place of the romance in American fiction—failed to demonstrate that the romance/realism dialectic did not exist prior to Hawthorne. Instead, as Thompson and Link develop in a careful study of nineteenth-century periodicals and literary essays, American writers have always been aware of, as well as deeply concerned with, theories of the romance and the novel.[44] However, the objections offered by Baym and others did put into relief the masculine grounding upon which the discussion of the romance (as well as many of the romances themselves) has been built. One important lesson to be learned from Baym is that, while there are many women working in the romance tradition,[45] there continues to exist a strong tradition of romances composed by male authors that engage with America's foundational mythological tradition. And it is this tradition that the present study seeks to explore, while also opening discussion to include nonwhite authors (for which I am indebted to Budick; see below).

Far from closing the book on the matter, however, Thompson and Link's work further highlights a problem—almost entirely unaddressed—in the development of the American romance. A study of the romance controversy and not a new reading of the literature, *Neutral Ground* concerns itself primarily with nineteenth-century texts. A study of the development of American fiction in general, and not just the romance, *The American Novel and Its Traditions* discusses early-twentieth-century works, but without making clear what, if any, influence the romance exerted after Henry James. Other major critical texts make vague stabs at discussing the twentieth century, such as George Dekker's *The American Historical Romance*, which briefly investigates twentieth-century American fiction of the South, answering Mark Twain's outlandish—though not entirely spurious—claim that Scott can be held responsible for the American Civil War. One must then ask, What happened to the romance during the twentieth century?

In *The Development of American Romance: The Sacrifice of Relation*, Michael Davitt Bell bases his reading of the romance tradition on Henry James's famous definition of the romance, taken from his preface to *The American*, as a "sacrifice" of the bonds that tie the "balloon of experience . . . to the earth. . . . The art of the romancer is . . . insidiously to cut the cable, to cut it without our detecting him."[46] In his readings of the romances of Brown, Irving, Poe, Hawthorne, and Melville, Bell attempts to show how this "sacrifice of relation" was fully achieved toward the middle of the nineteenth century, specifically in Melville's *The Confidence Man*. The final words of his study are ominous: "The sacrifice of relation has been fully and fatally realized."[47] This realization is both full and fatal because the American romance has seemingly reached its full development. Does this mean that there is no romance after Melville?

Certainly not. Joel Porte also offers an end date for the romance in *The Romance in America: Studies in Cooper, Poe, Hawthorne, Melville, and James*. Of Henry James's *The Golden Bowl*, Porte claims that "James's masterwork completes and culminates the genre with dazzling brilliance."[48] What these books show is that there is no singular, definitive "Romance Tradition" in American fiction; rather, there are many strains of romance fiction, depending on how one establishes its formal and thematic parameters. It is just as clear that universal claims should not be made based on readings of only a few authors, and I will attempt to avoid such claims in my own study.

To return to Thompson and Link, one reason why the critical community may see an end to the romance in the late nineteenth and early twentieth centuries is as a result of the rise of naturalism. As Thompson and Link demonstrate through their readings of Frank Norris's critical essays, especially those dealing with Émile Zola, both Norris and Zola (a founding influence on American naturalism) considered naturalism to be a development that arose from the romance as opposed to the realist novel.[49] Claiming that "naturalist fiction is the product of the contestatory negotiations of the rise of realism with a continuing romance tradition," Thompson and Link claim an unbroken development of the romance in American fiction.[50] As appealing an idea as this is for romance theorists (especially those who still cling to the Chase thesis, as Thompson and Link do), this argument is not convincing.

Thompson and Link amply demonstrate how Norris and other naturalists read Zola as a romancer; however, they ignore those contemporaries who read Zola as a realist. Indeed, they suggest that Norris's essays were attempts to challenge the popular reading of Zola as a realist, pointing out in "Zola as a Romantic Writer" that "it is curious to notice how persistently M. Zola is misunderstood . . . [h]ow strangely he is misinterpreted."[51] If, following Thompson and Link, one must accept a novel/romance distinction in the nineteenth century because writers of the time made such distinctions in their own works (a well-documented point), then one cannot accept naturalism as a twentieth-century reinvention of the romance by claiming that writers of the time were unable to recognize it for themselves. Although one may be reminded at this point that Chase—the critic whose work began this controversy—moves seamlessly from romance to naturalism, one should also keep in mind that Chase's thesis has been demonstrated to be needlessly narrow in its treatment. Wherever one situates oneself in this particular debate, however, what remains clear is the notion that the romance was an influential force in nineteenth-century American fiction, whereas its status in the twentieth century is, at best, unsubstantiated. I hope to demonstrate in the following chapters that, despite this confusion, the romance remains a popular genre through which authors successfully engage pressing sociopolitical concerns.

One critic who traces the development of the romance in American fiction into the twentieth century is Emily Miller Budick. In *Engendering Romance: Women Writers and the Hawthorne Tradition, 1850–1990*, Budick demonstrates how Carson McCullers, Flannery O'Connor, Toni Morrison, and Grace Paley inherit an antipatriarchal and skepticist critique of American culture by means of their participation in the "Hawthorne tradition." However, given the breadth and range of this tradition, studies engaging it must limit their scope by some criteria. Just as Dekker limits his discussion of the romance in the twentieth century to the South, Budick focuses on fiction written by women. Similarly, the present study is limited by considering only men. As such, these works should be read as participating in a larger conversation, with each study providing one important—but necessarily limited—piece of that conversation. Further, Budick notes that the four women she studies "write into an originally male, not female, tradition."[52] Budick thus asks her readers to ignore not only romances written by women in the nineteenth century—including popular texts by Lydia Maria Child, Catherine Maria Sedgwick, and Harriet Beecher Stowe—but also romances written by men in the twentieth century. That said, however, Budick is careful to note that "male authors may be just as sensitive to issues of gender as female authors."[53] I would like to go one step further, and note that white authors may be just as sensitive to issues of race as nonwhite authors, and as such I have included white, African American, and Native American authors in my study.[54]

In many ways, I hope my study works largely alongside, rather than against, Budick's substantial work. I certainly agree with her characterization of the romance as "skepticist" and "antipatriarchal"; the present study rests on the claim that the writers discussed are skeptical of the mythology of the American frontier, which is itself a very masculine (and as such, patriarchial) inheritance. However, Budick does not make clear what she means by a "male" (as opposed to "patriarchal") tradition, especially given her claim that her work does not rest upon a sex-based consciousness, even if her selection of authors for study does.[55] More importantly, Budick claims for the romance an "evasion of explicit sociopolitical reference" and suggests that "its antimimetic mode of representation produce[s] a text that insists . . . on challenging the reader to enter into an interpretive relationship with it."[56] Certainly the second claim is true: all literature can be said to challenge the reader to "enter into an interpretive relationship." However, her first charge—that the romance evades explicit sociopolitical reference—is simply false, both for the nineteenth-century romancers upon whose works she is basing her claims as well as for their twentieth-century counterparts, whom I argue explicitly embrace the sociopolitical in their participation in a larger critique of the foundational American mythology. Remembering that Perry Miller claims of romancers as a whole that "all of them were basically concerned with . . . the continent, the heritage of America, the wilderness," devoting "themselves heart and soul to portraying the uniqueness, the glory, the ordeal of America,"[57] it should not come as any surprise that, when the "glory" and "ordeal" of America came to be challenged by late-twentieth-century writers, the romance was the most useful choice for form, just as the frontier was the most fitting choice for setting and subject matter.

In a similar manner, my study works alongside—rather than against—the large body of work on "historiographic metafiction," a designation coined by Linda Hutcheon in her study of postmodern fiction, *A Poetics of Postmodernism: History, Theory, Fiction*. Arguing that "postmodernism in fiction be reserved to describe the more paradoxical and historically complex form that I have been calling 'historiographic metafiction,'"[58] Hutcheon (like many theorists of postmodernism) understands postmodern fiction as representing a sharp break with the past, specifically in terms of how it engages with the past and performs the work of historiography. However useful it has been to read some of the following works as examples of historiographic metafiction (Barth and Pynchon, especially), Brian McHale has reminded us that "it is in the nature of the periodizing enterprise that every gesture of temporal delimitation is a kind of thought experiment or enabling fiction," and that in selecting "a particular onset date or threshold moment, and particular continuities and discontinuities, causes and effects, themes and figures, leap into focus, while others recede into the background."[59] By selecting 1960 as a starting point, this study immediately calls to mind certain sociopolitical movements and specific aesthetic developments; a very different picture might emerge if I chose to begin in the 1950s, or in the 1980s.

So for all that Hutcheon's formulation works to situate writers like Barth and Doctorow within the context of authors who playfully engage with historical documents to radically subvert the act of historiography, such a context is less helpful in understanding writers like Cormac McCarthy. Perhaps defined most broadly, all of the works considered in my study could fall under the umbrella of "historiographic metafiction," if we focus on Hutcheon's definition of work that, in its engagement with history and the means of constructing historical knowledge, "cast[s] doubt on the very possibility of any firm 'guarantee of meaning,'"[60] and does so by "installing and subverting familiar conventions."[61] However, I will consciously avoid applying the label "historiographic metafiction" broadly because not all of the works under discussion in this study engage in the "postmodern fantastic historiography" that Fredric Jameson identifies in the "wild imaginary genealogies and novels that shuffle historical figures and names like so many cards from a finite deck" from which Hutcheon develops her definition.[62] (Neither Doctorow's nor McCarthy's works could be described in such a manner, for instance.) More importantly, however, I wish to show how these works participate in a larger tradition, one that dates back in America to the nineteenth century; while these works can certainly be read as marking a break with the past (with respect to our understanding of grand historical narratives), I hope to show that they can *also* be read as participating in—albeit as a reevaluation of—a larger narrative tradition. In short, I am taking for granted that these works are examples of "historiographic metafiction," in order to demonstrate how they also participate as paradigmatic examples of a recent development of the American Historical Romance tradition, and its continued commentary on America's foundational mythology.

The Frontier as Topos in the Post-1960s American Historical Romance

There are two major understandings of the American frontier inherited by the twentieth century. The first is characterized by Frederick Jackson Turner's comments addressed to an audience of historians in 1893, where he claims: "And now, four centuries from the discovery of America, at the end of a hundred years of life under the Constitution, the frontier has gone, and with its going has closed the first period of American history."[63] For Turner, the frontier is a thing of the past, a dead space whose closing marks the passing of an era in the history of the nation. With no more "West" to explore and conquer, America had no more frontier space. However, despite the official closing of the frontier by the Census Bureau in 1890—in which it was decided that "there can hardly be said to be a frontier line. . . . [I]ts westward movement . . . can not, therefore, any longer have a place in the census reports"—the more positive inheritance of the frontier mythology remains prominent in the definition of American values.[64]

On the other hand, in his acceptance of the Democratic Party's nomination for the presidency of the United States, Senator John F. Kennedy employed the familiar notions of the frontier as that space upon which the common good, the overcoming of hardships, and the exploration of horizons define America's mission, a modern reclamation of John Winthrop's vision of America as "a city upon a hill": "For I stand tonight facing west on what was once the last frontier. From the lands that stretch three thousand miles behind me, the pioneers of old gave up their safety, their comfort and sometimes their lives to build a new world here in the West. They were not the captives of their own doubts, the prisoners of their own price tags. Their motto was not 'every man for himself'—but 'all for the common cause.' They were determined to make that new world strong and free, to overcome its hazards and its hardships, to conquer the enemies that threatened from without and within. Today some would say that those struggles are all over—that all the horizons have been explored—that all the battles have been won—that there is no longer an American frontier."[65] Both of these notions—the frontier as dead history and the frontier as active topos—play against each other in much American literature published after 1960. This interplay is so pervasive that even while employing the frontier as positive space, Senator Kennedy recognizes that victories on the frontier came as a result of battles, referencing the violence implicit in the "taming" of the western lands. (One should recall a similar sentiment expressed by Theodore Roosevelt, another man who would become the U.S. president.)

The literature of the period will be shown to address directly the notion that the positive, progressive aspects of the frontier came as a result of the violence inflicted by warfare and attempted genocide. This far-from-neutral ground is the space whereby American values originated and have since been defined by American mythmakers. The social and cultural destruction caused by westward expansion was not systematically addressed in Turner's work. However, by the 1960s, the darker implications of the frontier mythology had begun to compete with its more positive associations, as evidenced by such slogans as "We didn't land on Plymouth Rock; Plymouth Rock landed on us."

As Richard Slotkin has already pointed out, "Kennedy's heroic myth derived much of its force and resonance from the symbolism of the combat film and the Western."[66] As such, we can see how a variety of films came to visually and narratively define "the frontier" for a generation of Americans. This is perhaps most strikingly and permanently witnessed in the popularity of John Wayne's westerns; as Slotkin notes, "by the end of the 1960s, Wayne would be so identified with the West that his presence in a Western was taken as a guarantee of authenticity."[67] The combat film and the western, of course, were strongly linked by means of the Cold War, an ideological battleground that—not unlike the later war in Vietnam, or the civil rights movement, and American Indian Movement—borrowed heavily from the rhetoric of the mythology of the American frontier.[68] However, as Stanley Corkin has noted in his study *Cowboys as Cold Warriors: The Western and U.S. History*, "after 1962 the reigning films in the genre tended toward irony and self-criticism."[69] This parallels the move in American literary history toward the ironic self-criticism employed by many writers associated with historiographic metafiction (including some of the writers considered in this study). Like Slotkin before him, Corkin uses the war in Vietnam as a marker of change for the development of the frontier mythology, claiming that "Vietnam . . . served as both the culmination of the New Frontier and an index of the slogan's dangers."[70] Beginning with E. L. Doctorow and John Barth in 1960, the contemporary romancers chosen for this study all reflect this dual inheritance of the frontier as it was complicated by the political and social unrest growing as the twentieth century progressed.

Even the scholarship on the frontier that was produced during this period shows signs of this dual inheritance. For all its remarkable attention to the vast amount of writings produced on and about the frontier, Slotkin's *Regeneration through Violence* demonstrates the impossibility of an objective account of the frontier mythology in post-1960s America. Claiming that "the cycle of the myth never really ends," and that the "subversive forces within society" are continually addressed by American mythmakers in terms inherited from the Indian captivity narratives, Slotkin brings into his analysis the contemporary sociopolitical environment. Alluding to McCarthyism, Slotkin writes that "wars are followed by witch-hunts." This reference is followed immediately by a more overt condemnation of the war in Vietnam. The inheritance of the "savage Indian," for Slotkin, reappears in the savagery of war: "So the Indians (no less "American" than Crockett) garnered trophies as proofs and reminders of their battle valor and as kernels around which to build their names and the myth-tales of their tribe. In Vietnam it was called the body count."[71] By equating the Indians with Americans of such mythic stature as Davy Crockett (a white masculine hero not unlike Daniel Boone), Slotkin can then attribute the notion of Indian savagery to American actions as part of the inheritance of the frontier mythology. This decidedly negative representation of the frontier topos serves as a reminder of the destruction that America's move west left in its path, a description that Slotkin employs as the conclusion to his study: "the piles of wrecked and rusted cars, heaped like Tartar pyramids of death-cracked, weather-browned, rain-rotted skulls, to signify our passage through the land."[72]

This reference to "wrecked and rusted cars"—seemingly out of place in a discussion of the frontier mythology—serves to remind the reader that the conflicts of the past continually resurface in the present, albeit in slightly different form. In other words, a nation cannot escape its past, even if its myths attempt to obfuscate or rewrite that past. The national myths will be continually reinvented for younger generations, reimagined in new terms, yet remaining fundamentally the same on certain grounds. Or, as Hayden White has succinctly put it: "There are no changeless truths, then, except that everything changes; and no absolute progress in human culture save the progress of the idea of progress itself."[73] The past continually exists in the present; this is especially the case with respect to the continual development of the national mythology. In fact, it is the national myth of progress, central to the American frontier mythology, that the writers of this study are challenging in their texts. Even the "progress of the idea of progress itself," it seems, is not free from critical investigation. White further argues that "the past . . . can be known only insofar as it has continued to exist in the present."[74] The only way to fully understand the past, then, is by studying the means through which the stories of the past resurface in the present. However, as I hope to demonstrate, this does not mean that myths cannot be challenged by those who would participate in their development. In fact, given the social and political forces operating in and after the 1960s, it is inevitable that writers of that period would challenge their inherited mythology.

This inevitability can also be seen in a parallel focus on the history of the American frontier in the works of the historians of the "New West" as well as those participating in what has come to be called "postwestern studies." New West historians—such as Patricia Nelson Limerick, Richard White, Robert V. Hine, and John Mack Faragher,[75] among others—explore the history of the American West by challenging popular misconceptions, providing new understandings of old events, and reconceiving the importance of the West in the development of American culture. And certainly, to do so they must grapple with the mythology of the frontier. On the power of mythology, Limerick writes: "Myths resting on tragedy and on unforeseen consequences, the ancient Greeks certainly knew, have far more power than stories of simple triumphs and victories."[76] Much of Limerick's work (which I select as merely one representative example of New West historians) explores how the mythology acted as a driving force for America's westward expansion. One such myth was "to believe that the times of scarcity were a fairly recent phase, that in the immediate past arrivals got what they wanted from the West." However, "the West promised so much that the promise was almost sure to be broken."[77]

In a similar vein, postwestern theorists engage in what Susan Kollin has called a "critical regional studies," insisting, however, that "we understand the region not as a closed or bounded space but as a continually changing and evolving entity."[78] Even when postwestern theorists attempt to dissolve the boundaries of our notion of "the West" and frame it—as Neil Campbell does in his study *The Rhizomatic West: Representing the American West in a Transnational, Global, Media Age*—as "a traveling or mobile discourse," the focus still appears to be on a particular geographic region: the contiguous United States west of the Rocky Mountains.[79] Just as Limerick demonstrates that Americans fooled themselves into believing the West (either as physical space or as ideological construct) promised them an endless horn of plenty, the writers in this study explore the various problems inherent in that promise. If the New West historians want us to understand the actual history of the West separate from the popular mythology, the writers discussed in the following chapters want us to understand why the mythology failed those of us who live in the wake of that history.

And, in a nod to the persistence of the frontier mythology, Limerick also notes that "false renderings of that past do not make it any less significant."[80] Just as I am situating my study parallel to, but certainly not contiguous with, New West historiography, I would like to similarly note the distance between my study and postwestern studies. With a nod to the work of Krista Comer, the following study does acknowledge that "the problem of specifying 'the west' is always with critics," and I would like to take her as literally as possible when she notes that "it might be advantageous in fact to begin and remain critically deterritorialized."[81] Although there are similarities in both subject matter and methodology, the following study does not take as its subject matter a specific place (the West), but rather a construct (the frontier), for the frontier was not one fixed location, but rather a moving zone, largely heading west (but also south) throughout the development of American history. Any study of the mythology of the American frontier must be "critically deterritorialized" because, even if the frontier is popularly thought of as "the West," the frontier—and, as such "the West"—did not exist in a stable, fixed position. For this reason, we can focus on seventeenth-century Maryland as a frontier, though clearly Maryland would not be a subject for the New West historians. Specifically, it is the frontier (regardless of its actual location) as it has been reimagined by contemporary writers with which I am concerned.

It is because "the frontier" is not coterminous with "the West" that the following chapters focus on a wide array of geographical locations, from Maryland to the Dakotas to the Mexican-American border. The frontier is not here conceived as a stable location but rather, following Mary Louise Pratt, a "contact zone" where "disparate cultures meet, clash, and grapple with each other, often in highly asymmetrical relations of domination and subordination."[82] The frontier, as I use the term in this book, is an area of conflict designated by the meeting (often violent) of two cultures. The frontier mythology, then, is the narrative developed by one of those cultures as a means of subordinating the other.

In chapter 1, we will see how E. L. Doctorow and John Barth critique the means by which this narrative is developed, in their challenging of the means of written transmission; both authors invent documentary evidence that creates the circumstances for and hints at the dual failure of the frontier romance mythology described above. Chapter 2 investigates Thomas Pynchon's more explicit challenge to the racism of the frontier mythology (as well as his implicit challenge of that mythology's underlying sexism). In chapter 3, we will explore the Loop Garoo Kid, a figure of frontier authority whose very presence poses both a challenge and a solution to the dual failure of the mythology explored in the first three chapters. In chapter 4, we will see that the frontier need not necessarily be a zone of violent conflict. Following Louis Owens's concept of the frontier zone as a zone of play, Gerald Vizenor explores a zone of productive as opposed to destructive contact. Finally, building off of such a definition of the frontier, chapter 5 looks at Cormac McCarthy's Border Trilogy and *Blood Meridian*, and argues that the dual failure of the frontier mythology is one from which our nation likely cannot recover. Certainly, as McCarthy demonstrates, the Mexican-American border was (and still is) a zone of violent conflict. The frontier, as these chapters demonstrate, is less a physical description than an ideological construct. Or, as David E. Johnson and Scott Michaelson write of the growing interest in border theory in their introduction to *Border Theory: The Limits of Cultural Politics*: "Borders everywhere, but a world where no geographer's or cartographer's science is up to the task of mapping."[83]

Given its importance in the construction of American identity, it is no surprise, then, that the frontier would reappear as a major topos in contemporary Historical Romances, particularly those that wish to provide "counterhistories" and "oppositional possibilities." Post-1960s American Historical Frontier Romances provide alternate narratives and counter-readings in order to challenge the conclusions traditionally drawn from the national mythology. In the 1960s, E. L. Doctorow and John Barth suggested the illegitimacy of historical documents as foundations of the frontier mythology. Twenty years later, Thomas Pynchon demonstrated the impossibility of mapping the boundary between civilization and savagery. Ishmael Reed gave voice to African Americans, whose participation on the American frontier has been effaced by many sources, literary and historical. Gerald Vizenor then showed how the American frontier myth actively attempted to exclude Native Americans from positively participating in America's cultural development, despite their undeniable presence and influence. Finally, Cormac McCarthy, engaging in several of the above projects simultaneously, suggested the failure of the frontier mythology as a source of progress.

As such, in addition to working within the nexus established by the vectors described above (the romance tradition, engagement with the American frontier myth, commentary on contemporary political issues, and representation of progressive cultural values), these authors have also penned works that themselves compose a loose narrative, documenting the challenges to this mythology and exposing its failures as exposed by the cultural and political uprisings of the latter half of the twentieth century.

Major social and political movements necessitate a reevaluation and rewriting of national mythologies in light of new understandings of the nation's history. The first step of this process is the critical reinvestigation of the historical record. Perhaps the most famous example of revisiting the historical record is Howard Zinn's *A People's History of the United States*. Published in 1980, and building upon Zinn's academic research and social activism (including but certainly not limited to his support of civil rights movements and protests against the war in Vietnam), *A People's History* both rewrites the historical record and exposes some of the major problems with traditional historiography. Alluding to the problems with both the historical record and maps (both of which are attacked by the authors in this study, as well), Zinn writes: "It is not that the historian can avoid emphasis of some facts and not of others. This is as natural to him as to the mapmaker, who, in order to produce a stable drawing for practical purposes, must first flatten and distort the shape of the earth, then choose out of the bewildering mass of geographic information those things needed for the purpose of this or that particular map."[84]

A People's History, like many of the works in this study, revisits major moments in American history from the perspective of those whose voices have not been heard and, akin to Ishmael Reed's *Yellow-Back Radio Broke Down* and Gerald Vizenor's *The Heirs of Columbus*, is "skeptical of governments and their attempts, through politics and culture, to ensnare ordinary people in a giant web of nationhood pretending to a common interest."[85] In the wake of the social and political movements that defined the 1960s, historians and novelists alike were revisiting American history for the purpose of critical and imaginative reevaluation. Many writers have challenged the cultural inheritance of the national frontier mythology—especially its implications for race relations in contemporary America—and they must first engage in the textual tradition that is employed to disseminate and codify this mythology, what Foucault has called "the questioning of the *document*."[86] Historical documents, Foucault reminds us, need to be questioned, for "history is that which transforms *documents* into *monuments*."[87] That is, such documents have been given authority by virtue of their having been composed in the past, one that is foreign but remains familiar through the persistence of the frontier mythology.

As we will see in chapter 1, Doctorow and Barth use their fiction to ask "not only what these documents meant, but also whether they were telling the truth, and by what right they could claim to be doing so, whether they were sincere or deliberately misleading, well-informed or ignorant, authentic or tampered with."[88] In other words, before we can consider the cultural implications of rewriting the American myth, we must first turn our attention to challenging the means by which the myth has been transmitted. As E. L. Doctorow and John Barth demonstrate, the medium is the message, and both have failed.

1 / Rewriting the Historical Record: The "False Documents" and Failed Frontiersmen of E. L. Doctorow and John Barth

Yet the telling of history is all that stands between human beings and the eclipse of history.

—EMILY MILLER BUDICK, *FICTION AND HISTORICAL CONSCIOUSNESS*

As Richard Slotkin demonstrates in *Regeneration through Violence*, the myth of Daniel Boone developed in large part due to the written accounts of his life and exploits by both American and European writers. The various treatments of Daniel Boone by John Filson in the late eighteenth century serve as the starting point to Boone's development as a key figure in the American frontier mythology. Numerous American and European authors contributed to the development of the Boone myth by adding, deleting, or changing aspects of the narrative.[1] Slotkin articulates the inseparability of literature and mythology, especially regarding the American frontier myth: "Great literature is at once the apprentice and the master of myth. Its sources are mythic, for its statements refer to the ultimate questions of human consciousness and human existence, and it employs metaphors appropriate to the experience of the writer and his audience, his culture, and his people."[2] Literature has long been the vehicle by which American mythology is conveyed. The Boone narrative grew into its role as the foundational American frontier myth *because* of its varied treatment in American literature.[3] And given the large number of biographies of Daniel Boone, including Robert Morgan's recent (2007) contribution to the field, the Boone legend shows no signs of losing its hold on the American imagination.

A second, and no less important reason for the persistence of the Boone mythology in American culture is Boone's status as an exemplar of white masculinity, a status built on his physical exploits. As R. W. Connell argues: "I have stressed that masculinities come into existence at particular times and places, and are always subject to change. Masculinities are, in a word, historical."[4] This is not to say that there is only one kind of masculinity, of course. Rather, Boone stands as one specific kind of masculinity, a figure of great strength and skill; one who can not only survive in the wilderness but provide for others; a figure for whom the difficulties of the frontier exist as challenges to be overcome; a figure embodying Manifest Destiny and the spread of European people culture across the American wilderness. Heroes of the American Historical Frontier Romance are cut from the same cloth. And as we will see in later chapters, the literary figure of the cowboy is a reimagination of this mythic hero. Because of Boone's status as the mythic figure representing American expansionism and the settlement of the frontier, Boone is arguably the first truly American embodiment of white masculinity; in short, Daniel Boone is the model against which men have defined themselves as men. In his taming of the frontier, Boone (as mythic hero) provided an example of mastery and control over savagery that Connell has noted lies at the heart of the history of masculinity in the United States: "Loss of control at the frontier is a recurring theme in the history of empires, and is closely connected with the making of masculine exemplars."[5] And so just as the frontier mythology gives the nation a creation story, so also does it provide the foundational figure for white American manhood.

Further, as American literature supports this national mythology, charting its sectional, regional, and national developments, American literature also expands it, helping to shape those developments. Writers occupy a unique nexus in the development of the American frontier myth: they serve as cultural barometers as well as shapers of the cultural consciousness, serving the changes that both Slotkin and Connell note in the development of American culture. As conduits of received wisdom, their works preserve traditional notions while also serving as the genesis for new interpretations and developments. American Historical Frontier Romancers writing after 1960, more than any other group before them, consciously used their dual role in order to critique the various inherited values of the national mythology.

Specifically, E. L. Doctorow and John Barth used their Historical Frontier Romances to challenge the values of the inherited American frontier mythology and the figure of the mythic frontier hero, as well as to highlight the fundamental flaw of basing this mythology on the documentary evidence. Just as there is no one "Daniel Boone narrative," but rather a collection of related narratives that together created a mythology, Doctorow and Barth show the dangers of accepting one written record over others. In Doctorow's *Welcome to Hard Times*, Blue's ledgers prove to be an imperfect account of the growth and destruction of a small Dakota Territory town, and Blue himself fails as a frontiersman in the tradition of Daniel Boone; in Barth's *The Sot-Weed Factor*, John Smith's narrative of the Pocahontas legend (as well as his other heroic exploits) are challenged by the recovered journal of Henry Burlingame, whose descendant serves as foil to the foppish and dandified Ebenezer Cooke, another failed frontiersman. These narratives attempt the dual function of deconstructing the American frontier myth—and the values and figures associated with it—and highlighting the difficulties of using written records for establishing a mythology. And as such, this chapter identifies the dual failure of the mythology of the American frontier: first, Blue and Ebenezer Cooke fall far short of the heroic model set by such figures as Daniel Boone; second, and more importantly, that very model is wrongheaded and proves to be inconsistent with the values of a progressive society.

As he makes clear in many of his works, E. L. Doctorow is concerned with, as he has repeatedly called it, "the theme of our lives."[6] By this, Doctorow means that his works—while situated in a very specific historical chronotope[7]—simultaneously address sociopolitical issues of the time and critique contemporary American politics and culture. In fact, for Doctorow, all writing addresses its contemporary world: "Because that of course is what writing about the past is all about: you are writing about the present."[8] Similarly, Doctorow believes that writing is itself a political act: "I think everyone writes political books, actually. . . . I don't see how it's possible for a novelist not to recognize the political implications of his work."[9]

And Doctorow's own political views are well known, if not always clear. Though many critics align him with the political Left as a result of the subject matter of his works and his favorable treatment of political revolutionaries, Doctorow himself is cryptic about his politics. When directly asked about his politics and their expression in his works, and to answer the charge that he is a "political novelist," Doctorow responded:

> A novelist is thought to be a political novelist only when the politics of his novel are not the prevailing politics of his society. Then the politics stand out. We could discuss as a proposition the idea

> that all novels are political; all art is political, which seems to be endorsed in most countries of the world where the profession of novelist or artist is slightly more dangerous than that of high speed automobile racing. We have novelists who are in insane asylums, who are tortured and put in cages, who are exiled. What does the rest of the world know that we don't know, about fiction and about art? I've often made the observation that this is one of the few countries in the history of western civilization in which artists are not seen to be a danger to the state.[10]

Although one would be hard pressed to characterize Doctorow as "a danger to the state," his point that art cannot ignore—and in fact must participate in—the politics of the age is well put. And one reason why Doctorow's politics, in particular, stand out is his active critique of postwar American society. In a 1978 interview with Paul Levine, Doctorow characterizes the skepticism of history that permeated America as it rolled into the 1960s: "A lot of people discovered after World War II and in the fifties that much of what was taken by the younger generations as history was highly interpreted history. . . . And it turned out that there were not only individuals but whole peoples whom we had simply written out of our history—black people, Chinese people, Indians. At the same time, there is so little a country of this size has in the way of cohesive, identifying marks that we can all refer to and recognize each other from. It turns out that history, as insufficient and poorly accommodated as it may be, is one of the few things we have in common here."[11] So for Doctorow, history must be engaged to strengthen those "cohesive, identifying marks" that unite Americans as a people. However, this history must also be critiqued because of past efforts (conscious or not) to ignore certain unpleasant events and to write ethnic minorities out of the historical record.

This dual engagement with history—participating in the transmission of the national myth and critiquing its inheritance—comes for Doctorow very naturally in the buildup to the 1960s, a decade marked by "the New Left, the anti-war movement, an amplification by a later generation of the torment of the 1950's."[12] In the same interview, Doctorow claims that "when I'm writing out of a spirit of transgression, I'm probably doing my best work."[13] For Doctorow, the 1960s represented a major cultural revolution on multiple fronts:

> It wasn't until the 1960s and the rise of civil rights and countercultural movements that Black Studies was created as a subject, as a discipline in the universities. Before that it was as if in the United States there has been no black people or no contribution of black

> people to the building of the United States. And what scholars discovered in the 60s was that there was an enormous literature of black testimony buried in the libraries: black biography, black autobiography, black scholarship, that had been totally neglected. To this day, there is no concerted or large effort to understand historically the tremendous contribution of the Chinese people to the developing of the United States. The role of women in our history has only recently begun to be defined in Women's Studies Programs in the colleges and the universities.[14]

The 1960s, as Doctorow remembers them, were a period of great social and intellectual upheaval, whereby various institutions (as well as institutionally supported limitations based on race and gender) were reexamined with a critical eye as to what was being ignored, what the historical record had effaced. Doctorow's awareness of and sympathies toward the various social movements of the second half of the twentieth century allow us to read his fiction as participating in the discourses of revolution in which other writers—particularly social activists and alternative historians—were engaged.

That he situated his first novel on the American frontier—a site often used to embody American identity and cultural values—is therefore not insignificant. In addition to the civil rights movement (which I will address in more detail in chapter 3), Doctorow gestures toward the women's movement in his comments about the radical social changes facing America in the 1960s. To note but one paradigmatic example of the discourses of revolution within which we should read Doctorow's fiction, 1963 witnessed the publication of Betty Friedan's landmark work *The Feminine Mystique*, the publication of which is seen by many as the first moment of second-wave feminism. Addressing "the problem that has no name" (as she titles her first chapter), Friedan explores the widespread problems faced by women (particularly housewives) in twentieth-century American society. Despite Doctorow's celebration of the formation of women's studies programs in the 1960s, Friedan reminds us that "women attending college in comparison with men dropped from 47 percent in 1920 to 35 percent in 1958" (although by 1983, Friedan would note "women's studies" and "more women now going to college than men" as positive developments over the twenty years since her book was first published).[15]

Speaking about these various movements simultaneously, Doctorow alludes to the ways these movements were interconnected; often the same activists were engaged with multiple civil rights efforts. However, even within those movements and the resulting laws that were passed, the 1960s at times only gestured toward equality. Friedan reminds her readers that "the sex discrimination part [of the Civil Rights Act of 1964] was tacked on as a joke";[16] Howard Zinn has also noted that "in the civil rights movements of the sixties . . . [w]omen took the place they customarily took in social movements, in the front lines—as privates, not generals."[17] The war analogy is telling, as it reminds us that acceptance to changes in the roles of women, particularly as they have been developed by the narratives employed to disseminate cultural values (the frontier mythology in many ways working similarly to the developing narrative of the American soldier),[18] were slow in coming, as were the resulting reevaluations of hegemonic masculinity that came out of the 1960s. Doctorow has similarly noted in interviews that no small amount of the upheaval in the 1960s was due to what "we were all going through [in] Vietnam," the "anti-war movement" being "an amplification by a later generation of the torment of the 1950's."[19] *Welcome to Hard Times* inaugurates this period of cultural upheaval by directly challenging both the foundational national mythology and the notion that our past has been accurately transmitted to us through the documentary evidence.

Doctorow's first romance reaches back to the nineteenth-century American frontier of the Dakota Territory and grapples with accepted American history and myth. Although one should be careful not to confuse history with myth, Doctorow argues that the two operate perilously close to one another. In explaining the necessity of "multiple witnesses" to history, Doctorow warns of the dangers of perspectivism: "if you don't [employ 'as many testimonies as possible'], history turns into mythology. If you don't constantly recompose and re-interpret history, then it begins to tighten its grip on your throat as myth and you find yourself in some kind of totalitarian society."[20] Reading this in light of his comments regarding the countercultural movements of the 1960s, one can see that Doctorow participated in the recomposition and reinterpretation of the history of the American frontier, challenging the inherited view that the frontier experience led to the betterment of those who pioneered America's westward expansion. And it is for this reason that he consciously wrote in the romance tradition; of *Welcome to Hard Times*, Doctorow notes: "I had been trying without success to write a realistic novel until I conceived of this one. I realized I was, like Hawthorne, not an exemplar of realism but a writer of romances. I was interested in imagery as a kind of moral data. And I was at home in the past."[21] The romancer is not writing history; rather, he is focusing on moral truth over historical fact.

He reimagines the past in order to provide a counterhistory, one that presents the reader with a representation of the frontier that does not sit comfortably with our accepted mythological inheritance: the frontier town of Hard Times is not the home of heroic frontiersmen.

Similarly, just as Filson's Boone narratives are not the sole source for the Boone myth, no one account of the West should be accepted as the sole source of the American frontier myth. Rather, all accounts—historical, fictional, sociological, psychological—participate in the construction of the myth. Doctorow's concern with the multiplicity of written accounts of history is the subject of his essay "False Documents," in which he explains

> why history has to be written and rewritten from one generation to another. The act of composition can never end.
>
> What is a historical fact? A spent shell? A bombed-out building? A victory parade? A long march? Once it has been suffered it maintains itself in the mind of a witness or victim, and if it is to reach anyone else it is transmitted in words or in film and it becomes an image, which, with other images, constitutes a judgment. . . . [H]istory shares with fiction a mode of mediating the world for the purpose of introducing meaning, and it is the cultural authority from which they both derive that illuminates those facts so that they can be perceived.
>
> Facts are the images of history, just as images are the facts of fiction.[22]

Fiction—especially the romance—is not a corrective to historical accounts; rather, the historian's account and the romancer's creation work in conjunction with one another in order to give as wide a lens as possible on the historical moment, where both mediate the world in very different ways, giving meaning to the multiple (but not competing) accounts. And it is for this reason that Doctorow's text is presented as the journal of the town's only official, Blue.

Welcome to Hard Times is the written chronicle of Blue, unofficial mayor of Hard Times, a small town on the Dakota frontier to which miners come in order to spend their wages on alcohol and prostitutes, buy supplies, and post letters. Blue becomes mayor of this town as a result of the records he keeps. Trained in law before moving west, Blue acquired ledger books from the supply train and began keeping property records. Originally kept for the purpose of someday applying for statehood, Blue's ledgers become the only official record of the town, and as such Blue becomes the town's only official, promoted by chance rather than through heroic exertion or innate skill. All disputes, even those unrelated to property, are addressed to Blue. This is why, when the Bad Man from Bodie ravages the townspeople and destroys the town in the opening chapter, it is to Blue that the townspeople turn. Because Blue keeps the ledgers, he has become the representative of law in Hard Times, despite being clearly unqualified (he doesn't even own a gun). Blue is called mayor for lack of any other official title.

For the purposes of Doctorow's critique, the records of primary importance are those that comprise the book. Divided into three "ledgers," *Welcome to Hard Times* is a personally composed history of the town. Where the employment of ledgers would allow for the account to appear objective, Blue's "ledgers," in fact, read more like a diary. Although Blue attempts an objective voice, trying at various points to be a truthful witness to the town's cycle of growth and destruction, the reader is continually reminded that his is a very subjective account. As Hayden White asked in his essay "The Question of Narrative in Contemporary Historical Theory": "How else can any past, which by definition comprises events, processes, structures, and so forth, considered to be no longer perceivable, be represented in either consciousness or discourse except in an 'imaginary' way? Is it not possible that the question of narrative in any discussion of historical theory is always finally about the function of imagination in the production of a *specifically human truth*?"[23] It would appear, then, that the kind of truth that writers such as Doctorow are attempting to expose can only be addressed through fictional narratives. Further, the kind of political and social critique that Doctorow and others achieve is possible as a result of their participation in a larger sociopolitical critique of established authority. In other words, this kind of critique is only possible through the romance, in this case by means of the invented counterhistory of a failed mining town, as presented by a decidedly failed frontiersman.

At various points, Blue is self-reflective in his narrative, remarking, "Now I'm trying to write what happened and I wonder, does a dream come under that?"[24] Blue also has the benefit of hindsight, and can open the *Second Ledger* with the cryptic foreshadowing statement: "That was the way it ended and began again," hinting at the impending destruction that Blue has witnessed just before he composed these ledgers (71). Further, Blue can editorialize on the process of writing itself, as when he laments: "Now I would write about that spring in its every minute if I could, using up my strength and time and going no further through the pain of seasons. But it is no pleasure to me now; and it is all I can do to remember it for my purposes which is to tell the way things happened" (113). Blue may believe in his objectivity, but he also recognizes that he makes subjective choices as to the content of his narrative. Writing on his deathbed, Blue attempts to provide an account of the actions that have taken place and of the actors themselves; the implications are that history is an account of what happened and that his ledgers accurately reflect the "account" of Hard Times. However, Blue here embodies Doctorow's primary objection to historical accounts: no one record can be complete. Blue recognizes the incompleteness of his project, and realizes he has neither the time nor the strength to provide more than he has.

As the narrative nears its conclusion, the reader is made aware of Blue's impending death. Opening the *Third Ledger*, he writes: "I have been trying to write what happened but it is hard, wishful work. Time is beginning to run out on me, and the form remembrance puts on things is making its own time and guiding my pen in ways I don't trust. In my mind's eye is an arch of suns multiplying the sky—or a long flickering night of one moon turning over and over into its shadows. I know this is trickery but I can't blot it out. . . . And I see something that never happened" (147). Knowing his time is short, Blue becomes increasingly distrustful of his objectivity, and for good reason. Where before he questioned whether or not he can include dreams under the heading of "what happened," he now includes a description of a hallucination (Molly and Fee planting a cross over the grave of Fee's father), something that certainly did not happen, at least according to Blue's account. Further, he admits to losing control over the guidance of his pen; rather than being guided by his own memory, Blue believes that "remembrance"—the controlling force of what has been preserved, as opposed to Blue's faulty means of preservation—is in control.

Though this may appear objective—as if history itself is directing the course of his narrative—Doctorow uses "remembrance" instead of history so that the reader does not lose sight of the role that individual memory plays in any account of historical documentation. Even if Blue is fooled into believing that he may be capable of objectivity at this point (where before he was not), the reader is not so fooled. Also, in accepting that his death is near, Blue turns his attention away from the account and to its potential audience, looking now for the first time not to the past—which he comes to realize he could not have escaped—but to the future: "Of course now I put it down I can see that we were finished before we ever got started, and our end was in the beginning. I am writing this and maybe it will be recovered and read; and I'll say now how I picture some reader, a gentleman in a stuffed chair with a rug under him and a solid house around him and a whole city of stoned streets around the house. . . . Do you think, mister, with all that settlement around you that you're freer than me to make your fate? Do you click your tongue at my story? Well I wish I knew yours. Your father's doing is in you, like his father's was in his, and we can never start new, we take on all the burden: the only thing that grows is trouble, the disasters get bigger, that's all" (184). Blue is now beginning to recognize the personal nature of his narrative, and has almost completely dropped all pretense of objectivity. He also imagines not only the survival of his text, but its enjoyment as a text; like all good romances, his will provide excitement for future readers.

Further, Blue notes that what he is telling is very clearly his own story. He may have been a witness to the events in the book; however, no one witness is sufficient for any narrative account to be taken as the only true account. Finally, Blue comes to believe that his tale is simply a retelling of an oft-repeated story, even if this recognition is addressed by way of allusion to the life story of his imagined reader. The only difference between his story and the one he inherited is the scope of the disaster. In this regard, Doctorow is hinting toward what we might call metaromance, suggesting that the romance tradition—and in particular, the American Historical Frontier Romance tradition—has done little more than find new ways of telling the same story. It is in this regard that Doctorow is providing (with John Barth, discussed below) the opening work for the reevaluatory phase of the development of the national mythology.

This move away from his previously positive view regarding his work as unofficial town historian is characterized immediately after the address to his imaginary reader: "I know it, it's true, I've always known it. I scorn myself for a fool for all the bookkeeping I've done; as if notations in a ledger can fix life, as if some marks in a book can control things. There is only one record to keep and that's the one I'm writing now, across the red lines, over the old marks. It won't help me nor anyone I know. 'This is who's dead,' it says. It does nothing but it can add to the memory. The only hope I have now is that it will be read—and isn't that a final curse on me, that I still have hope. I would laugh if I could, who will come here to find my ledgers of scrawls" (184–85).[25] It is at this point that Blue comes to realize that he has no authority over either Hard Times or the telling of its history. The title's pun, though clear from the first mention of the town's name, is now recognized as darkly ironic. For if Blue does not have the authority to relate the history fully and objectively, then *Welcome to Hard Times* as a document welcomes its readers into the "hard times" of remembered history.

Blue has lost all conviction of his worth as both mayor and storyteller, the two roles he attempted to play in welcoming his readers to both Hard Times and *Hard Times*: he scorns himself for a fool as a bookkeeper (the reason he was advanced to the position of mayor), and would laugh at himself in his hope that someone (such as the aforementioned imaginary reader) would read his story. And just after Blue realizes that he has kept a poor account of the town, he acknowledges that he does not now have, nor has he ever had, a clear and objective narrative. As his account catches up to his present situation, he writes: "I'm trying to put down what happened but the closer I've come in time the less clear I am in my mind. I'm losing my blood to this rag, but more, I have the cold feeling everything I've written before doesn't tell how it was, no matter how careful I've been to get it all down it still escapes me: like what happened is far below my understanding beyond my sight. In my limits, taking a day for a day, a night for a night, have I showed the sand shifting under our feet, the terrible arrangement of our lives?" (199). Doctorow provides a dark double entendre; the "rag" Blue is losing his blood to is both the rag keeping him from bleeding out and a reference to his own writing, which is no longer a ledger of great importance but a worthless piece of hack journalism. Blue has lost all faith in his objectivity. And as Christopher D. Morris has pointed out, "Blue's narration conceals, to the point of undecidability, his own complicity in the events."[26] The reader should not fall into the trap that Blue has: focusing on his role as chronicler and not as participant. Blue repeatedly underscores his own (in)actions in his narrative, especially as those (in)actions fail to help the town to avoid destruction at the hands of the Bad Man from Bodie.

Because Blue is incapable of objectivity, truth escapes him, below his understanding and beyond his sight. That is, the truth of historical fact escapes Blue; he is no longer able—or he realizes he was never able—to keep his narrative from providing anything more than a subjective account of events. This is the difference between Blue's narrative project and Doctorow's; where Blue fails to keep an objective rendering of the facts of history, Doctorow succeeds in using this failure to accurately explore "the theme of our lives." And even if Blue could sufficiently record the truth of what happened, he no longer has any faith in his ability to even comprehend the events. However, as he dies, Blue fears not that he has lost the truth, but rather that he has captured it: "And now I've put down what happened, everything that happened from one end to the other. And it scares me more than death scares me that it may show the truth. But how can it if I've written as if I knew as I lived them which minutes were important and which not; and spoken as if I knew the exact words everyone spoke? Does the truth come out in such scrawls, so bound by my limits?" (210). Blue's authorial expectations and fears have been reversed: where before he believed that he was writing the truth but feared he was not, now he believes to be writing something inaccurate that may in fact turn out to be true.

But what is this truth he fears will come out of his narrative? Clearly not the objective truth of historical fact, as he recognizes that his memory of the events—even his ability to select important events—is subjective and cannot possibly reflect "which minutes were important" or "the exact words everyone spoke." Rather, Blue has exposed "the theme of our lives." The cause of the fear, then, is not in his text, but in the truths that it exposes. If Blue has, despite any factual errors he may have committed, recorded the "truth" of Hard Times, then *Welcome to Hard Times* exposes a very grim truth about the American frontier. Additionally, Doctorow—through Blue—demonstrates the failure of *Author*-ity, undercutting his own narrative just as he undercuts Blue's. This leaves the reader with the impression that all such documents are "false documents."

Blue fails at more than record keeping, however. He also fails as a frontier hero in the tradition of Daniel Boone: that through hard work and self-sacrifice, American pioneers achieved a level of social and economic independence on the American frontier. As noted in the introduction, Doctorow (and the others participating in the reevaluatory stage of the development of this mythology) demonstrates the dual nature of the failure of the mythology of the American frontier: the mythology fails because of the difficulty of living up to an idealized mythologized figure; further, the mythology is itself a failure because it does not account for progressive notions of race and gender. In other words, even if such figures as Blue were successful in their exploits, their success would only have calcified the figure of the white, male hero as the embodiment of progressive American values. As the sociopolitical situation of the second half of the twentieth century in America has demonstrated, the mythology of the frontier spectacularly failed America, first in terms of the unrealistic standard set by such mythic figures as Daniel Boone, and again in terms of the latent racism and sexism of the mythology itself.

Blue is hardly cut from the same cloth as Daniel Boone.[27] As a pioneer who came west and assumed a position of moral and legal authority, Blue literally attempts to write himself into the Boone legend with his ledger. However, where Boone was a knowledgeable pioneer and woodsman, Blue is incapable even of digging graves or fetching wood without assistance. Where Boone was brave in the face of dangers—environmental and human—Blue cowers from both. When the Bad Man from Bodie first comes to Hard Times, Blue watches others—including the prostitute Molly—attempt to bring him down, without acting himself. By the time the Bad Man returns at the end of the book, Blue has divested himself of any power over law enforcement, instead backing a newly appointed sheriff who also fails to stop the Bad Man. Rather than moving West for personal advancement and fame, Blue admits that "when I came West with the wagons, I was a young man with expectations of something, I don't know what, I tar-painted my name on a big rock by the Missouri trailside. But in time my expectations wore away with the weather, like my name had from that rock, and I learned it was enough to stay alive" (7). Blue attempted to practice law out West, showing his opposition to Boone: where Boone is often characterized as embodying natural/wilderness law and succeeded in his pioneering aims, Blue attempted to bring law with him onto the frontier and failed.

Their relative successes can be seen in Boone's establishment as a figure of moral and natural authority, where Blue is unable to gain the respect of—much less command authority over—Hard Times. Blue's distinction from Boone is best characterized by Blue's own statements near the end of his account, where he tells his readers: "Like the West, like my life: The color dazzles us, but when it's too late we can see what a fraud it is, what a poor pinched-out claim" (183). If, as the Daniel Boone myth demonstrates, the hero is the embodiment of the frontier mythology, then Blue embodies only failure. Referencing fool's gold—worthless iron pyrite that, on the surface at least, resembles gold—Blue comes to represent the failure of his own settlement as well as the West in general: like fool's gold, the West dazzles people, only to be found a false dream, a "poor pinched-out claim"; and like fool's gold, Blue may resemble a hero from a distance, but up close one recognizes him for the coward he is. Finally, unlike Daniel Boone's attempts at settlement, which still exist, even if as tourist attractions, Blue's settlement—the town he attempted to found and make prosperous—twice burns to the ground over the course of his short narrative.

Blue also lacks any of the traditionally masculine qualities associated with Boone. The biographer Robert Morgan notes that, in addition to his adult exploits, Boone possessed traditional frontier masculine virtues even as a boy: "From an early age he could walk miles without getting tired and swim any river or pond. He could outrun other boys and he always seemed to win fights and wrestling matches. With bow and arrow he always seemed to win shooting matches, and with a rifle he was without peer."[28] In short, Daniel Boone as a child already possessed more manly attributes (as they are defined by the frontier mythology) than Blue. Molly, the town prostitute who comes to live with Blue after her injuries, often complains that had he been more of a man, perhaps he could have saved Hard Times. In a halfhearted attempt at embodying the kind of masculinity he thinks can save the town, Blue takes in Molly and Fee, living as a family (even introducing Molly to the prostitutes as his wife).[29] However, Blue is no husband to Molly and no father to Fee, and their "family" is little more than a show. Blue is a husband/father in the same way that he is a mayor: in name only.

As such, Blue represents the "crisis of masculinity" that Robert Bly later famously championed. Discussing Bly and Barbara Ehrenreich, Judith Kegan Gardiner notes "the decline of patriarchy" that leads to "men's decreasing interest in children" specifically, and the family generally. Given the prevalence of the family as a central social unit in America generally and the western genre specifically, I'd argue here that Doctorow is subtly challenging the "breadwinner ethic" that dominated postwar American definitions of masculinity.[30] However, Blue's seeming lack of sexual desire for Molly may also stem from Blue's inability to imagine procreation. As much as he operates as a booster for the town, he does not realistically consider a second generation, and offspring seem not to be part of his own personal goals. As Susan Jeffords has argued about "masculine identification" during the Vietnam War, "women as sexuality must be excluded from warfare, for they are reminders of the body and its possible death."[31] Although Blue is not a soldier in a war, it is not much of a stretch to read him that way; in particular, he is a soldier in an unwinnable war, whose makeshift "family" will not provide him with a legacy. Whether in the home, in the office, or on the "battlefield" facing the Bad Man from Bodie, Blue failed to embody the masculine values that the western expects of its heroes.

As Roger Horrocks notes in his study of traditional western male icons, "the patriarchal framing of the western is not in doubt: men have come to the untamed west to create homes and build empires."[32] Blue's purpose in coming west was to help tame the wild frontier (through the practice of law) and participate in the building of the American empire (by establishing a recognized town). The more traditionally masculine figure, as his name suggests, is the Bad Man from Bodie: in addition to being a hard drinker (he "drank down a half bottle of the Silver Sun's best"), he is also physically impressive ("Florence had never seen a man so big" [3]). Further, none of the men in town—Blue, Ezra the shopkeeper, Hausenfield with his gun, or the sullen Indian John Bear[33]—are able to successfully stand up to the Bad Man from Bodie, whose very presence cows the men into submission. The only townspeople who do stand up to him are the women; one is raped and the other is badly burned in the fire that consumes the town. In short, the figure who most closely resembles the mythic frontiersman—the large, capable man who stands unopposed in his quest to subjugate those who stand in his way—is the villain of the story. Doctorow here turns the traditional mythology on its head, exposing heroic masculinity as a destructive force. By contrast, Blue's more tame sensibilities—learned, thoughtful, reflective, gentle—are of no use in this frontier town, which ultimately fails in large part because Blue was incapable of protecting it.

Hard Times thus represents the much larger cycle of growth and destruction on the frontier. Blue notes that the frontier, far from being a space for progress, is itself a cycle of failure: "we can never start new, we take on all the burden: the only thing that grows is trouble, the disasters get bigger, that's all." Further, the town itself was rebuilt from multiple markers of previous failure. Although hopeful at the prospects of a new town, Blue tells Ezra the shopkeeper, "We got a cemetery. That's the beginnings of a town anyway" (28). Similarly, even though Blue does help in rebuilding Hard Times, the first buildings in this new Hard Times were constructed out of wood "garnered from dead towns in the territory" (58). Finally, when Blue has built up Hard Times to have it included on the map—written into existence, carrying with it the authority of a government ledger—the government agent complains about the worthlessness of most frontier towns: "Every time someone puts a little capital into the territory I'm called in by the Governor and sent on my way. . . . If a man files a claim that yields, there's a town. If he finds some grass, there's a town. Does he dig a well? Another town. Does he stop somewhere to ease his bladder, there's a town. Over this land a thousand times each year towns spring up and it appears I have to charter them all. But to what purpose? The claim pinches out, the grass dies, the well dries up, and everyone will ride off to form again somewhere else for me to travel. Nothing fixes in this damned country, people blow around at the whiff of the wind" (146).[34] The hard work that goes into the establishment of frontier towns comes to naught in the eyes of the government agent, who aligns their work with urinating.

Though he thinks it aptly named, the government agent cannot accept that Hard Times is a town, especially now that it lacks both sheriff and jail, for which purpose Jenks is hired. As is seen in the Bad Man's imminent return, neither has any effect. Hard Times fails as a town despite these measures. And that foreshadows similar failures in the future, as Blue explains in the closing words of his narrative:

> The mortal stench is everywhere, especially on me, and there is so much carrion in this town I wonder every buzzard on the land won't be here before the sun sets. It has crossed my mind to set the street afire—that would scatter them. But there's no wind and it would be hard work, harder than I can do.
>
> And I have to allow, with great shame, I keep thinking someone will come by sometime who will want to use the wood. (212)

Blue knows that Hard Times is not the first town to fail, and he intimates here that it will not be the last. Just as Hard Times was built out of the ruins of another town, so a third settlement will eventually be built out of the remnants of Hard Times. The implication that such a town will fail is clear. As Hard Times has demonstrated, constructing a town from ruin will inevitably lead to more ruin; there is no progress on this frontier. Just as Blue has lost all hopes for the positive aspects of life on the frontier, he has also lost what attributes of the frontier hero he may have possessed. And the only work a fire may do—aside from scattering the buzzards—is to encourage another hapless victim of the frontier myth to settle there, as Zar did after the first town burned to the ground.

Even the land itself will not live up to its apparent promise. After Hard Times first burns down, Doctorow increasingly makes clear that "this place here is not much country" because "none of it is" (29). Hard Times, in other words, is just as doomed to fail as any other prospect. Blue later repeats this idea when he claims that "only a fool would call anywhere in this land a *place* and everywhere else a journey to it" (66). It is not that individual towns fail, but rather that the experience itself is doomed to failure. And no matter how successful a town may be, it cannot become so large that it is immune to the destruction inherent on the frontier. Blue comes to realize that the Bad Man returns because he is a part of the frontier, a natural part of the landscape itself. The Bad Men "take to this land, they don't need much to grow, just a few folks together will breed 'em, a little noise and they'll spring up out of the empty shells" (165). A visit from the Bad Man is inevitable because the frontier is hostile to settlements. Blue knew this the first time the Bad Man came, claiming at the start of the narrative that "they came with the land, and you could no more cope with them than you could with dust or hailstones" (7). His lack of preparation against the second visit, then, should not be condemned: the Bad Man was destined to return, again bringing with him the ruin of Hard Times.

Welcome to Hard Times demonstrates that if the mining claim doesn't pinch out, and the water flows, and the game is abundant, the Bad Man will still come and burn it all to the ground. But more likely, all of the above will occur. Ruined, rebuilt, and ruined again, Hard Times stands as a symbol for the violence and destruction on the frontier not accounted for by the positive inheritance of the American frontier mythology; the destruction of the town represents the failure of this myth. Contrary to this myth, hard work does not bring success, successful towns do not bring stability, and numbers do not bring security. Hardworking men seeking to bring order will ultimately die, watching their efforts burn. Even the romantic notion of the heroic gunfighter bringing order to the frontier is seen as a lie.

Near the start of the narrative, Blue remarks that "the saying is common that Sam Colt made men equal. But if that is true then our town wouldn't have burned up in the rain; instead that Bad Man would have been buried with due honors and a proper notice sent to the Territory Office. . . . Colt gave every man a gun, but you have to squeeze the trigger for yourself" (32). Gunmanship has long been associated with masculinity, particularly on the frontier (going as far back as Natty Bumppo and his long rifle), and the connection between guns and manhood was reinforced during the conflict in Vietnam. Writing about various representations of the conflict in literature and film, Susan Jeffords claims that "technology is the (male) body";[35] essentially, a man is his weapon. Despite this traditional association, however, Jenks painfully demonstrates that just owning a gun does not make one a man. Duly appointed and properly armed as sheriff—whose marksmanship was well known and often tested against inanimate objects for the enjoyment of onlookers—Jenks fails in his duty to protect Hard Times. As a symbol of authority, stability, and order—and as a man whose identity is almost entirely established by his gun—Jenks should be able to protect the town from Bad Men. However, because good does not always win on the frontier, and because he had no practical experience as sheriff, Jenks loses this gunfight to the better man.

Blue remarks about Hard Times at the start of his ledgers, "Really there was no excuse for it except that people naturally come together" (4).

Doctorow shows in *Welcome to Hard Times* that the myth of the American frontier is itself "no excuse" for the construction of such towns and the continued belief in the myth's positive inheritance. Not only is the myth built upon flawed premises, but even on its face the myth fails to usher in progress. Blue fails as mayor, historian, and storyteller because, in the case of Hard Times, those who put their faith in the American frontier mythology failed, and it was this failed mythology to which Blue had hitched his wagon as a model of success.

In "The Writer as Independent Witness," a 1978 interview with Doctorow, Paul Levine notes, "In the 1960's, one had a series of novels that revised history, such as John Barth's *The Sotweed Factor*."[36] However, Doctorow and Barth are rarely discussed in tandem.[37] Where Doctorow is generally read as an overtly political writer, Barth's politics are hardly ever addressed by the critical community. Both writers have been referred to as postmodern writers, sharing such traits as complex and inventive narratives, multiple narrative voices, and challenges to reason and authority (including the authority of history). Though both authors share the label "postmodern," Barth (unlike Doctorow) was first read as a "fabulator"[38] and later as a paradigmatic example of "historiographic metafiction." As a result, Barth's fiction has at times been read as escapist, in that it does not directly comment on contemporary sociopolitical issues, as opposed to Doctorow's, which critiques important aspects of America's sociopolitical history. As we have seen, Doctorow's politics—"perhaps reformist Democratic with anarcho-socialist pretensions," as he once claimed[39]—inform his novels, which serve as vehicles for his commentary on the development of the American frontier myth. Barth's works, on the other hand, do not regularly engage major moments in American history.

In many of his works, Barth reworks classical mythology, showing how the values embedded in these myths continue to be engaged by contemporary society, and specifically how contemporary cultures accept a positive inheritance from these myths without (much) critical analysis. Throughout his career, Barth has repeatedly returned to both ancient Greek mythology and *1001 Arabian Nights*. However, one cannot fault the critical community for its failure to tease out the ways that Barth has written his immediate sociopolitical world into his fiction. Barth himself rarely addresses politics in his essays and other nonfiction works, and such brief moments are often carefully embedded in very detailed discussions of form. Because such instances are few and far between in his writings, as recently as 2005 scholars have comfortably discussed Barth's "eager[ness] to put aside the entanglement of the everyday world in order to define fiction as something that transcends its occasions."[40] Similarly, Barth's explicit focus on the formal qualities of his work and the various possibilities open to storytellers often allows readers and critics to focus exclusively on the complex textuality of his works, bolstered by such comments as "I wanted to write a novel that would consist of documents,"[41] which encourages critics to chase him down the rabbit hole of textual self-reference.

As a writer of Historical Romance—and particularly as a participant in the reevaluatory stage of the development of the mythology of the American frontier—Barth cannot escape completely from the cultural influences that led to and characterized the 1960s, even if many read Barth as seeking to avoid "the entanglement of the everyday world." As Kurt Müller has noted of the development of historiographic metafiction, "It was certainly the political situation of the 1960s which was conducive to the re-emergence of historical interest."[42] One characteristic example of the seemingly insignificant, yet pervasive centrality of politics in Barth's work appears in his oft-cited study of postmodern fiction, "The Literature of Replenishment: Postmodernist Fiction." Taking to task the usefulness of "critical categories," Barth claims that "actual artists, actual texts, are seldom more than more or less modernist, postmodernist, formalist, symbolist, realist, surrealist, politically committed, aesthetically 'pure,' 'experimental,' regionalist, internationalist, what have you."[43] In this list, Barth includes "politically committed" within a grouping of stylistic categories by which literature can be classified or evaluated. I argue that Barth's fiction operates similarly: although the stylistic aspects of Barth's work are more clearly articulated and explored than its political implications, those political implications are embedded in his work.

In fact, just as in his list, political implications may in fact be central. Barth rarely addresses his own politics in print, and when he does write on political subjects, he attempts to remain objective (though not neutral). Rather than discussing his own political views, he describes situations generally. In his most overtly political piece of nonfiction to date, "A Poet to the Rescue," Barth focuses his attention on the work of his friend and former student, the poet John Balaban. Originally published in 1972, this essay discusses the importance of poets such as Balaban, who traveled to Vietnam in the midst of war in order to save the native poetry. However, despite his clear sympathy for Balaban and his work,

Barth does not openly criticize the war or the United States government. In the introduction to this essay that appears in *The Friday Book: Essays and Other Nonfiction* (1984), Barth explains that "during the period of our war in Vietnam I remained apart from, though sympathetic to, the great antiwar demonstrations in our cities."[44]

However, in his 1973 commencement address to the graduating class at Western Maryland College, Barth overly critiques the "military-industrial complex": "public and private education get by on austerity budgets, while General Motors, as the saying goes, could still buy the state of Delaware if DuPont would sell it. Most maddening of all, while veterans of the Pentagon's war on southeast Asia go on relief and/or turn to crime to support a drug habit picked up in service, the budget for the Department of Defense crazily *increases*, to make the world safer for no one except the military-industrial complex. Talk about addiction! The Pentagon is the most expensive habit in the world, and apparently the hardest to kick. It has turned us into death-freaks, mugging and burgling our other priorities to pay for a dreadful militarist fix that fixes next to nothing."[45] And while this clear invective led to charges, as Barth recalls, that he was "a flaming socialist whose return to the Free State of Maryland was to be regretted,"[46] he points out in the essay itself (albeit parenthetically, as if as an aside) that he is not a socialist, but rather a person who "certainly prefer[s] life in this country to life in the large socialist countries."[47]

It would appear that although Barth has on occasion—and generally in either small public addresses or small-print circulations[48]—made scathing attacks on the social, economic, and political world of 1960s America, he has done so without specifically addressing his own political tendencies as did his contemporary E. L. Doctorow. This does not mean, however, that one must guess at Barth's politics. Aside from his implied critiques of established authority, Barth has on occasion made reference to his politics in print, though the works in which they appear are not overtly political. For example, Barth closes "The Literature of Exhaustion" with a lament that it is "distressing . . . to *us liberal Democrats* [that] the commonality, alas, will *always* lose their way."[49]

In a 1980 interview, Barth makes another reference to the sociopolitical climate in which he wrote, arguing:

> History exists in the documents and our knowledge of history exists only in the published interpretations of the documents. Where the events are in history, they're kind of removed and behind all that.

> Therefore, history in an almost literal way, is a dream that we keep re-dreaming. What went on in black life from the days of the first slaves up until the 1960s would depend on which generation is understanding the dream that somewhere back there we became independent. But we keep re-dreaming the dream generation by generation. And the changing of the perception does not concern even the subjects of the dream.[50]

What Barth here is addressing, as Heïnz-Joachim Müllenbrock noted, is "the question of whose history deserves to be handed down to posterity."[51] Although the rhetorical shift that allows Barth to associate himself with the black dreamers of the 1960s may appear odd to readers unfamiliar with the way he uses his fiction to assume and manipulate perspective and authorial voice, what is important here is that he identifies the 1960s as a major turning point in the political life not just of one group of people but of the nation as a whole. Further, Barth here addresses the importance of documents in our understanding of history; knowledge of history comes not from the facts of history, or from the documents that record those facts, but from the interpretations of those documents. As different people interpret these documents, different interpretations will arise. As significant changes in the sociopolitical climate affect the ideological assumptions of a nation, major changes to the interpretation of such documents are inevitable.

As such, in his 1960 American Historical Frontier Romance *The Sot-Weed Factor*, Barth is (along with Doctorow) prefiguring the kinds of critiques of history and the value of historiography that will come to characterize much of the social and political work of American fiction throughout the period. Similarly, he is also (again with Doctorow) inaugurating the reevaluatory stage of the development of the mythology of the American frontier. I am not arguing here that Barth carefully incorporates his political agenda into an otherwise powerful statement of narrative limitation and artistic freedom. Rather, I claim that the times were such that writers could scarcely avoid participating in their political development, similar to what Barth once noted as the "much greater likelihood . . . that the author will project his/her contemporary sensibility back onto our ancestors."[52] Instead of overwhelming his readers' senses with the political atmosphere, in Barth's texts one can—as he once commented—"sniff traces of tear gas in its margins."[53] Barth, like Doctorow, challenged the establishment of authority in general by challenging the establishment of *Author*-ity, calling into question the power that authors—and the documents they produce—have in the establishment of a national mythology.

As Linda Hutcheon has now famously stated: "The intertextual parody of historiographic metafiction enacts, in a way, the views of certain contemporary historiographers (see Canary and Kozizki): it offers a sense of the presence of the past, but this is a past that can only be known from its texts, its traces—be they literary or historical."[54] I will go one step further and suggest that Barth's romance does not suggest that the past can only be known from its texts; rather, he suggests that it cannot be "known" at all. All that can be known of the past is the texts, and the texts (as Barth will demonstrate) may be inaccurate, will likely be misread, and will certainly fail to give us a true picture of the past.

In order to provide his critique, Barth selects the chronotope of the Maryland frontier of the late 1600s for his epic work of reevaluation. In a 1971 interview, Barth discussed the hold that colonial Maryland had on him while researching for *The Sot-Weed Factor*, alluding to Stephen Dedalus's famous comment in *Ulysses* that "History is a nightmare from which I am trying to awake." For Barth, history is "in many ways nightmarish, but reading the documents [of Maryland's colonial history], one laughs in one's sleep."[55] Maryland's history includes such events as pirate captures, sexual escapades, and political intrigues, all of which Barth treats humorously in *The Sot-Weed Factor*. However, Barth also alludes to the fact that he "was deep into the idea of the mythical America by that time."[56]

And as all great myths require mythic characters—who in all likelihood will be white men—Barth presents his readers with Henry Burlingame III, friend and tutor to Ebenezer Cooke, hapless protagonist (cut from the same cloth as Doctorow's Blue) of *The Sot-Weed Factor*. Early on, Burlingame explained to Cooke that "we sit here on a blind rock careening through space; we are all of us rushing headlong to the grave. Think you the worms will care, when anon they make a meal of you, whether you spent your moment sighing wigless in your chamber, or sacked the golden towns of Montezuma? Lookee, the day's nigh spent; 'tis gone careening into time forever. Not a tale's length past we lined our bowls with dinner, and already they growl for more. We are dying men, Ebenezer: i'faith, there's time for naught but bold resolves!"[57] Coming at the end of a personal history that borders on the mythic in its scope (including treacherous affairs and adventures at sea), Burlingame argues that because the larger world cares not for the actions of man, then neither should he. Further, given the continued need to satisfy one's physical desires, one should do all in one's power to both gratify those desires and explore their depths. Such seemingly amoral behavior has its source; as the reader comes to learn as the narrative unfolds, Burlingame's lack of footing—moral, national, political, and even physical (given his ability to alter his features at will)—comes from his being an orphan, a seemingly "self-made man" in the tradition of Daniel Boone and his inheritors of rugged individualism.

In attempting to uncover his personal history, Burlingame discovers two lost documents: *The Privie Journall of Sir Henry Burlingame*, whose author Burlingame believes to be his grandfather, and Captain John Smith's *A Secret Historie of the Voiage Up the Bay of Chesapeake From Jamestowne in Virginia*, believed to be a first draft (and more honest account) of the adventures recorded in Smith's *The Generall Historie of Virginia, New England, and the Summer Isles* (1624), one of the first documents to characterize the American frontier in mythic terms. These documents, pure inventions by Barth—and so "false documents" that, like Blue's journal, remind the reader of the loose relationship that documentary evidence has with historical fact—are the major source of his critique of the American frontier myth and its inheritance as passed down through such documents as Smith's *Generall Historie*.

The first of the two "false documents" that Barth introduces into his narrative—*The Privie Journall of Sir Henry Burlingame*—is an account of Captain John Smith's travels in Virginia by one of his shipmates, a fat, clumsy, and comic figure whose presence on the journey brings more harm than good to the company. Often chastised by Smith himself, Sir Burlingame keeps his own "privie journal" as a corrective to Smith's boasting and, as is suggested, false record of the journey. The most significant variation from Smith's published journal is his account of his relationship with Pocahontas. Smith's official record of the incident (which Burlingame III has appended to his grandfather's journal), reads as follows:

> At his entrance before the King, all the people gave a great shout. The Queen of *Appomattoc* was appointed to bring him water to wash his hands, and another brought him a bunch of feathers, instead of a towel to dry them: having feasted him after their best barbarous manner they could, a long consultation was held, but the conclusion was, two great stones were brought before Powhatan: then as many as could laid hands on him, dragged him to them, and thereon laid his head, and being ready with their clubs

> to beat out his brains, Pocahontas the King's dearest daughter, when no entreaty could prevail, got his head in her arms, and laid her own upon his to save him from death: whereat the Emperor was contented he should live to make him hatchets, and her bells, beads, and copper; for they thought him as well of all occasions as themselves.[58]

This story, commonly taught in history classes and the subject of much subsequent art, Cooke finds to be "a marvelous rescue!"[59] Burlingame, having read his grandfather's account, corrects Cooke, replying, "'Tis a marvelous romance . . . not so wonderous heroic after all" (148). Though Pocahontas does save Smith's life in Sir Burlingame's account, claiming that she "wd rather she loose her owne head, then that they shd dash in his," that event only begins Smith's trials as opposed to ending them.

Pocahontas, whose name Sir Burlingame translates as "she of the smallnesse and impenetrability" (153), is discovered to be a virgin, whose maidenhead could not be taken by any of the men in her tribe, resulting from her "tympanum therein so surpassing stout as to render it infrangible." Because Pocahontas has saved Smith's life, and as no man has yet been able to take her virginity (though not for lack of trying, Sir Burlingame points out), Smith is named as her fiancé and is set to yet another trial. Pocahontas, we are told, "heard with greate joye" this proclamation, due to her taste for carnal sport (154).[60] But should he fail, Powhatan warns, Smith shall be clubbed to death. This fragment of the *Privie Journall*, ending at Smith's acceptance of his new trial, distorts the famous rescue scene, changing it from an example of heroism and self-sacrifice (befitting the mythology of the American frontier) to one of carnal lust. Pocahontas's efforts at saving the life of an important Englishman (itself often read as a sign of white English superiority, to say nothing of a woman sacrificing herself for a male authority figure) are thus recast to show her as an opportunistic harlot, described by Sir Burlingame as "deprav'd as was her consort" (152). Of course, one should not be surprised that in both accounts, Smith's masculinity is defined in opposition to Pocahontas's femininity. Both Smith's original account and Barth's politically informed critique uphold the characterization befitting what Connell has defined as "men of the frontier."[61]

Pocahontas has been recast, but not in any way that as yet challenges the gender politics of the mythology. The more significant recasting is that of Smith, who is shown to be anything but the heroic adventurer that his journal proclaims him to be. Sir Burlingame recounts Smith's proclamations regarding his "fanc[ying] him selfe a Master of Venereall Arts, and boast[ing] to have known carnallie every kind of woman on earth" (148). Further, he is seen as headstrong and foolish (for ignoring Sir Burlingame's warnings about Indians, and thus walking them into capture, "as had been predicted by men wiser than our Capt"); cowardly ("our leader, for his part, shrewdlie pull'd that Ganelon our Guide before him for a shield, and retreated in all haste" [149]); and gluttonous ("gorg[ing] himself very like a swine in the slaughterhouse" [151]). Of the Pocahontas episode, Sir Burlingame later remarks that "yet he cannot contain his lewd exploit, but must still catch privilie my eare, and declare that hers was the most succulent flowr ever he pluckt" (734). Far from being the bold, heroic, and a capable leader history (by means of his journal) remembers him as, Captain John Smith is described by Sir Henry Burlingame as decidedly unheroic.

And here we see where the Smith mythology shares many characteristics with the Boone mythology; in both cases, certain values (hard work, heroism in the face of danger, etc.) are to be revered, as they lead to success on the American frontier. To be discovered as common may not sound damnable, except that through such a description Barth works to strip Smith's mythic inheritance from him. Such myths, based on "false documents," end up doing more harm than good as they may shield the truth of the events from those who inherit the mythic tales and employ them as cultural standards. Even on its face, in other words, the mythology of the American frontier fails to provide an accurate sense of the past, instead providing a highly skewed construct supporting an ideology that accepts the superiority of white men.

However, substituting Sir Henry Burlingame's journal for Captain John Smith's as the source text for the true events of the Pocahontas myth is just as disastrous as uncritically accepting Smith's. Without corroboration, one should argue, the new document may be just as false as the original. Worse yet, the reader comes to learn—from both Sir Burlingame's journal and Captain Smith's *Secret Historie*—that neither may be accurate accounts, given the enmity between the two writers. The existence of multiple, contradictory accounts of historical events highlights the potential fallibility of all such documents. With respect to the Pocahontas episode, however, Captain Smith's *Secret Historie* shows Sir Burlingame's account to be, if not true, at the very least corroborated. The published version, therefore, is revealed to be false, a self-serving account meant more for the establishment of Smith's mythic stature than for the recording of historical events. With this revelation,

Barth shows how written texts have been used by others to consciously establish a mythology. Smith's *Generall Historie* is a false document in that it does not accurately reflect history, but rather establishes a mythic tradition that is used to hide the factual events from the reader. But, as Burlingame points out when he first discovers this journal, it is only such false documents that provide such "marvelous romance," the stuff from which myths are created.

More importantly, at least for the characters in the narrative, the *Secret Historie* also exposes the truth behind Sir Burlingame's disappearance, and the reason he is not accounted for at all in the *Generall Historie.* Having been captured by the Ahatchwhoops, and facing the possibility of execution, Smith offers Sir Burlingame to the Indians as a proxy for an upcoming trial to determine authority over the tribe. Leadership, absent a direct line of ascendancy, is determined by the Ahatchwhoops according to appetite: he who can eat the most is the most fit to rule. Sir Burlingame, being larger than anyone in the company or any of the Indians, becomes a participant in this farcical trial for the kingship of the Ahatchwhoops.[62] Without being informed that his participation will cost him his life should he lose or his freedom to leave should he win, Sir Burlingame wins the contest. Afterward, as Smith's *Secret Historie* records, Burlingame "in all innocence," is surprised when "the Salvages lay'd hands on him, and mauger his whoops and hollowings, bore him back to the Kings hutt, to reign over them with Wepenter [the Ahatchwhoop with whom he shared power] for ever." With this episode, Smith ends his *Secret Historie*, writing of the "scurvie, barbarous countrie," "whither (God wot) I shall never return, nor yet (God grant) any other Englishman." Further, Smith swears his crew to secrecy, and comments that this episode shall never "appeare in my greate *Generall Historie*" (565). Not only does Smith make the conscious decision to produce for the public a false document of his travels, but he plans on its being "greate," a source of mythic importance, which is already censored to eliminate events that cast an unfavorable light on Smith.[63]

By introducing counterfeit documents into his text, Barth questions his readers' knowledge of the American frontier and the mythic heroes who explored it, as well as the authority of the documents from which their knowledge is inherited. However, where the presumed existence of the *Privie Journall* and the *Secret Historie* challenge the historical record and the mythic inheritance, it is the interpretation of such documents that provides the most distortion. Barth has commented on the fact that "history exists only in the published *interpretations* of the documents."[64]

Such interpretations, as Barth demonstrates with Smith's *Secret Historie*, may be flawed. The section of the *Secret Historie* discussed above is that which was held by the Ahatchwhoops, who call it *The Book of English Devils*, a sacred text in their tribe that recounts the trials that brought to them the great leader Sir Henry Burlingame, whose son the Tayac Chicamec still holds power. The reader learns, as does Henry Burlingame and Ebenezer Cooke, that Sir Burlingame inspired the Ahatchwhoops to become a scourge upon the English, no doubt as a result of his anger at being left behind, given his earlier condemnations of the "salvages." Sir Burlingame is so inflamed that, although his son bears the name Henry Burlingame II, Sir Burlingame will only call him by his Ahatchwhoop name, Chicamec. Further, "every day he would read *The Book of English Devils*, and further inflame the Ahatchwhoops to murther any white man who fell into their hands" (569). Sir Burlingame's inflaming the Ahatchwhoops to a hatred of the English—which hatred is the impetus for their coming war against the English in Maryland—was done, in part, through a conscious misreading of the *Secret Historie*. Because the Ahatchwhoops could not read English—even Sir Burlingame's son needs a translator to speak to Henry Burlingame III and Ebenezer Cooke—their knowledge of the book's contents could come only from Sir Burlingame.

Sir Burlingame's intentional misreading of the *Secret Journal* is apparent when Chicamec explains of *The Book of English Devils*: "Its tale you know: how my godlike father, the Tayac Henry Burlingame One, did best the Attonceaumoughhough as champion for Wepenter, and drove the English devils from our land" (568). As the reader knows, the *Secret Historie* does not show Sir Burlingame driving away Smith and his companions; rather, there is an account of Burlingame uttering "whoops and hallowings" upon his being dragged back to the village. Burlingame's interpretation of the events (events of which we cannot ever know the truth), therefore, became the basis for both the Ahatchwhoops' understanding of the historical events, as well as for their elevating Sir Burlingame to mythic stature in their tribe. Burlingame is thus a failed frontiersman, whose self-perpetuated mythic stature was built upon the misreading of a false document (perhaps as a nod to metaromance, as we saw with Doctorow). However, despite his importance as a mythic heroic figure, Burlingame is not the protagonist of this tale; that honor belongs to the hapless Ebenezer Cooke.

Loosely drawn from the life of a historical personage, Ebenezer Cooke is a minor poet sent to America to run his father's sot-weed (tobacco) plantation in Maryland. Poet by temperament if not by actual vocation, Cooke seeks to gain the official, written recognition of Lord Baltimore as poet laureate of Maryland, in which service he will attempt to write an epic attesting to the glory of the province, his ill-fated *Marylandiad*, a false document of a different sort. Among the other important false documents of the text are the minutes of the 1691 Maryland Assembly, which, due to the shortage of paper in the colonies, were recorded on pieces of both of the lost journals by Burlingame and Cooke. These documents are also sought after to quell a rebellion by one John Coode, a shadowy political intriguer who appears to operate as an all-purpose enemy to established authority, and who has tried on multiple occasions to capture Ebenezer Cooke (though his motives, like his actual identity, are never discovered).

The various documents, therefore, serve multiple purposes and have multiple meanings, depending on who is seeking them and for what purpose. For Henry Burlingame III, these documents will inform him of his personal history and establish his place in the world; further, because Burlingame is a spy for Governor Nicholson, these documents will help establish the political order he is working to secure in Maryland. For Governor Nicholson, John Coode, and Lord Baltimore (who is seeking to reclaim authority over Maryland after it was revoked by King William), possession of these documents will aid in each establishing the possessor as Maryland's political leader. And for Ebenezer Cooke, who is interested in both the personal and political implications of these documents, the journals serve primarily as sources for a wondrous adventure—a romance, if you will—exposing the private stories of major figures in American history, whose actions have become the backbone of America's founding mythology. Although all of the seekers of these documents intend to use them to establish some sort of authority, Barth shows that such documents—if not the act of writing itself—have no inherent authority; as such, all documents used to establish authority are false. In the end, any authority is granted *despite* the existence of such documents.

Barth's critique of the use of documents to establish authority permeates all of the book's subplots, as well as the main story line focusing on Ebenezer Cooke, and allude to his failure as a frontiersman. To begin with, Cooke is by no means a laudable poet; his comical failures remind one of Blue's: neither failed frontiersman possesses talents similar to Daniel Boone's. Both are by turns cowardly, indecisive, ignorant of the native populations, and incapable of surviving long by one's own means.

Both are (slightly) more successful as chroniclers, but, as both learn (albeit in in different ways), they are incapable of accurately chronicling their adventures. The very first thing the reader learns of Cooke is that he is a "rangy, gangling flitch" who is counted among "the fops and fools of the London coffeehouses" (3). If we compare descriptions of Boone and Cooke, we can see just how unheroic a figure Cooke embodies. Boone was once described as follows: "His large head, full chest, square shoulders, and stout form are still impressed upon my mind. He was (I think) about five feet ten inches in height, and his weight say 175. He was solid in mind as well as in body, never frivolous . . . but was always quiet, meditative, and impressive, unpretentious, kind, and friendly in his manner."[65] By contrast, Cooke is described as "a Heron of a man, lean-limbed and long-billed, he walked and sat with loose-jointed poise; his every stance was angular surprise, his each gesture half flail. Moreover there was a discomposure about his face, as though his features got on ill together: heron's beak, wolf-hound's fore-head, pointed chin, lantern jaw, wash-blue eyes, and bony blond brows had minds of their own, went their own ways, and took up odd postures" (3). Although such a description might suggest how memorable Cooke should be (though as a figure to be mocked rather than admired), one should remember that throughout the story Cooke is impersonated by a variety of men, of vastly different appearances.

Unlike Boone, whose positive impression lasted upon the many who met him, Cooke is both unimpressive and forgettable. And his poetry—the work he performs on the frontier—is as awkward as his bearing: Cooke is "more ambitious than talented, and yet more talented than prudent," and his poetry is "aclang with jarring rhymes, and string-taut with similes stretched to the snapping point" (3). Cooke's application to Lord Baltimore for the post of poet laureate of Maryland—a request in keeping with his ambition if not his talent—is approved, but not on the basis of his poetic genius; in fact, during the long interview Cooke has with Lord Baltimore, never once is he asked to produce an example of his verse for inspection, nor is it important that Cooke has yet to publish so much as a couplet. In other words, unlike the mythic frontiersmen who earn their successes based on their efforts, Cooke is granted a meaningless sinecure. This oversight occurs, both the reader and Cooke eventually learn, because it is Henry Burlingame III who approves the appointment, not Lord Baltimore.

Burlingame, posing for Lord Baltimore in order to help advance his own political intrigues, pens for Cooke his commission to write the *Marylandiad*. This commission becomes instrumental (in appearance, at least) for establishing the identity of the laureate. Numerous of Cooke's acquaintances assume his identity and use the commission as their proof. Both Burlingame and Burton confess to having drafted copies of the "original" commission to aid them in establishing themselves as laureate. As such, the laureate's identity was fraudulently established by multiple people, using forged copies of a document that, even in its original, was a forgery. In fact, as Cooke is reminded at the end of his interview with Lord Baltimore, the Calvert family no longer has political authority in Maryland; the king has instituted a governor on his own behalf. Lord Baltimore reminds Cooke that "I have no authority . . . and so can no longer confer dignities and titles" (92). So not only is the official commission itself a forgery, but one penned by the true Lord Baltimore himself would have had no more legal authority than any of the forgeries. This official commission, to which many appealed with respect to the identity of a person and his title, proves to be a "false document" indeed, and by the end of the work is useless in establishing Cooke's position as laureate. Rather, it is Cooke's satiric verses on Maryland—rather than his intended epic—that win him the fame he originally desired.

The notion of a *Marylandiad* might be, to many readers, comic in its own right, given that "Barth chooses a location that, as Leslie Fiedler says, has little mythic import for us, and a period of history that is generally skipped over in history books." However, as much as it may add to the comic nature of the work as a whole, Linda S. Bergmann has argued that "Maryland is a fine choice if . . . Barth intends to destroy our myths in general, to suggest that history itself is impossible." Because Barth is using historical figures that are not generally well known, and dealing with a political battle that is similarly obscure, many of his readers are learning about this history for the first time. Barth's readers are no more informed than his characters, of whom Bergmann claims, "the more his characters learn about Maryland, the more impossible they find it to establish casual connections, prove responsibility, tell which side anyone is on, or distinguish good from evil." Bergmann also notes that "facts are but little help" for either the characters in the story or the readers.[66] Because the reader is likely ill-equipped to challenge Barth's use and misuse of history, one is able to appreciate the humorous aspect of the text as well as recognize its challenge to the historical record.

After having recounted Maryland's messy political history to Cooke, Burlingame (in the guise of Lord Baltimore) instructs him to "put her history out of mind and look you at her peerless virtues" (92). Although

Cooke interpreted this charge to mean that he should look past the political squabbling, the reader comes to learn that Cooke takes this instruction far too literally. Cooke ignores Maryland's history in the composition of his *Marylandiad*, and even manages to ignore Maryland itself, taking his cues instead from his own idealistic notions of what such an epic should describe. Cooke's first rhymes for his *Marylandiad* describe the majesty of the *Poseidon*, the ship on which he is scheduled to sail:

> *Let Ocean roar his damn'dest Gale:*
> *Our Plank's shan't leak; our Masts shan't fail.*
> *With great* Poseidon *at our Side*
> *He seemeth neither wild nor wide.* (168)

Though Cooke is later criticized by Burlingame for the quality of the verses, what is most important to note are the circumstances preceding their composition. Cooke has not so much as seen the "*great* Poseidon," let alone set foot on any such vessel. From its very beginning, Cooke's *Marylandiad* is less a true record of his journey to Maryland and an investigation of its virtues than a rehearsal of generalized poetic conceits, fitted only circumstantially to certain aspects of his voyage. In this regard, the *Marylandiad* is not unlike the mythology of the American frontier: a narrative whose idealized notions reflect more accurately the prevailing ideology than the historical events on which they are loosely based.

The rest of the *Marylandiad*—what little of it was actually written—is similarly composed, serving as Barth's criticism of the tendency of the epic poem (or any "official" text) to mythologize historical events and agents. Cooke writes further verses on the glory of the "*noble Ship, from Deck to Peaks*," as well as on her captain, "*like a briny God*," whom he has yet to meet (176). He sings the praises of all aspects of his yet to be undertaken voyage, down to the quality of the meals: "*Ne'er were such Delights . . . / E'er served to* Jove *and* Junos *Breed*" (177). Cooke will later learn the state of affairs regarding the ship itself, her dishonorable captain (who is in league with pirates serving Coode), and the quality of the food served. However, his most startling education comes at the hands of the ship's crew, whom he originally praised as "*noble, salty* Tritons *race, / Who brave the wild* Atlantics *face*" (176). After suffering a blow to the head during a storm and being nursed to health by the crew, Cooke is nearly raped by his would-be saviors. Unable to fight them off, Cooke is rescued only by a cry on deck, summoning the crew to respond to a pirate attack. In his confused condition, and not yet informed of the situation above decks, Cooke composes (but does not write down) his first honest verses of his voyage: "Hell *hath no fouler, filthier Demon: / Preserve me,* LORD, *from English Seamen!*" (234).

His last attempt at poetry for some time, this couplet reinforces for the reader the falsity of the *Marylandiad* as a document attesting to Maryland's virtues. The *Marylandiad*—though unfinished—is a "false document," and as such cannot establish the kind of authority or have the effect that Cooke had in mind when he asked for his commission: to help restore Lord Baltimore to power. And given Coode's various attempts at capturing Cooke, it would appear that there would be great power indeed in such an epic. The falsity of Cooke's text is further established by the physical document itself. Early on, Cooke attempts to purchase a journal for his poetry in London before shipping to Maryland. Because he has never made such a purchase before, he is confused at all the options; and being unable to decide—and frustrated at the bookseller's inability to help him—Cooke grabs the first volume he can and storms out of the shop. Later, he learns that he mistakenly grabbed the bookseller's account ledger, amusingly paralleling Blue's own ledgers (which are written into, the reader assumes, the ledgers he keeps for the town's water usage). What Cooke steals is a document whose purpose is to accurately record business transactions;[67] what he writes into this book, on the other hand, is a romantic fantasy.

Once the falsity of Cooke's document is sufficiently established for the reader, Barth is then able to turn that document to the frontier itself. After glimpsing an Indian, Cooke proceeds to write a very long series of rhymes with respect to both the character of the "salvage" as well as his history. The Indian is described as "*wild*" and "*Barb'rous*"; his character is damned as a result of his "*Lewdness, Lust, and Fornication*" (377). A representation of the very opposite of civilization, in Cooke's opinion, the "salvage" races' history is recounted in the lines that follow, offering such absurd suggestions as their descent from the lost tribes of Israel to their genealogical connection to Cain. At the end of his speculations, however, Cooke simply asserts that they were "*engender'd in the Fires of* Hell" (379). Because the reader already knows his *Marylandiad* to be a false document, Cooke's philosophizing on the nature and history of the Indians is to be similarly discarded. Barth here shows the reader the ignorance of even the supposedly learned English settler with respect to the natives in America.[68]

Ultimately Ebenezer Cooke, whose childhood reading consisted of such romantic, mythic adventures as "the *Odyssey* and the

Metamorphoses... [and] the tales of Robin Good-Fellow" (5), found himself unable to complete his task as poet laureate of the Province of Maryland. His intention to "sing of the heroic founding of that Province! The courage and perseverance of her settlers in battling barb'rous nature and fearsome salvage to wrest a territory from the wild and transform it to an earthly paradise" fails; in its stead, Cooke composes a satire on his lot, which he later publishes under the title "The Sot-Weed Factor" (75). Returning to his poetry after some weeks, Cooke describes Maryland and its inhabitants as nothing but "scoundrels and perverts, hovels and brothels, corruption and poltroonery" (457), and instead decides to sing of his true experiences:

Condemn'd by Fate, to wayward Curse,
Of Friends unkind, and empty Purse,
Plagues worse than fill'd Pandoras Box,
I took my Leave of Albions Rocks,
With heavy Heart, concern'd that I
Was forc'd my native Soil to fly,
And the old World must bid Good-b'ye. (458)

The rest of "The Sot-Weed Factor," from what little Barth supplies in the text, shows Cooke's complete reversal of attitude with regard to Maryland, his voyage thereto, and the people he meets along the way.

From this opening, however, the reader can see how the myth of the American frontier has failed, at least for Ebenezer Cooke. Forced to leave England, Cooke's journey runs contrary to the aspect of the American frontier myth that inspires hope in those who would willingly come to seek out their fortunes by working the land, Boone-like, in the "heroic founding" that Cooke wrote of earlier. The New World, far from being the hospitable land of plenty and ease promised by Smith, ends up nearly destroying Cooke physically, emotionally, and financially. He discovers that the New World is not a welcoming land of opportunity, but rather a refuge for those who, like him, had to flee the civilized Old World. What Cooke learns through his adventures is that the myth of the American frontier is just that: a myth, not a reality.

To make his point regarding false documents one final time, Barth has Cooke express surprise upon learning that his poem was hailed in London as "a fine example of the satiric extravaganza currently in vogue" (753). Just as the Ahatchwhoops misread Captain Smith's *Secret Historie*, Cooke's London audience misreads his poem. As such, the one "real" document incorporated into this text—Barth quotes the historical

Cooke's 1706 poem for his own fictional purposes—is misread, showing that the intention of the writer is less important than how his audience reads his work and the use to which that text is eventually put.[69] The historical texts that Barth mentions—Smith's *Generall Historie* and Cooke's "The Sot-Weed Factor"—are intentionally misread in order to challenge the authority of written documents. Similarly, Barth introduces into his text fictional documents—Smith's *Secret History* and Sir Burlingame's *Privie Journall*—in order to challenge the notion that any one document can be appealed to for authority.

Finally, various characters forge, copy, and misread (intentionally or otherwise) all of these documents, by which Barth demonstrates to his readers that the myth of the American frontier is built upon romance, fantasy, and lies, rather than on accurate accounts of true events that have been correctly understood by succeeding generations of Americans. And if this were not complicated enough, Barth's *The Sot-Weed Factor* as it exists today is a revision of an earlier work by the same title, "a farcical rewriting of his former parody of an earlier literary text."[70] Barth's work thus buries the historic texts within three levels of literary invention, all of which the reader must negotiate, at every stage forced to come to terms with the document-based nature of history. Barth frames his work with the only two accurate (if such a distinction is still possible) historical instances unchallenged by the text: Ebenezer Cooke's birth in London and his eventual publication of "The Sot-Weed Factor." Barth's Historical Romance demonstrates that the "truth" of the myths we inherit, if such truth is to be found at all, lies buried within the history that has been passed down to us, just as we saw that Barth's politics lie buried within his discussions of form and style.

Although Earl Rovit appears to get Barth's joke when he comments that "I do not think that *The Sot-Weed Factor* is the novel that John Barth intended to write," the rest of his essay shows that he did not.[71] Rovit notes that the work may hold some "interest" for students of contemporary literature, but is otherwise little more than a "prolonged kind of academic joke."[72] Rovit notes that Barth likely misuses the historical record, but he brushes aside his own comment by also claiming that only a scholar of colonial Maryland could call him on his abuses. Of course, Barth's text was not intended to replace the historical record; rather, it points the readers back to that record. Barth does not ask his readers to rely on his text for Maryland's colonial history. Just the opposite; *The Sot-Weed Factor* calls into question our reliance on "the historical record" and highlights the fact that all such records and narratives are subjective documents composed out of fact, fiction, hypothesis, and intentional mythologizing. Barth himself admits to having misused history, admitting to doing "a respectable amount of homework on the historical periods involved. But it was a novelist's homework, not a historian's."[73]

Barth's use of history in *The Sot-Weed Factor* is not meant to be as faithful to the historical record as possible (especially considering the use he makes of historical documents). His intention is not to simply re-create the historical record for the purposes of creating fiction, but rather to draw from it details that help him to address his "real concerns, which will be the *passions of the human breast* and the possibilities of language."[74] And as if the reader has not yet come to doubt the authority of the written text, Barth reminds us elsewhere of such a necessity, when he alludes to himself as "an author who imitates the role of Author."[75] Like his contemporary Doctorow, Barth shows his readers the falsity of all documents, all acts of Author-ity, by reminding us of the difference between an author (one who writes) and an Author (one in whom we invest authority by means of written documents).

Barth also echoes Doctorow's interest in the "theme of our lives" in his intention to record the "passions of the human breast." Barth's primary goal, as he mentions in nearly all of his "Friday pieces," is to tell stories. As he explains in "Historical Fiction, Fictitious History, and Chesapeake Bay Blue Crabs, or, About Aboutness": "Rule #1: *Fiction about history almost never becomes part of the history of fiction*. . . . The trouble with much official history . . . is that it is poetry: It tells us how its sponsor wishes things had been. 'History is the propaganda of winners,' etc. And the trouble with much historical fiction is that it's so concerned with getting the 'facts' straight—as given in the documents of history—that the artistic truth gets lost. The data might be correct, but the hearts and minds and souls of the characters come from Hollywood, not from human history."[76] What Barth has provided, in other words, is a romance in the tradition of Hawthorne, a world someplace between the "Actual" and the "Imaginary."[77] He is primarily interested in a truth that can only be apprehended once we get past traditional historical documents which, as he continually asserts, often prove to be false.

As such, Barth provides a very early example of what Linda Hutcheon would later term "historiographical metafiction," in the way that it "works to situate itself within historical discourse without surrendering its autonomy as fiction," though recognizing that such work is also at the very heart of the tradition of the Historical Romance tradition in American letters.[78] With his contemporary Doctorow, Barth inaugurates a new fictional mode (as Hutcheon has noted) as well as a new turn in the development of our national mythology, using his fiction to provide a reevaluation of the frontier myth as a response to the social and political developments of his own time. And like Doctorow, Barth constructs a narrative that highlights the dual failure of the mythology of the American frontier: first, Ebenezer Cooke fails to live up to the mythic role provided by such figures as Daniel Boone. More important, however, is the failure of the mythology to provide a socially progressive narrative. As we will see in chapter 2, Barth's epic adventure sets the stage in many ways for Thomas Pynchon's later work along these same lines. However, as we will also see, Pynchon's critique of the frontier mythology will extend beyond notions of the historical record and characterizations of the failed frontiersman to the mythology's racist underpinnings (to which Doctorow and Barth merely alluded).

2 / "Crimes of Demarcation": Spatial and Cultural Transgression in Thomas Pynchon's *Mason & Dixon*

There is no line, straight or crooked, suitable for a national boundary, upon which to divide.

—ABRAHAM LINCOLN, "MESSAGE TO CONGRESS, DECEMBER 1, 1862"

Along with his contemporary John Barth, Thomas Pynchon has produced dense, complex works that challenge readers and critics alike with their formal and thematic convolutions. Just as the works of both writers are now widely considered to belong to the canon of historiographic metafiction, both writers were labeled early on as "black humorists," a critical categorization that predated postmodernism and included many who became leading postmodern writers.[1] For the purposes of the present study, *The Sot-Weed Factor* and *Mason & Dixon* read as parallel texts in many ways, despite the nearly forty years that separate their respective composition: as exemplary instances of historiographic metafiction, both employ fictionalized versions of real historical figures whose legacy of mythic frontier masculinity is transmitted by the texts they inscribe; both make use of "false documents" to challenge textual authority and confuse their readers' assumptions about early America (specifically in their creation of the *Marylandiad* and *Pennsylvaniad* as fictionalized national epics); both writers return to important periods in the development of the American frontier in order to challenge the frontier mythology; and finally, both works are set in Maryland.

Although this last point may seem minor, one should not forget how Barth employs colonial Maryland as a microcosm of American colonialism in general; nor should one forget the importance for later generations of the boundary between Maryland and Pennsylvania that Mason and Dixon inscribe onto the landscape; the Mason-Dixon Line became the cultural and political marker between the slave and free states during the American Civil War, providing an instance of inscribing the "color-line" onto the landscape, with serious social and political consequences.[2] The colonial impulse in America, Pynchon demonstrates, can be read as an attempt to impose the order of civilization onto the complexity of the frontier. One key means of imposing order was through the imposition of a racial order, whereby ethnic minorities would be barred (in practice if not always in law) from full participation. America's political lines are drawn, quite literally in this instance, with respect to color: are African Americans free or slave? As I will demonstrate below, one of the many tasks taken up by *Mason & Dixon* is the demonstration that we cannot have social or political order when we segregate and enslave any part of the population. And because America's foundational mythology refuses to accept this truth, those who actively participate in its lies are doomed to failure. This is but one of the negative results of such impositions in "the reinvention of myth as a viable attitude in relation to the past" that Monika Fludernik identifies as a central component of historiographic metafiction.[3]

Recent scholarship continues to pair Barth with Pynchon, as evidenced in Gary Thompson's claim that both writers use their work to demonstrate how "official histories repress or edit the past into a blessing of their enterprise," offering a corrective that is "not a 'correct' interpretation, but an account of the processes of knowing."[4] In his recent study *Thomas Pynchon & the Dark Passages of History*, David Cowart notes that "both Pynchon and Barth remind the reader that truly disinterested discourse does not exist—least of all for historians."[5] Similarly Amy J. Elias's *Sublime Desire: History and Post-1960s Fiction*, which "examines late-twentieth-century examples of the historical novel in relation to recent postmodern cultural assumptions and the traditional historical novel form,"[6] ends with a discussion of *The Sot-Weed Factor* and *Mason & Dixon*, reading these "huge, baggy monsters of novels" as "reenergiz[ing] the historical romance genre by inverting its dominant, melding fantasy, anachronism, metafictionality, and other fabulatory techniques with the facts of history."[7]

I would argue, however, that one cannot take for granted any such notion as "the facts of history." As Barth has shown in *The Sot-Weed Factor*, what has been taken for historical fact may well be a combination of arbitrary textual selection (which narrative do you read?) and willful misinterpretation (does that narrative conform to your existing world-view?). In fact, it is the very notion of "the facts of history" that post-1960s American Historical Frontier Romancers are out to challenge.[8] As the proliferation of narratives—fictional and factual, textual and oral—increased in the late twentieth century, the very notion that "the facts of history" can be acknowledged and disseminated itself became a myth. This is why Pynchon works within the romance tradition: while working with historical figures, he is not bound to historical fidelity. And like Doctorow and Barth before him, Pynchon engages with the romance tradition to reevaluate the nation's founding mythology.

However much it shares with John Barth's, Thomas Pynchon's career has been significantly different, particularly given Pynchon's lack of public essays, addresses, and even a public persona. A known recluse, Pynchon does not deliver commencement speeches, teach creative writing at the university level, or write many articles for popular periodicals.[9] As such, it may appear to be difficult to identify Pynchon's politics, and specifically his response to the social and political developments of the 1960s that I argue characterize his discussion of the American frontier mythology. As with E. L. Doctorow, Pynchon's politics are often read with respect to his sympathetic treatment of characters who participate in the counterculture, such as the oft-recurring Pig Bodine, a seaman with no respect for military (or any other) authority; Tyrone Slothrop, the sympathetic protagonist of *Gravity's Rainbow,* who acts as unwitting guinea pig for various experiments in human behavior by a complex of forces best described as the military-industrial machine; Zoyd Wheeler, ex-hippie and countercultural hero of *Vineland*; Doc Sportello, private investigator and pothead protagonist of *Inherent Vice*; or Webb Traverse, a known anarchist and the likely bomber targeting railroad and mining operations in *Against the Day.* However, unlike Doctorow, Pynchon has not publicly addressed politics at large, and certainly not the political implications of his fiction.

This is not to say that one must guess at Pynchon's politics, or come at them merely through an understanding of his fictional characters and their sympathies. One could also look at who reads Pynchon and for what reasons. Some critics who work with Pynchon's texts are admittedly sympathetic to the counterculture of the 1960s, and were drawn to Pynchon in no small part because of their own political leanings. Two such critics who have produced book-length studies on Pynchon's work are Molly Hite and Stefan Mattessich. In her preface to *Ideas of Order in the Novels of Thomas Pynchon*, Hite claims: "I became interested in Pynchon's work in 1966, when I first read *V.* My immediate reaction to that novel tends to contradict one of the charges most commonly leveled at Pynchon's writing: whether or not Profane, Stencil, and the Whole

Sick Crew are 'round' or 'flat' characters, I was convinced I *knew* them, traveled in some of the same circles, and could recognize the rhythms of their speech in Pynchon's uncannily precise dialogue."[10] Although one may have difficulty imagining anyone traveling in the same circles as the Whole Sick Crew—a perpetual party-on-the-move whose alcohol and drug binges are financed in part by participating in an alligator-hunting expedition in the sewers of New York City—I believe that Hite is trying to establish that she moved in countercultural circles, that she was familiar with those who, in the 1960s, worked to defy tradition and establishment in cultural and political affairs. That she "could recognize the rhythms of their speech" shows that she had direct communication with and sympathy for anti-establishment individuals.

Stefan Mattessich, speaking of his own "countercultural life," claims that his book, *Lines of Flight: Discursive Time and Countercultural Desire in the Work of Thomas Pynchon*, "grew out of a desire to explore the relation between the double nature of writing and the 'personal' dimension of the countercultural moment in American life—personal not only for Pynchon but for me as well, since my parents 'went north' (to Mendocino) in the early 1970s, catching me up in a movement of escape from the exigencies of modern urban and technocratic life."[11] Where Hite traveled in the countercultural circles represented by the Whole Sick Crew, Mattessich was caught up more generally in the wake of the 1960s. His family's desire to escape the problems of urban and technological development in their move to Mendocino drew them to the locale of Wanda Tinasky, whose letters to such Mendocino Valley weeklies as *Commentary* and *Anderson Valley Advertiser* (a well-known leftist publication) are believed by many to have been written by Pynchon.

Wanda Tinasky's letters appeared between 1983 and 1988, the same years Pynchon spent in California working on his novel *Vineland*. Tinasky and Pynchon each critique "the failure of the counterculture and the ongoing depredations of our capitalist society's 'tyrants and proprietors and monopolists' (as Emerson calls them in *Vineland*)."[12] Although addressed to a local audience, the letters betray the same sweep of national and historical issues that often permeate Pynchon's works, with the same political sympathies. This is not the place to comment on whether or not Pynchon did in fact write these letters; nor is it particularly relevant. What is important to my study is why many scholars and readers hold this belief. Aside from the circumstantial evidence that Moore provides in his foreword (both stylistic and biographical), Moore claims that the writer of Tinasky's letters shares with Pynchon "his countercultural roots [and] his leftist/populist politics."[13] Mattessich, for example, describes Pynchon as working in the "cultural crucible" of the 1950s and 1960s.[14] This "crucible" includes such political movements as "the New Left, the women's movement, the civil rights movement, and the gay rights movement."[15] And although Pynchon cannot be directly identified with any of these movements, his works—especially *Vineland*, which Cyrus R. K. Patell claims "is Pynchon's most openly political novel"[16]—certainly show sympathies for a wide spectrum of anti-establishment cultural and political movements. It is for this reason that David Cowart can claim that "Pynchon's novels and other short stories revolve in planetary orbits around the sunlike moral intensity of the sixties."[17]

While surveys of the political landscape of Pynchon's work have already been provided by such critics as Patell and Mattessich,[18] I would like to look briefly at Pynchon's now-famous *New York Times Book Review* article "Is It O.K. to Be a Luddite?" This article—which narrates a history of Ludditism and its application to those living in a world equipped with nuclear weaponry—may be Pynchon's clearest attempt at political self-identification. However, like many of Pynchon's writings, its clarity is murky at best. Early in this article, Pynchon describes the original Luddites—those who "flourished in Britain from about 1811 to 1816"—as "the counterrevolutionaries of that 'Industrial Revolution.'"[19] By characterizing Luddites as "counterrevolutionaries"—a revolution against a revolution, and thus counterculture by two degrees—Pynchon is setting himself up to be read as a "counterrevolutionary" when he later identifies himself with the modern manifestation of King Ludd's followers.

In closing his essay, Pynchon follows "well-known President and unintentional Luddite D. D. Eisenhower" in his belief that "there is now a permanent power establishment of admirals, generals and corporate CEO's, up against whom *us average poor bastards* are completely outclassed."[20] Pynchon's identification with those "average poor bastards" who are displaced by the military-industrial machine, or, as Patell terms it, the "technopolitical order,"[21] justifies those critics like Mattessich who characterize Pynchon's corpus as "a meditation on post-war society and its own countercultural desire."[22] Further, one can assume Pynchon's audience to be sympathetic to his casual reference to Karl Marx: "It took no German philosopher, then or later, to point out what this [the development of knitting machines, against which the original Luddites raged] did, had been doing, to wages and jobs."[23] Although Marx and his political philosophy have become common knowledge, I would suggest that Pynchon here intends to make this reference as an insider would, suggesting to his readers his own political sympathies.[24]

Pynchon similarly alludes to an association with the New Left of the 1960s in his introduction to his collected early stories, *Slow Learner.* And in another of his rare acts of political self-identification, he notes that, in opposition to the traditional university life of the 1950s, "*we* had begun to get a sense of that other world humming along out there. Some of *us* couldn't resist the temptation to go out and see what was happening . . . a preview of the mass college dropouts of the '60's."[25] As with his "Luddite" essay, Pynchon does not use this time to engage in a thorough discussion of the political scene, instead making quick references while introducing his first attempts at fiction. Interestingly enough, one of these short pieces, "The Secret Integration," represents Pynchon's earliest efforts to address race relations in America. *Mason & Dixon* thus continues his efforts to expose America's troublesome issues with race relations. He critiques America's problematic relationship with Africans and African Americans by both narrating fictional scenes of racism based on colonial American (and European) views of slaves and native populations, as well as suggesting—through its focus on a marker of great sociopolitical significance—that these concerns continued to reappear throughout major moments of American history, in particular the Civil War and the 1960s.

In another of his rare nonfiction works, Pynchon explored racism in America in the 1960s for the *New York Times Magazine* in 1966, in "A Journey into the Mind of Watts." Writing this piece after the unprovoked killing of Leonard Deadwyler, a black resident of Watts, by a white police officer—who was later acquitted—Pynchon describes for his readers the socioeconomic condition of Watts, and attempts to expose the reasons for past (as well as upcoming) race riots in that area. In language that now seems to echo his discussion of race relations in *Mason & Dixon* in terms of physical geography, Pynchon writes of "their landscape, both the real and the emotional one": "Watts is a country which lies, psychologically, uncounted miles further than most whites seem at present willing to travel." One can read Mason and Dixon's expedition to chart the boundary line between Pennsylvania and Maryland in colonial America as a journey into America's racial frontier, as Pynchon's attempt to have whites travel that psychological distance in order to expose them to America's dark racial subtext. That Pynchon is aware of both the racial conflict as well as the culture of Watts's inhabitants, is implied by his references to both "the Muslim and civil-rights movements,"[26] as well as to "the dirty dozens."[27]

These various attempts to tease out Pynchon's political leanings—to suggest his sympathies with respect to the sociopolitical movements of the 1960s—will hopefully serve as useful background in understanding Pynchon's fiction, which is where all discussions of his politics always begin and end. In many ways, he shares the sympathies of his contemporaries Doctorow and Barth, particularly with respect to a desire to frustrate notions of order and challenge the unquestioned inheritance of grand historical narratives. Further, Pynchon shares with his contemporaries the need to expose the dual failure of the myth of the American frontier: first, by showing the ways that frontiersmen—in this case, actual historical figures—failed to exemplify the mythology as defined by such figures as Daniel Boone; and second, by highlighting the ways that the mythology itself has failed subsequent generations of Americans. In this regard—as one can see from Pynchon's comments on Watts as well as the selection of America's most famous "colorline"—one would rightly expect that *Mason & Dixon* should address issues of race more explicitly than did either *Welcome to Hard Times* or *The Sot-Weed Factor.* Although many of his works allude to the frontier mythology and explore various borders, *Mason & Dixon* is the work in which he most directly addresses the myth of the American frontier.

In *Mason & Dixon*, Pynchon fictionalizes the meeting of Charles Mason (1728–1786) and Jeremiah Dixon (1733–1779), the British astronomer and surveyor who were assigned to chart out and map the boundary line between Pennsylvania and Maryland (1763–67). Narrated by the Revd Cherrycoke to his family during the "Christmastide of 1786,"[28] the narrative of Mason and Dixon's adventures interweaves numerous other historical personages, such as George Washington and Benjamin Franklin, with fictional figures, such as a talking dog and a mechanical duck, in order to provide a humorous commentary on the Age of Reason, exposing it less as a hallmark for rational thought and more as a time of great confusion. Such confusion is aptly represented in the assignment given to Mason and Dixon; their findings were to settle disputes about the location of the border between the two states, which had been hotly contested by the Calvert and Penn families, which had each received grants from King Charles II for overlapping pieces of land.[29] However, although Pynchon situates the text on the frontier chronotope of the Maryland/Pennsylvania boundary in the 1760s, he begins his narrative much earlier in order to introduce his major characters and begin his critique of the racism inherent in assigning arbitrary political boundaries.

Before Mason and Dixon draw the boundary between Pennsylvania and Maryland, they are first paired to mark the Transit of Venus, bringing them to Africa. There they are presented with a lush, wild landscape, whose exoticism is matched only by the daughters of their hosts, the Vroom family. Both the landscape and the women, Pynchon demonstrates, are considered wild frontiers to be conquered and tamed by men. Overwhelmed by the landscape and all it provides, Dixon exclaims one morning that "One feels as Adam felt,—even better, as Eve" (84). Initially ignorant of the social atmosphere of this new Eden, Dixon characterizes Sumatra as a garden of earthly delights, including the sins of the flesh. And just as Dixon is the first of the geometers to sample the varied native delights, he is also later the first to feel shame at the treatment of blacks in Cape Town, just as Eve was the first to taste of the forbidden fruit and to feel the subsequent shame that accompanied her knowledge. Dixon's comment aptly demonstrates the various assumptions based on sex that run throughout the narrative but are rarely addressed explicitly. Here, Dixon suggests that Eve has the better part of the bargain in the Garden of Eden, despite the details of the story: Eve is created as Adam's subordinate, fails to adhere to the rules of the Garden, and her actions cause their fall and subsequent expulsion from Paradise.

As this one offhand comment reminds the reader, the adventures recounted by Revd Cherrycoke are tales of men, told for the enjoyment and edification of the younger generation.[30] As we will see throughout, the aspects of the frontier mythology to which Pynchon attends are those that involve manly exploits; this, of course, is because of the sex-based limitations of the mythology itself. In this myth, women were secondary figures and window dressing. (Or, in the case of Tenebrae, part of the audience for such tales, along with the children.) As such, we should read into Astronomer Royal Nevil Maskelyne's suggestion that "the Reign of Reason [will] cheerily dispose of any allegations of Paradise" a tinge of irony, as Pynchon will demonstrate that the Age of Reason was built upon the oppression and enslavement of dark-skinned peoples as well as the oppression and exclusion of women (134).

The allure of the frontier myth does not infect Mason and Dixon alone (discussed in detail below), who as newcomers cannot be expected to understand the rich cultural history of Sumatra and its relations with European colonizers. Even those who live in Cape Town, the center of civilized (European) authority, come to read the frontier as an idealized space. Soon after Mason and Dixon's arrival, Police Agent Bonk, perfectly characterizing Albert Memmi's description of the colonial seeking "an easier life . . . , adventure, the picturesque surroundings" of the frontier, gives up his position to strike out as a farmer.[31] Calling to mind later images of the move west across the American landscape in the nineteenth century, Bonk is ready to "put my Family in an Ox-waggon, and start North. Perhaps over the Mountains. Out of the reach of the Company. . . . The Mountains beckon'd, the vast Hottentot Land beyond." Seeking to escape the overwhelming control of "the Company"—the East India Company that attempts to define the socioeconomic boundaries of the geographic spaces within its reach—Bonk has invested the African frontier with all of the positive aspects that remind the reader of the American frontier mythology: "Out there are green rolling Leagues of farmland and Range, Bushmen for the most part docile, I am assur'd, wild Game ev'rywhere, and best of all no more Company orders to obey" (154). Willfully misreading the frontier in ways reminiscent of those described by Doctorow and Barth in chapter 1, Bonk assumes that an easier life exists beyond the boundary of the civilization that up to this point he has presided over but never crossed. With no experience as farmer or hunter, he expects an easy time given the abundance of land and game. However, as police chief, one of his previous duties was to quell native unrest; he is perhaps the last person who should anticipate the docility of the natives, demonstrating how easily one can be seduced by this mythology.

Contrasting Bonk's assumptions of native docility, upon hearing that their father is off to his own frontier adventure in America, Mason's sons imagine natives in a much different light.[32] Excitedly exclaiming that their father will explore lands dominated by "Snakes! Bears! Indians!" (201), the boys exhibit the European racist attitude that Native Americans are equivalent to other species of dangerous animals found in the wild. Mason himself acknowledges the need for strength in his frontier adventure when he tells his boys, while carrying one in each arm, that "I'll need to be at least this strong, in America" (212). That male pioneers need to rely on their physical strength to overcome the dangers of the frontier represented by the savage native inhabitants (be they animals or men) is a stock characteristic of the national mythology based on the legendary exploits of Daniel Boone, and suggests as well that Mason will be engaged in such manly exploits, even though his actual employment is more intellectual than physical. In fact, much of this physical labor will be performed by ethnic minorities.

The sentiment is echoed by Rev[d] Cherrycoke's audience, many of whom are children. After Brae comments on the difficulty of economic success in America, her father corrects her, claiming that "anyone with the necessary Drive can make a go of it here." Adding to this sentiment is DePugh, who comments that, "in thinking of the West . . . in those Wilds,—so 'tis said,—ev'rywhere to be found . . . and the Powers being already long known to the Indian medicine-men, Business opportunities await the alert Practitioner." The necessity of physical strength is here expanded to the broader notions of strength of character, by which trait all may succeed, for in America, "Competition is of her Essence!" (217). Of course, business concerns are also a traditionally masculine affair, as we also saw in Blue's desire to practice law on the frontier and Ebenezer Cooke's appointment to his father's sot-weed farm in Maryland. The characters in *Mason & Dixon* all appear to accept such gendered assumptions, likely based on their acceptance of the mythology.

Dixon, representing failure differently, feels trepidation for his upcoming adventures. His dream of America brings to light his foremost fear: the natives. Although Dixon was the one who most openly embraced the native culture of Africa, Pynchon here shows his readers the dominance of Native American stereotypes in the European mind-set (a stereotype we briefly encountered in *The Sot-Weed Factor*). In his dream he pictures "a Score of Savages," all "shouting strange jibber-jabber, the words incomprehensible, yet the vowels unmistakably North British" (243).[33] Not quite people, these "Savages" are imagined as living beyond reason. Further, Dixon shows that he is incapable as yet of defining reason in terms other than his own; the "Savages" here are employing Dixon's own "North British" dialect, but are unable to make any sense with it. Other references to the savagery of the Indians are dropped throughout the text, as in the comment made by R. C., one of the Americans whom Mason and Dixon meet while working on "the Line." After swallowing Dixon's chronometer, R. C. remarks that such a move makes him incapable of "sneak[ing] up on an Indian someday" (325). One would only need to "sneak up on an Indian" if one has malicious intentions.

Such intentions are echoed years later by the young boys in Revd Cherrycoke's audience. Pitt, hungry for the romance he assumes must have characterized Mason and Dixon's adventures, reminds Cherrycoke that "You *did* mention Indians." Pliny immediately follows this reminder with what he believes to be an appropriate question: "Do the Surveyors get to fight anyone, at least?" (316).[34] Pynchon is here demonstrating that even after a full generation of social advancement in the New World, Indians are still thought of as a savage force to be exterminated, particularly by means of the brute masculine strength that European men will bring to the frontier. The implication is clear: the advancement of civilization does not include a more humane understanding of race relations.

This is not to say, however, that change is impossible. Soon after beginning their task of drawing "the Line," Mason and Dixon are told of the "first Connestoga Massacre." After reflection, we learn that "Mason did note as peculiar, that the first mortal acts of Savagery in America after their Arrival should have been committed by Whites against Indians." Further, as the narrative voice (presumably that of Rev[d] Cherrycoke) reminds the reader: "They saw white Brutality enough, at the Cape of Good Hope. They can no better understand it now, than then. Something is eluding them. Whites in both places are become the very Savages of their own worst Dreams, far out of Measure to any Provocation" (306–7). Having witnessed it once before, Mason and Dixon are better prepared to recognize white brutality when they meet it again. One may argue that this is why Pitt and Pliny remain ignorant, as they have yet to encounter such brutality outside of the stories read to them.

That this recognition comes at the start of Mason and Dixon's mapmaking project is telling. As the pair come to realize, their work is part of the larger project of cultural domination promoted by Europe under the guise of political and economic authority. This is the "Something" that eludes them, and that comes to light only after they have participated in the European effort to inscribe authority onto the American landscape. Or, as Henk van Houtum has aptly put it: "Looking at the world, describing the world, is to a large extent also the art of learning to read space that cannot be put on a map."[35] It is in this respect that Mason and Dixon can come to represent "American Adams," as David J. Greiner reads them, in relation to Natty Bumppo, the most recognizable literary American Adam with respect to the frontier (and one of the more memorable figures in the later development of the Daniel Boone mythology). As Greiner points out, "whereas Natty turns west to escape the sound of axes, Pynchon's bonded males bring the axes with them."[36] And just as Mason and Dixon must learn through their wilderness experience what Natty seemed to always know, they must similarly learn Natty's racial tolerance and respect for the chaotic landscape.[37]

Speaking to his family members in the winter of 1786—the year that Charles Mason died—Cherrycoke describes the work on the now-famous Mason-Dixon Line as follows: "what we were doing out in that Country together was brave, scientifick beyond my understanding, and ultimately meaningless,—we were putting a line straight through the heart of the Wilderness, eight yards wide and due west, in order to separate two

Proprietorships, granted when the World was yet feudal and but eight years later to be nullified by the War for Independence" (8). Of course, readers know that the line was neither meaningless, nor entirely nullified by the War for Independence, given its continued use as a marker on America's cultural landscape and as a means through which history is often remembered with respect to American slavery.[38] But in his denunciation of the importance of this line, Cherrycoke does introduce to the reader the various aspects of the American frontier myth that Pynchon will be addressing in the rest of the work. By moving "due west," "through the heart of the Wilderness," Mason and Dixon represent in microcosm the exploration and settlement of the American West that will come to embody the narrative of the American frontier myth. That their work was "brave" despite their living in a world "yet feudal" (precivilized, according to European standards) links this party to other explorers of the American West, like Daniel Boone, who have come to represent the positive aspects of the American frontier mythology. Finally, that the work—"scientifick beyond my understanding"—involved inscribing a "straight" line, allows one to read Mason and Dixon's task as part of the larger work of the Enlightenment in general and American colonization in particular, a bringing of order to complexity.[39]

However, despite my assertion that the Mason-Dixon Line continues to carry significant meaning in the contemporary world, it is Cherrycoke's characterization of the Line as "ultimately meaningless" that will come to dominate Pynchon's text by demonstrating that man-made boundaries either are meaningless or they produce only negative effects on both the land and the people. Such boundaries are not an indication of reason and order, and ultimately demonstrate the failure of the mythology of the American frontier by showing how the civilizing efforts brought about by Boone and his followers wreaked havoc upon succeeding generations of Americans. One instance of the former involves Charles Mason, who has recently lost his wife, as he continually attempts to cross the boundary between this life and the next. Early on, Mason seeks the advice of the Learnèd English Dog, who "has led him to presume there exist safe-conduct Procedures for the realm of Death." Mason's ultimately unfulfilled desire to transgress this line will haunt him throughout the book in the various dreams of Rebekah that follow him from England to Africa to America. Mason—"Mopery" as Rebekah calls him in his visions—never recovers from his "Hyperthrenia" ("Excess in Mourning" [25]) due to his inability to cross the boundary between life and death, a boundary that necessarily exists only in his mind, as he has no understanding of what, if anything, lies on the other side. As a metaphor for the frontier, Mason here learns that we can never truly know what lies on the other side of the border. One could also read in this episode a not-so-subtle suggestion that women don't belong on the frontier adventures of their husbands, not unlike the belief that women brought bad luck on sailing vessels, and were generally barred from participating in the kinds of exploration we see throughout the narrative.

Pynchon's characters invest meaning in other arbitrary lines existing on maps; this is, of course, their job. One such meaningless "surveyor's line" is the equator. Long before Mason and Dixon are assigned to map out the boundary between Pennsylvania and Maryland, they cross another imaginary boundary en route to their African assignment. As a result of the "recreational Vacuum" that is an eighteenth-century oceanic voyage: "the Prospect of crossing the Equatorial Line soon grows unnaturally magnified, as objects in certain Mirages and Apparitions at Sea,—a Grand Event, prepared for weeks in advance. Fearless Acrobats of the upper Courses and hardened Gunners with prick'd-in black-powder Tattoos are all at once fussing about, nitter-nattering like a Village-ful of housewives over trivial details of the Ceremony of Initiation plann'd for those new to this Crossing" (55). Though Cherrycoke only hints at the details of this initiation—little more than the harmless, simple pranks of sailors[40]—Pynchon uses this preparation to highlight how much meaning these men have invested in a line that exists only on a map.

In other words, though the equator may well be "the single shadowless Moment" the sailors believe it to be, it is itself only identifiable on a map. In lieu of other entertainment, the sailors have decided to ritualize the "Crossing" of an arbitrary boundary, one that may stretch around the globe, but has no inherently political, legal, cultural, or even physical significance. Even if the sailors believe the Southern Hemisphere to possess "a newly constellated Sky"—showing why this line would be important to astronomers like Mason—such can be said for any line of either latitude or longitude. Further, that the sailors use this line to mark "all-unforeseen ways of living and dying" hints at Pynchon's later critique of the racist cultural implications of such arbitrary lines as the one later inscribed by Mason and Dixon (56).

Jeremiah Dixon, the one whose surveying work is more closely related to the landscape than the heavens, often recalls the teachings of one Emerson, from whom he learned the craft of surveying as well as the "tellurick" secrets of the earth. In one such recollection, Dixon is told that "Right Lines [give] a clear sign of Human Presence upon the Planet." These lines, as Dixon was taught, convey "Force," and as such occupied the minds of "The Romans" in their various applications, "hydraulic, or military, or architectural" (219). Pynchon here connects the act of inscribing lines of cultural force to the development of the military-industrial culture that Pynchon's works are often read to counter.[41] In addition to the repeated reminder of Pliny, this reference to the Roman Empire—the first great military-industrial colonizer of the Western world—links the act of linear inscription to colonization and empire building specifically, as well as to human presence generally, as if military-industrial development were man's primary work, or at the very least the most telling sign of his presence. Just as important is the implication that this process of colonization and empire building based on the act of manipulating these lines of force is a European process. As Dixon comes to learn in his travels to Africa and America, mapmaking is centrally concerned with establishing a "colorline."

One of Dixon's earliest encounters with a native nonwhite population is during his stay in Cape Town, during his visit to "the Company Brothel at the Slave Lodge," once again subtly linking together natives and women as oppressed populations on the frontier. In this community of "Sylphs of mixed race," Dixon begins to enjoy the various pleasures of the flesh, particularly those associated with the natives. Unlike Mason (whose memory of Rebekah keeps him from many sexual possibilities), Dixon enjoys the erotic pleasures of the natives along with their peculiar cuisine, developing a near-addiction to the *ketjap*. However, Dixon is all too aware that the white community and the slave community are "two distinct Worlds, the Company maintaining their separation" (81). This reference to the East India Company, which not only runs the brothel but also manages most of the interactions between Europeans and natives, hints at the segregation promoted by economic ventures into Africa (and later America), which in large part led to the enslavement or destruction of native peoples. Further, this separation is described geographically, a physical separation of two worlds, not unlike the geographic separation hinted at by the sailors aboard the *Seahorse* when they crossed the equator, and the later geographic separation between free and slave states represented by the Mason-Dixon Line.

That the act of line drawing has economic benefits is not lost on Dixon, who makes his living as a surveyor, drawing out lines that separate property. It comes as no surprise, then, that General Washington suggests to him and his partner that there is "no reason you fellows shouldn't turn a Shilling or two whilst you're over here . . . and have ye consider'd how much free surveying ye'll be giving away,—as the West Line must contribute North and South Boundaries to Pieces innumerable?" (276). That this question comes from George Washington—former surveyor, military leader, Founding Father, and first president—only highlights the connection between the economics of surveying and the political impulses of colonization and empire building. Washington also employs the metaphor of the line in recounting his own economic expeditions on the frontier, for while lost "in the wild Anarchy of the Forest" with the Ohio Company, he and his brothers were "as deep in the savage state as man have been known to venture, [with] often no clear line of Retreat" (281). Here Washington hints at what Mason and Dixon will later discover, and which Pynchon implies throughout to be the mentality of Europeans: civilization and savagery are considered to be geographically separable. Washington's "clear line of Retreat" could be the path taken to extricate oneself from the savage forest. However, it could also be the "colorline" between the states of savagery and civilization, beyond which one can retreat to comfort and safety.

However useful such lines may be for military and economic ventures, defining the boundaries of what is savage and civilized for the purposes of economic exploitation, Pynchon suggests that focusing too much on the lines themselves leads not to the order they are meant to inscribe onto the world, but rather madness and destruction. R. C., a local American surveyor who swallowed Dixon's prized chronometer—a watch that kept perfect time and never needed winding, an Enlightenment dream of order through perpetual motion—has been driven mad by surveying. First becoming "the kind of mean, ornery cuss his neighbors associated with years of Maturity," R. C. later renounces the scientific aspects of his trade in favor of "walking the Terrain, and making noninstrumental guesses." Believing himself to have internalized his work as a surveyor—undoubtedly linked to his earlier "internalizing" of the chronometer—R. C. later develops what others call an "accustom'd Madness" when he "turn'd his hand to the Problem of the Tangent Line" (324).

Nor is the turn to madness a problem only for surveyors. Maskelyne, with whom Mason marks the Transit of Venus, also eventually wanders beyond the line of sanity. Successor to Bradley as Astronomer Royal, Maskelyne eventually stops his scientific work to revel in his own position. His madness is hinted at by his rejection of science (as anti-Enlightenment, and thus opposed to reason and intellect) as well as in his manner of dress. Mason learns that Maskelyne's "Observing Suit" (in which he makes no observations) is "a garment of his own design that his brother-in-law the famed Clive of India sent him from Bengal, where the Nabob had had it cut and sewn with painstaking fidelity to a thirty-page List of Instructions from Maskelyne. It is a three-piece affair, everything quilted, long jacket, waistcoat, and trousers, which have Feet at the ends of them, all in striped silk. . . . It is usually not wise to discuss matters of constume with people who dress like this,—politics or religion being far safer topicks" (728). If Maskelyne is not exactly insane, he is at least childish and obsessive. (What instructions could possibly require thirty pages of explanation?) Further, it is important that Maskelyne received this suit from Clive, his brother-in-law and head of the East India Company. The Company is intimately involved in the economic exploitation of indigenous peoples, and Pynchon here hints at the exploitation of such peoples for the manufacture of unnecessary markers of wealth and idleness in Maskelyne's colorful, oversewn pajama-like suit. Maskelyne's connection to Clive also implies the connection between business interests and scientific exploration. And that it is Maskelyne who must ask favors of Clive and not the other way around implies that scientific advancement is at the mercy of the business community.

Mason and Dixon themselves, however, never suffer from the insanity that others in their profession have, despite the former's bouts with "Hyperthrenia." Rather, it is through Mason and, primarily, Dixon that Pynchon levels his charges against the use of arbitrary lines to segregate populations and thereby mar both the physical and cultural landscape of America. Although most important for Mason and Dixon is the map that they must draw with the proper positioning of the line, they are not ignorant of the physical line that they are cutting across the landscape in order to measure it. Among the first of their obligations is to hire out a company of axmen to chop through whatever stands in their way, cutting a perfectly straight line between Pennsylvania and Maryland as a visual reminder of the line for the area's inhabitants as well as an economic reminder of Mason and Dixon's budget, considering the mounting costs of their venture. Despite these—or rather, because the implications of each have not yet set in for the geometers—Dixon is able to joyfully describe their job as a "pure Adventure" with "Each day impossible to predict" (340). Like Ebenezer Cooke, Mason and Dixon easily slip into the romance of the mythology despite their lived experiences.

This is not to say, however, that Mason and Dixon were not presented with difficulties early on. Their first challenge was finding the Tangent Line, from which they were to begin: "One reason given for bringing

Mason and Dixon into the Boundary Dispute was that nobody in America seem'd to've had any luck with this fiendish Problem of the Tangent Line, which had absorb'd the energies of the best Geometers in the Colonies, for more Years than would remain to some, their lives to the Great Cypress Swamp a Forfeit claim'd. Field parties had gone out in '50, '60, and '61, ending up east and west of various Tangent Points by as much as four tenths of a mile" (344). The problem is that the political powers behind the decision to parcel out land made their judgments not on science, but rather on whim. Mason and Dixon are shown to be merely the latest examples of the use of "Royal Astronomers to tidy things up," suggesting that science is often used to clean up the very real messes made by political authority. In this particular instance, Mason and Dixon are confronted with solving the riddle of "all this Geometrickally impossible territory,—as unreal, in a Surveying way, as some of the other Fictions that govern'd that unhappy Monarch's life."

If the political boundaries such as those drawn by "the dead Hand of the second James" have no basis in the landscape of the region—are in fact impossible to map out on the actual landscape—then such lines can have no clear meaning (336). This is, of course, the case with those who live near this border, those who repeatedly approach Mason and Dixon to find out in which territory they actually reside. James's line of political expediency has no inherent meaning for those who live upon it, because meaning is ascribed after the fact for the local population. Similarly, Mason and Dixon's line will come to have no meaning to the English authorities given the impending revolution. It is for this reason that Cherrycoke can claim to his audience that "there exists no 'Maryland' beyond an Abstraction, a Frame of right lines drawn to enclose and square off the great Bay in its unimagin'd Fecundity, its shoreline tending to Infinite Length, ultimately unmappable,—no more, to be fair, than there exists any 'Pennsylvania' but a chronicle of Frauds committed serially against the Indians dwelling there, check'd only by the Ambitions of other Colonies to north and east" (354). The colonies are not defined by the physical space they inhabit, but rather by what means they are drawn onto the cultural landscape of the colonists. It is here, then, on the boundary between Maryland and Pennsylvania, that the meaninglessness of arbitrary political boundaries meets the negative implications of early America's racial problems.

Although the line is used to critique Enlightenment reason as applied to the complex American landscape, Pynchon shows how it also created local difficulties, on the familial as well as the national level. One such instance occurs "At 3 Miles 49 Chains, [where the Line] went through Mr. Price's House" (446). Mrs. Price, amused by the incident, begins to tease her husband. She reasons that, as they were married in Pennsylvania, their marriage license is not binding in Maryland: "So from now on, when I am upon this side of the House, I am in Maryland, legally not your wife, and no longer subject to your Authority" (446–47). Marriage is another such imposition of order used to oppress, and the housewife here overtly alludes to the "nameless aching dissatisfaction" that Betty Friedan famously explored in *The Feminine Mystique*.[42] Although presented comically, this discussion soon turns to taxes, a very real concern for local residents. Mr. Price's decision to roll the house on logs to Maryland (because it is downhill, and thus an easier move) comes as a result of both the tax issue and the joke about their marriage that Mrs. Price initially raised.

As such, the Line quite literally cuts through the Price household. By the end of the commission, however, Mason and Dixon see that the Line, and all of the conflicts that it raises, are not at all comic. Having witnessed local problems firsthand, Dixon remarks to Mason that the people want "to know how to stop this great invisible Thing that comes crawling Straight on over their Lands, devouring all in its Path"; specifically, the Line has become "a tree-slaughtering Animal, with no purpose but to continue creating forever a perfect Corridor over the Land. Its teeth of Steel,—its Jaws, Axmen,—its Life's Blood, Disbursement. And what of its intentions, beyond killing ev'rything due west of it? do you know? I don't either" (678). The Line has become a force of its own, a living representation of Manifest Destiny, an unconscious will to power, marching west across the American landscape, fueled by economic motivation whose sole purpose is destruction. Dixon also points out that as the Line cares not for the harm it inflicts upon the environment, "imagine how little we care for Indians" (679). The Line becomes symbolic of the destruction that accompanies the myth of the American frontier, the eventual loss accompanying Boone's westward march.

Where "the Line" should represent, as Arthur Saltzman suggests, an "unconflicted vision for the landscape," such "unconflicted vision" does not represent "purposeful progress, reliable boundary, and stabilizing accuracy." And if, as Saltzman states, the Line "indicates a moral vector," it does so only by suggesting a line that should not have been crossed.[43] Where Dixon once saw his chance to work his way into the American frontier as an adventure, he now learns that his work has been purely destructive. Further, Dixon is not wholly unaware of the later cultural symbolism his line will have. If the Line for Dixon has become a force of destruction with respect to its treatment of the environment and the native populations, how much worse has it become to Pynchon's readers, who know it as the dividing line between slavery and freedom? That it negatively affects all who come into contact with it is seen in the later characterization of the Line as "a conduit for Evil" (701). As a conduit, a line whose purpose is transmission, its "Evil" does not stop when Mason and Dixon stop drawing it. Rather, its negative influence is carried through succeeding generations, a permanent reminder of the failed attempt to inscribe order on the complex American landscape, a failure of the mythology of the American frontier.

If lines in general—and the Mason-Dixon Line in particular—are markers of political and cultural problematics, then maps must be worse, being collections of such lines. Speaking of King James's "Geometrickally impossible territory" that Mason and Dixon must accurately survey along the Tangent Line, Cherrycoke tells his audience that "Kings and Princes are so stupid, they pretend maps that can't be drawn, and style them 'Pennsylvania'" (336). As Mason and Dixon learn through their efforts at following the Tangent Line, maps often more accurately express political will than geographical reality. The order that a map imposes is very different from the order it proposes to represent. Finally, mapmaking makes explicit the racism that arises out of Mason and Dixon's attempts at inscribing order on the American frontier.

Pynchon's first reference to maps in *Mason & Dixon* comes with the introduction of his titular characters to Africa. That Mason and Dixon do not remember their passage clearly, it "having pass'd like a sailor's hasty dream between Watches," highlights their inability to understand "the unreadable Map-scape of Africa." Africa is an unreadable map precisely because it is uncivilized, outside of the boundaries of European culture; Africa is in "this new Hemisphere, this haunted and *other* half of everything known" (58). Just as Mason and Dixon's crossing of the equator brought them into a racially defined world of savagery filled with "all-unforeseen ways of living and dying" (56), so does this movement to Africa bring them into the savage land of the "*other*," that which is unknown, that which is beyond reason. That natives are both dangerous as well as beyond reason is implied by Police Official Bonk's reactions to Mason when he first arrives. When Mason launches immediately into a discussion about his mission, his inability to restrain himself offends Bonk, who remarks that this is "precisely the sort of English Whiggery . . . that here is much better left unexpressed." Bonk is concerned because Mason does not yet understand the racial conflict, and is acting "so unrestraint'd . . . , how much more dangerous may his rattling be in the hearing of others,—even of slaves?" (59). Although Bonk never explains why such "English Whiggery" may be dangerous around the slaves, his fears alone mark the racist culture that Mason and Dixon have just entered. I would argue, however, that Bonk's concern comes from a fear of exposing the slaves to reason because, as Mason and Dixon learn and as Pynchon's readers already know, slavery is unreasonable.

The Dutch of Cape Colony, the reader shortly thereafter learns, are kept "behind a Boundary" established by the Company, which, as we have seen, attempts to control all aspects of Europeans' contact with the colonized populations (68). As Stacey Olster reminds us, "by the time that Mason and Dixon make their 1760s expedition to America, the East India Company has shifted from a trading to an armed power, mirroring the British empire's own shift from the pacifist trade policies of Robert Walpole to the militaristic one of William Pitt."[44] This "Boundary" is both a physical and a cultural marker. Dixon, who early on learns that "'tis Slavery, not any form of Desire, that is of the essence" of the culture of Cape Colony, must make special efforts to interact with the native population (68). Traveling at night, Dixon must go increasingly farther from the safety of the Vroom household in order to sample the local pleasures of the flesh, culinary as well as carnal. And although Dixon describes his movement spatially—"I'm seldom all the way outside their Perimeter,—yet do I make an effort to keep to the Margins close as I may"—the cultural implications are made clear, as it is "*their* Perimeter," referencing "the Company" (69, emphasis mine). Dixon continues in his explorations, in time acquiring a "nasal map of the Town," internalizing the physical geography (78). That such internalization does not drive him mad, as a similar internalization will later push R. C. beyond reason, can be attributed to Dixon's growing sensitivity to racial tensions. It is Dixon's desire to celebrate native culture, as opposed to the efforts at segregating it from the European colonies, that keeps him sane. And because of Dixon's efforts to erase the cultural lines of force that represent their political counterparts of official maps, he is able to recognize the racist effects of his later work in America.

In addition to being employed by those in political power for the purpose of inscribing order onto the complexity of the frontier, or an objectification of an abstract idea, maps are also used as a metaphor with respect to the transmission of knowledge. Mason evidences this belief in his discussion with Bonk, as well as in various places where he extols the virtues of stargazing. Dixon, himself a mapmaker and as such aware of his own use of mapmaking as a metaphor, is instructed by the Rabbi of Prague and his followers about the secret behind America. Speaking of religion, and specifically of "God's project of Disengagement" with respect to America, Dixon is told that "the Secret was safe until the choice be made to reveal it. It has been denied to all who came to America, for Wealth, for Refuge, for Adventure. This 'New World' was ever a secret Body of Knowledge,—meant to be studied with the same dedication as the Hebrew Kabbala would demand. Forms of the Land, the flow of water, the occurrence of what us'd to be called Miracles, are all Text,—to be attended to, manipulated, read, remember'd" (487). America itself is here a text, one that if read properly can expose its secrets to the reader, not unlike the texts of Blue's ledger or Cooke's epic.

The map that Mason and Dixon will eventually draw of their Line will thus become an important text in exposing America's "secret Body of Knowledge" for its readers, presumably the powers-that-be (read military-industrial complex) who commissioned Mason and Dixon's work. Those who wish to control that "secret Body of Knowledge"—those political and economic forces that exert their influence on the colonies—can do so by ordering an accurate textual representation of the landscape. Further, this knowledge is specifically kept from the colonists. Those who would wish to understand America, therefore, must learn to read the "Text" of America's map. Those colonists who came to America in order to participate in the American dream, which offers up the American frontier as a place of economic advancement, safety from oppression, and the excitement of adventure, are not told of America's secret. I would argue that this secret is the truth of the frontier myth, that those reasons for coming to America are bogus. As we are shown throughout *Mason & Dixon*, only the Company seems able to take economic advantage of America. The adventure of the frontier often leads to violence or madness, and America is certainly no refuge for anyone not white, male, and European.

The importance of maps as a marker of knowledge, especially as a tool in early American politics to aid in the project of nation building, is implied by the specific historical personages Pynchon selects to represent in *Mason & Dixon*. As Stacey Olster has noted:

> It is worth remembering how many of those who later became known as Founding Fathers assumed similar roles [as surveyor] over the course of their careers. George Washington chose surveying as

> his first profession and over one hundred maps either surveyed or annotated by him exist today. Benjamin Franklin produced his own map of the boundary between Maryland and Pennsylvania in 1733 and, in collaboration with his cousin Timothy Folger, later prepared the first accurate chart of the Gulf Stream, based on thermometer readings. Thomas Jefferson, whose father was also a surveyor, published his "Map of the Country between Albemarle Sound and Lake Erie, 1787" in England after the Revolutionary War.[45]

The Founding Fathers worked to identify and fortify the borders that defined America as a space, geographically as well as politically. One should note that Washington, Franklin, and Jefferson (white men all) also authored numerous texts defining the boundaries of the American physical and moral character, as well as pieces of political legislation. Further, all three participated in the American Revolution. Washington, Franklin, and Jefferson represent, for Pynchon, the complex forces—literary, military, political, cultural, spatial—that created America. That Franklin was also a leading businessman (and Washington himself had economic interests in the frontier)[46] only helps the reader to identify the three characters as representing the "military-industrial machine" which, similar to the East India Company (itself a "military-industrial machine" of a different order), failed in its attempts to impose order on the complexity of America.

The political implications of mapmaking are brought to full relief in the map that Dixon draws upon the completion of their task. Dixon is given the job of textual inscription, having had years of experience and possessing a professional mark. This mark, "the 'Flower-de-Luce.' A Magnetickal Term," has a different meaning for Mason. Where for Dixon this mark, "among Brother and Sister Needle-folk in ev'ry Land" is "known universally," Mason points out that others may read it as "a reassertion of French claims to Ohio" (688). Mason here recalls all of the political implications of the Line, domestic and international. Local magistrates on both sides of the Line were interested in using it to settle claims, just as King James commissioned it to settle a political dispute. The reader will also here remember the other various political claims made with respect to the Line during its inscription, from the Swedish irredentist who was looking to reclaim America for his Viking ancestors, to the Chinese *Feng Shui* master who attempted to foil the Jesuits' master plan of American domination. Eventually settling for Dixon's explanation that "it does not generally benefit the Surveyor to debase the Value of his North Point, by lending it to ends Politickal" (688–89). Mason asks, "So this is the Line as all shall see it . . . and all History remember?" (689). Although Mason here assumes that the work of the "Map of the Boundaries" is completed, the reader of *Mason & Dixon* knows better. The inscription of this line as a political boundary between Pennsylvania and Maryland is only the start with respect to the Line's importance as a marker of cultural difference, and as a geopolitical reminder of America's exploitation of African and African American slave labor.

In his study *Negative Liberties: Morrison, Pynchon, and the Problem of Liberal Ideology*, Cyrus R. K. Patell claims that both Morrison and Pynchon "set their fractured narratives against the grain of official narrative," and as such "dramatize the failings of Emersonian liberalism by dismantling the official story that it promotes." Specifically, "both novelists recognize that Emersonian individualism and U.S. individualism more generally remain marred by an old pathology, namely, the country's historical tolerance for, even its dependence on, slavery and the subjugation of nonwhite peoples. Their novels depict both the phenomenological horror of the slave's experience and the continuing perversion of the practice of individualism by the ideological residue of slavery and subjugation—a residue that includes not only racism but also both the relentless materialism of twentieth-century consumer culture and the continuing power of the myth of rugged individualism."[47] Patell here links the "residue of slavery" to the "myth of rugged individualism," one of the cornerstones of the masculine American frontier myth as embodied by Daniel Boone. Further, Patell bundles together these two issues with the "relentless materialism" that many have identified as a major concern in Pynchon's texts and is most clearly addressed in his "Luddite" essay. For Patell, *Mason & Dixon* is "a story about the eighteenth-century American frontier from the vantage point of twentieth-century border studies" and "a revisionist narrative that uses the historical novel to expose the underside of European and American history."[48]

However, Patell's discussion of *Mason & Dixon* is slight compared to the developed analyses to which he subjects Pynchon's other works, just as Mattessich devotes less time to *Mason & Dixon* than to any of Pynchon's other texts, especially with regard to its response to the countercultural movements of the 1960s. I propose, however, that it is in *Mason & Dixon* that we can most clearly see Pynchon's response to these countercultural movements, particularly the civil rights movement. Pynchon specifically sets his frontier romance on the Mason-Dixon Line, the political boundary that served to separate slave states from free states in the cultural imagination (as opposed to any of the other numerous boundary disputes that characterized America's nation building). This "boundary" only lost its national political implications after the Civil War. However, as Pynchon demonstrates throughout his fiction, the twentieth century inherited an institutionalized racism that could not be resolved by the erasure of arbitrary political boundaries. In other words, the racist inheritance that was marked by the Mason-Dixon Line persisted up through the twentieth century; Pynchon is reminding us that slavery has inscribed itself onto the American cultural landscape permanently.

One reason for Dixon's sensitivity to racial issues may be his religious background. As he explains to one American he meets, Blackie: "''Tis not how British treat Americans,' Dixon amiably rubescent, ''Tis how both of You treat the African Slaves, and the Indians Native here, that engages the Friends more closely,—an old and melancholy History . . . My allegiance, as a Quaker born, would lie, above all Tribes, with Christ'" (568). Dixon here elevates the cause of freedom for the slaves—still barely in its infancy with respect to American history—above the cause of independence from Britain. Pynchon reminds his readers that, for all their talk of freedom and independence, the heroes of the American Revolution did not free the slave from his bondage. Although Pynchon does not get into the many social and political issues that attend this claim, this reference calls to mind the fact that America has always been plagued by the dark stain of slavery, even before its political independence.

Further, highlighting his Quaker roots, Dixon also implies that oppression is not Christian. Significantly, his Quaker aversion to physical abuse—especially abuse directed toward a slave—is soon overcome when he encounters a slave driver, in what may be Pynchon's clearest and most damning invective against America's inheritance of slavery: "The Driver's Whip is an evil thing, an expression of ill feeling worse than any between Master and Slave,—the contempt of the monger of perishable goods for his Merchandise,—in its tatter'd braiding, darken'd to its Lash-Tips with the sweat and blood of Drove after Drove of human targets, the metal Wires work'd in to each Lash, its purpose purely to express hate with, and Hate's Corollary,—to beg for the same denial of Mercy, should, one day, the rôles be revers'd. Gambling that they may not be. Or, that they may" (696). This description of one of the most easily recognizable tools of racial oppression sets the stage for Dixon's chance meeting with a slave driver who is in the act of employing it.

Noticing the "twenty Africans, Men and Women, each a flower of the Tribe they had been taken from," Dixon also marks that the slave driver "is calling them by names more appropriate to Animals one has come to dislike." Now fully aware of the racial tension in America to which he has been slowly awakening, Dixon's peaceful Quaker background is so disturbed that he "feels the need, strong as thirst, to get up, walk over to the fellow and strike him." Dixon's ire is fully aroused when the barker announces that his slaves are "useful in any number o' ways, cook and eat 'em, fuck 'em or throw 'em to the Dogs" (696).[49] Fighting back the urge to attack him, Dixon simply reminds the slave driver that "Sooner or later . . . —a Slave must kill his Master" (697).

Encountering the same slave driver the next day, Dixon sees him "screaming, having abandoned all control, and Striking ev'rywhere with the Whip" (698). Finally pushed over the edge, Dixon accosts the slave driver, strips him of his whip, and proceeds to beat him with it. Begging for his life, the driver must then watch as Dixon allows the slaves to unchain themselves. Knowing their fate if caught, the Africans quickly flee and advise Dixon to do the same. However, despite all his religious convictions, "Dixon still greatly desires to kill the Driver, cringing there among the Waggon-Ruts. What's a man of Conscience to do?" And here Dixon must squarely face the moral problem of slavery in America. His conscience tells him that he may not kill a man. However, that same conscience tells him that he cannot allow slavery to continue. Though unable to actually kill him, Dixon does threaten to, and takes the whip with him when he leaves: "And dead *you'll* be, ere *you* see again that Instrument of Shame. For it will lie in a Quaker Home, and never more be us'd" (699).

This passage follows what could well be the central argument of *Mason & Dixon*. Discussing their adventures to date, Dixon comments to Mason that the "Element common to all" has been "Slaves. Ev'ry day at the Cape, we lived with Slavery in our faces,—more of it at St. Helena,—and now here we are again, in another Colony, this time having drawn them a Line between their Slave-Keepers, and their Wage-Payers, as if doom'd to re-encounter thro' the World this Public Secret, this shameful Core . . . Pretending it to be ever somewhere else, with the Turks, the Russians, the Companies, down there, down where it smells like warm Brine and Gunpowder fumes, they're murdering and dispossessing thousands untallied, the innocent of the World, passing daily into the Hands of Slave-owners and Torturers, but oh, never in Holland, nor in England, that Garden of Fools . . . ? Christ, Mason" (692–93). Here Dixon expresses both his new awareness of slavery as the central evil of the Western (civilized) world, as well as their own complicity in its furtherance.

Dixon knows full well that they have done more than simply participate in the slave trade; they have helped to define it, codify it, make an official entry of it on the Map of America. If they who have slowly been made aware of this problem throughout the text can do nothing to stop it, they are left to wonder: "Where does it end? No matter where in it we go, shall we find all the World Tyrants and Slaves?" Further, recalling the American national mythology—which claims to provide freedom to all who test their merits upon the frontier—Dixon laments that "America was the one place we should *not* have found them" (693). America should have been the place described by the myth of the American frontier, that land where freedom was inherent and no man suffered, where men were judged not by the color of their skin but by their individual merits. But the myth of America has proven to be a lie.

By the end of *Mason & Dixon*, the titular characters have died; in fact, the Rev[d] Cherrycoke's story of their adventures comes upon learning of Mason's death. However, despite all of the lessons learned by the two geometers, and the transmission of these lessons to the audience (both Cherrycoke's and Pynchon's), it would appear that nothing has been learned. The text ends on a conversation between Mason's sons, William and Doc, and his wife, Rebekah. Though Mason would later return to England, "Rebekah's Sons," the reader learns, "would stay, and be Americans" (772). What this means to them is revealed in their final conversation:

> "Since I was ten," said Doc, "I wanted you to take me and Willy to America. I kept hoping, ev'ry Birthday, this would be the year. I knew next time you'd take us."
>
> "We can get jobs," said William, "save enough to go out where you were,—"
>
> "Marry and go out where you were," said Doc.
>
> "The Stars are so close you won't need a Telescope."
>
> "The Fish jump into your Arms. The Indians know Magick."
>
> "We'll go there. We'll live there."
>
> "We'll fish there. And you too." (773)

Speaking down to their father in his grave, William and Doc sound very much like Pitt and Pliny in their desire to hear about adventures with the Indians.

However, this boyhood desire to partake of the romance of America does not die with age, nor does their understanding of the myth of the American frontier change with the knowledge of their father's trials.

Their vague reference to both jobs and spouses—work and marriage defining manhood for these boys—belies the ease with which they expect to acquire them (both being a form of property and a marker of prosperity in this masculine mythology), much like the ease with which one can sustain a living if the fish "jump into your Arms." America is still envisioned as a land of plenty, the frontier a space where such dreams are realized. Further, that they believe the Indians know magic exposes their inability to see them as people; though not the savage animals they are for Pitt and Pliny earlier in the text, they are here nothing more than a stereotype.[50] If Mason finally came to learn what Dixon was trying to teach him about racial oppression, that knowledge was not passed on to his sons.

Pynchon here demonstrates America's inability to learn from its mistakes with respect to the myth of the American frontier and its implications for the continuing problems that slavery has left on the American cultural landscape. That William and Doc don't learn from Mason's adventures suggests that each generation has to come to terms on its own with the failure of the frontier myth to accurately describe the American experience, especially with respect to America's strained racial relations. Unlike Doctorow and Barth, who suggest that we have been unable to learn from the past because we have not had a true representation of what our past actually was (if such truth can even be faithfully represented), Pynchon is here suggesting that we are simply unable to learn from our past at all.

According to Captain Zhang, the Chinese *Feng Shui* master: "To rule forever . . . it is necessary only to create, among the people one would rule, what we call . . . Bad History. Nothing will produce Bad History more directly nor brutally, than drawing a Line, in particular a Right Line, the very Shape of Contempt, through the midst of a People,—to create thus a Distinction betwixt 'em,—'tis the first stroke.—All else will follow as if predestin'd, unto War and Devastation" (615). Along with everything else produced by the Line, Mason and Dixon have also produced "Bad History," an impulse from which will inevitably follow "War and Devastation," two signs of the kind of complexity that the activities of line drawing and mapmaking attempt to avoid. This act, Pynchon suggests, is more than just consequential; it is defining with respect to America's social fabric. In participating in America's involvement with the slave trade—in helping to inscribe it onto America's physical and cultural landscape—Mason and Dixon have set America on a course of social destruction from which it cannot escape. If *Mason & Dixon* is, as Gary Thompson claims, a work that "enacts . . . the indeterminacy of our knowledge of the past,"[51] it clearly also alludes to the negative effects of that past on our present, which include, as Samuel Cohen notes, "the Civil War and the postbellum years as well as the turmoil of the 1960s and the years between that turmoil and the time of the novel's publication."[52]

We have thus seen the various ways that Mason and Dixon fail as frontiersmen in their own right. Even though they succeed in drawing the "Map of the Boundary," they do so only by learning to ignore—or failing to alter—the various acts of oppression they encounter along the way. Far from being a marker of Enlightenment progress, the Line has brought only discord to those who worked on it or those whose lives were disrupted by it. Just as importantly, however, is the reader's knowledge that such discord will only increase, as later generations of Americans will know this line as the boundary between slave and free, between ugly and repressive racism and equality under the law (if not always in practice, unfortunately). Mason's sons have not learned that the frontier is not a place of wild adventure and promise for the future. Instead, they—and the succeeding generations they represent—will continue to promote the mythology of the American frontier and uncritically accept the lie it promotes. And it is telling that it is Captain Zhang—and not any of the white characters—who notes that the drawing of such lines will produce nothing but bad history; it will only be those who are negatively affected by the "colorline" who will note both its presence and its destructive effects. "Colorlines," like the American frontier, promote a lie: that the men of the frontier lived up to Daniel Boone's promise and that the mythology itself would assist America in reaching its dream of equality for all people.

The social protests of the 1960s demonstrated that the racism infecting America at its birth had not been resolved. Kyle Smith reminds us that *Mason & Dixon* is set in a time when "America is constructing itself as a nation-state. This is the point where America may have chosen new routes to freedom, but is also both a supplement of the British Empire and a community striving towards its own delusions of universality and imperialism."[53] As a "supplement" of England, Smith argues, America inherited the ideology of "Whiteness" inherent in the process of colonization. This ideology was perpetuated in America's own imperial impulse (the "technocratic order"). Further, it leads to the "great horror of *Mason & Dixon*," which is "a pre–Cold War one, but also a post–Cold War fear. It is not that Whiteness will destroy everything, as much as the effect of the continuity of Whiteness's power in the everyday world."[54]

As a result of inheriting and perpetuating this ideology, America has worked to erase from its cultural discourse the involvement of minority voices, particularly those of African Americans. Because these wounds were reopened in the 1960s, many writers who came of age during that period used their works to provide a corrective. Writers like Pynchon employed the American Historical Frontier Romance to demonstrate how the nation's failed race relations in the twentieth century had their roots in the racist implications of the American frontier mythology. And in the next two chapters, we will investigate works by African American and Native American authors who engage the masculine mythology of the American frontier as a means to expose its inherent racism.

3 / The Signifyin' Cowboy: Ishmael Reed's Wild Western Reimaginations

One cannot escape history as such, but one can rethink, contest, and revise it.
—MICHAEL K. JOHNSON, *BLACK MASCULINITY AND THE FRONTIER MYTH IN AMERICAN LITERATURE*

In his landmark essay "The Significance of the Frontier in American History," Frederick Jackson Turner noted of the American frontier: "In the settlement of America we have to observe how European life entered the continent, and how America modified and developed that life. . . . The wilderness masters the colonist. It finds him a European in dress, industries, tools, modes of travel, and thought."[1] In a now-classic case of the erasure of African Americans from the American landscape, Turner cannot see the African American contributions to the development of the American frontier. The frontier is peopled by Europeans who, once mastered by the environment, become Americans. Nearly eighty years later, Houston A. Baker references Turner in his own comments on African Americans and the American frontier: "Any black American might paraphrase Countee Cullen and ask: 'What is America to me? / Spacious sky / And land of liberty?' The answer history supports is that America is something apart. Black Americans were driven through the amber waves of grain, their stars and stripes the engravings of cat-o'-nine-tails on black flesh. The legends of men conquering wild and virgin lands are not the legends of black America . . . and the tales of pioneers enduring the hardships of the West for the promise of immense wealth are not the tales of black America. When the black American reads Frederick Jackson Turner's *The Frontier in American History*, he feels no regret over the end of the Western frontier."[2] Baker argues that African Americans have no inheritance of the mythology of the American frontier due to their lack of participation in the historic circumstances involved with the "winning of the West."

Instead, Baker claims that African Americans were "driven through" this history, suggesting that slavery prohibited African Americans from any significant participation in the development of the American frontier mythology, particularly that masculine mythology derived from the legend of Daniel Boone and other pioneers who prospered on the frontier. Both positions, I would contend, are shortsighted with respect to their understanding of the role of African Americans on the American frontier.[3] Both positions are also dangerous in that they are still referenced by scholars and historians, and thus continue to promote a limited understanding of African American frontier history. In his early American Historical Frontier Romance *Yellow Back Radio Broke-Down*, Ishmael Reed suggests that African Americans must reclaim their complex role in the mythology of the American frontier and challenge their erasure from its composition, a work of cultural reclamation also now being addressed by academics.

As Michael K. Johnson has demonstrated in *Black Masculinity and the Frontier Myth in American Literature*, African Americans did more than just participate in the development of the American frontier; they also recorded their accounts in both fiction and nonfiction, thereby contributing to the canon of frontier literature and expanding the frontier imagination. Johnson's detailed analyses of works by such writers as Nat (Deadwood Dick) Love and Oscar Micheaux make clear how African Americans were able to participate in the white, European mythology of the American frontier as a space for men to express their masculinity and tame the savage frontier. With hard work and courage, as they were being tested against the elements and hostile others—white Americans as well as Native Americans, who competed against one another in acts of savagery—African Americans proved that they can succeed on the frontier, even by white, European standards.

In fact, Nat Love (as Deadwood Dick) became a popular hero in western dime novels, even if his character was bleached to satisfy the white reading public.[4] I am not here suggesting that African Americans participated in the frontier mythology to the same degree as did Euro-Americans, or that the African American inheritance of the frontier mythology is the same as for Euro-Americans. Rather, as Johnson has demonstrated, a critical reevaluation of the frontier mythology in African American literature proves enlightening to both African American and frontier literature canons as a result of African American authors' "alter[ing] frontier mythology so as to accommodate black experience."[5]

Specifically, just as E. L. Doctorow, John Barth, and Thomas Pynchon participated in a critical reevaluation of the masculine frontier mythology inspired by such figures as Boone and others, Ishmael Reed challenged the inherited idea that the frontier was a space for only Euro-American men to participate in the building of the nation and the establishment of national values. As Johnson claims, "the frontier myth both offers the African American writer a set of motifs for exploring self-making possibilities and restricts those possibilities through a dominant discourse that associates the black individual with the racial other and not with the white subject of the myth."[6] In *Yellow Back Radio Broke-Down*, Reed critically reimagines the American West and creates an African American frontier hero whose exploits connect him to the larger mythology of the American frontier—specifically the heroics of the American cowboy, another iconic figure of American masculinity[7]—and simultaneously work to reevaluate those positive values that have become associated with success on the frontier. Further, Reed argues against the notion that African Americans were not significant participants on the American frontier, and for the idea that the positive frontier values of success through hard work and self-sacrifice were still available to Americans in the wake of the civil rights movement and protests against the war in Vietnam.[8]

However, even those politicians who opposed the war in Vietnam are subjected to Reed's criticism. Simply opposing the war, for Reed, was not enough. The larger problem in American society is that American politicians are more concerned with looking outside of America rather than solving internal cultural problems. Specifically, Reed indicts those who refuse to recognize the development of America's rich multicultural heritage: "You know, our Congressman can do things about stuff like [funding multicultural arts] instead of making speeches about how the troops shouldn't go to Viet Nam or whatever's happening thousands and thousands of miles away. We also need multi-cultural movie houses in every town."[9] Cultural development, specifically in multicultural arts, is far more important to Reed than a war on the other side of the world. The implication here is double-edged: African Americans are the ones fighting in this war; if they are used as cannon fodder, they will be unable to contribute to American culture.

As Reed sees it, the war in Vietnam was used to exterminate African American culture by sending a generation of young black men off to war and killing them before they could contribute to America's multicultural heritage. Reed identifies this as a problem that will continue to haunt the

African American community, particularly in areas of poverty. Writing about his adopted home of Oakland, California, Reed claims that "this Fifty-Third Street neighborhood, as well as black neighborhoods like it from coast to coast, will supply the male children who will bear the brunt of future jungle wars, just as they did in Vietnam."[10] Vietnam has thus become a model for how white American politicians can continue the cultural genocide of African Americans. It is for this reason that Reed calls for activism on the part of the African American community, and often looks back to the 1960s as an example of aggressive social activism.

In recalling the 1960s, Reed tends to focus on one of two issues: either the violence that resulted from the social and political protests or the rich multicultural arts movements that were led, in large part, by African Americans. For Reed, the 1960s were characterized by "the smell of protest, anger, tear gas, and the sound of skull-cracking billy clubs, helicopters, and revolution."[11] Not surprisingly, given his earlier comments about the war in Vietnam, Reed's memory of the 1960s is often negative. The anger was physically palpable, and the aura of revolution was inescapable, so much so that it affected the day-to-day lives of all involved: "In 1968, during the bombing of the campus with tear gas and anti-personnel weapons, as well as three gases outlawed by the Geneva Convention, I wrote a letter to James Hart, then head of the English department. I said when I signed up to teach a course, I wasn't volunteering to fight in a war. There was a difference. My contract did not say anything about war or being trained for combat, so I cancelled one summer course."[12] This episode serves to highlight two aspects of the 1960s that directly affected Reed. First, as John Barth also noted, the social and political upheavals were played out on college campuses, often to the detriment of academic pursuits. Second, and just as importantly, this episode shows how Reed himself was in a way drafted into a war that he chose not to fight. And although he did cancel his course—choosing to be a noncombatant in a war he did not believe in—he lost his job.[13]

Reed demonstrates to his audience that African Americans were not able to determine their involvement in the war at home, just as they were unable to determine their involvement in the war in Vietnam. Additionally, 1960s African American art is only part of the larger multicultural artistic community in America. It is this advancement, and not the efforts at political change, on which America needs to focus in order to achieve any meaningful cultural progress: "The civil rights movement not only led to political reforms in the United States, but inspired a multiethnic revival in literature. No longer was the main concern of many

Afro-American writers that of imitating the prevailing literary styles, but of setting the styles of the oral tradition to the page and delivering poetry from the drawing room to the streets."[14] The 1960s witnessed African American writers developing their own style, reflecting their own cultural and artistic traditions, as opposed to attempting to succeed according to the dominant, white artistic standards. One such stylistic adaptation to writing was the incorporation of the oral tradition into fiction. And while Henry Louis Gates may remind us that the "speakerly text" and use of oral tradition were aspects of African American literature before the 1960s in such texts as Zora Neale Hurston's *Their Eyes Were Watching God*, we should remember that Hurston's text was largely forgotten and out of print for several decades.[15]

However, this post-1960s multiethnic revival was not, according to Reed, widely accepted: "Many critics have denounced the multi-ethnic revival that occurred in the 1960s with the arrival of a new generation of Afro-American, Asian American, Native American, and Hispanic writers."[16] Although Reed believes this revival to be inclusive, and working within the larger tradition of American art and culture, "many critics" approached it as an opposition, a confrontation, and appeared to treat it with scorn. Despite the rich contributions of multiethnic art in America, Reed claimed that the larger artistic community refused to recognize the artists and their works. In language reminiscent of Thomas Pynchon's condemnation of the military-industrial complex and its implications for minorities in America, Reed further argues: "We are not crude writers engaged in ugly rhetoric against things we disapprove of. We're merely requesting that the literary industrial complex face up to the important changes that have occurred in American literature since the 1960s."[17] Just as the military-industrial complex determines the social, economic, and political fate of the nation, so does the "literary industrial complex" determine the artistic fate of the nation. In both instances, a minority population is attempting to wrest control of their own cultural and artistic development from a large, institutionalized governing body. In an effort against this complex, Reed founded the Before Columbus Foundation and *Yardbird*, both of which were committed to publishing works that reflected America's rich multicultural heritage.[18]

Reed's "signifyin'" on the concept of a military-industrial complex, however, is more than just a play on language; it represents Reed's belief that art and politics are intimately connected. In response to an interviewer asking if his work is political, Reed replies similarly to how his contemporary E. L. Doctorow would reply, that he does not know "how this opinion that art can be divorced from politics came about."[19] More specifically, Reed's body of work demonstrates that art is intimately engaged with the community at large. In fact, Reed's position concerning art's influence on politics may best be characterized by his understanding of the roots of the Black Panther Party, one of the most vocal and militant efforts toward African American sociopolitical revolution in the 1960s. Reed's claim that "the Black Panthers came out of a theater movement in San Francisco" shows that artistic developments can have significant political ramifications. Just as importantly, Reed hints here that failure to recognize the development of artistic communities can have violent results. And in a nod to the continued importance of the frontier mythology in contemporary America, Reed later claims that "they had to put covered wagons around the White House" when the Black Panthers protested the Nixon administration.[20]

Reed's characterization of the White House's response to the Black Panther Party is only one example of the way that America has not yet outgrown its reliance on the mythology of the American frontier. Much of Reed's writing references this mythology, particularly the masculine figure of the cowboy; it is this aspect of the frontier mythology that Reed specifically addresses in *Yellow Back Radio Broke-Down*. Reed may have employed frontier imagery in attacking the White House, but he also recognizes the importance of the mythology from which the imagery is drawn: "I think the western experience ["cowboys and the West"] is obviously significant in the American mind and you (the artist) should try to tap some of the things in the culture which most people don't perceive, which by the way is a way of illuminating or enlightening them."[21] Reed thus employs the frontier mythology as a pedagogical tool, educating the reader about the pressing cultural tension facing his readers. And although Reed has worked to educate his readers about racial tensions throughout his career, *Yellow Back Radio Broke-Down*, as Todd F. Tietchen reminds us, was written "at the height of the Vietnam War."[22] In this early work, Reed taps into the mythology of the American frontier in order to expose the racism inherent in the American Dream of progress and cultural development that helped fuel the American military-industrial complex, while also educating his readers about many of the cultural and artistic contributions made by African Americans over the course of American history. And a major part of Reed's program of reeducation for his readers lies in his exploration of hoodoo influences on African American culture.

This reeducation, like that provided by his contemporaries Doctorow, Barth, and Pynchon, comes by means of participation in the tradition of the American Historical Frontier Romance in order to reevaluate the mythology of the American frontier. And like that of his contemporaries, Reed's work also demonstrates the dual failure of the frontier mythology for America in the latter half of the twentieth century, even if his presentation of such failure differs from what we have seen in the previous chapters. Regarding the failure of the frontiersmen with respect to their comparison to figures like Daniel Boone, Reed creates a character who embodies all of the positive qualities of the frontier; however, this figure is black. For Reed, it's not that frontiersmen fail; rather, it's that *white* frontiersmen fail. Regarding the second failure of the mythology, Reed demonstrates how the monoculturalism behind the mythology fails later generations of Americans by not providing the kind of progressive social thinking required of later generations. This failure culminates in the racial tensions of the 1960s. And like his contemporaries, Reed also participates in the romance tradition so that he may not be bound to historical fidelity and the tropes of literary realism.

As implied by my title, I wish to frame my discussion of Reed in the larger development of African American literary history as established by Henry Louis Gates Jr. Space constraints prevent my providing a detailed reading of *The Signifying Monkey*, and reducing "signifyin'" to one definition would undermine Gates's project.[23] However, a brief overview of Gates's work may prove useful. In this cultural and linguistic study, Gates traces the influence of the "Signifying Monkey"—a trickster figure originating in African folklore—on African American literature and culture. The figure is one who plays with language, testing its elasticity and the bounds of meaning, often with humorous consequences, forcing the participants in the game to challenge their own understanding of language. "Signifying," then, deals with the plasticity of language, and itself is a difficult act to define, as Gates reminds his readers: "Signification is a complex rhetorical device that has elicited various, even contradictory, definitions from linguists."[24] Gates then moves to a study of the trope of "the talking book" in African American literature, as "the first repeated and revised trope of the tradition, highlighting the problematics of the intersection of oral and written means of communication."[25]

My own indebtedness to Gates, then, is largely based on his methodology of reading, allowing me to demonstrate how Reed "signifies"—that is, problematizes through participation in—the mythology of the American frontier, using his text to create a trickster figure[26] that works to expose the cultural and linguistic erasure of African Americans from the foundational national mythology. I begin my reading of Reed's narrative below by means of Gates's reading of *Mumbo Jumbo*, a work he understands "to be concerned to critique and to revise the modes of representation fundamental to the canonical texts that comprise the tradition of the Afro-American novel." Where Gates understands Reed's work to be "an extended commentary on the history of the black novel," I intend to show how Reed simultaneously works "to critique and to revise the modes of representation fundamental" to the mythology of the American frontier.[27] I further argue that *Yellow Back Radio Broke-Down* operates as a contemporary commentary on the American frontier myth, exposing its racist inheritance and exploring the positive possibilities of African American participation on the frontier.

Henry Louis Gates Jr. characterizes Reed's third novel, *Mumbo Jumbo*, as "a critique of black and western literary forms and conventions, and of the complex relationships between the two."[28] One of the "complex relationships" that he addresses is the use of Haitian voodoo or what Reed has often called his "Neo Hoo-Doo aesthetic." "Neo Hoo-Doo" is a category that describes his use of an African tradition in America (by way of Haiti) that emphasizes both multiculturalism and multimedia artistic explorations. In one of his many definitions of the Neo Hoo-Doo aesthetic, Reed claims that "it doesn't begin with me. There is much in the art of the Afro-American past to suggest that people have been using this kind of gumbo approach all along. Look at the quilts that Black women made in the South. Also hoodoo involved art, people made conjure balls, they made dolls, they used many techniques that we associate with the artist, in making what they call their grisgris. Hoodoo involved dancing, painting, poetry, it was multi-media, the kind of effect that I try to get in my work and not only to describe what I'm doing, but so no one can put me in any other kind of bag."[29] Reed includes himself in this tradition for a number of reasons. Most importantly, this tradition is rich in artistic and cultural importance, and not at all influenced by white, European culture. In fact, despite the years of cultural assimilation that Reed addresses in many of his nonfiction works, hoodoo persisted, as evidenced by the quilt work Reed references.

The quilt visually represents what Reed means by "gumbo approach," a reference to both a food and a style of cooking that involves the inclusion of multiple ingredients, changing from recipe to recipe, creating a dish that serves many people. Reed's writing similarly reflects the inclusion of multiple ingredients—various narrative voices, a pastiche of several types of documents, and the inclusions of tropes from disparate genres (as we also see with Doctorow, Barth, and Pynchon)—in order to reach a wide audience. As Gates demonstrates, Reed's "Neo Hoo-Doo aesthetic" links him to the "divine trickster figure of Yoruba mythology, Esu-Elegbara."[30] This figure, known by the Fon people of Benin as Legba, was brought to the Americas in many forms; it is known in Haiti as a voodoo loa (divine spirit) called Papa Legba (pronounced La-Bas), and exists in America as the hoodoo trickster figure Papa La Bas. Reed employs this figure as the hero of two of his novels, *Mumbo Jumbo* and *The Last Days of Louisiana Red*, where he is a hoodoo practitioner and detective, solving crimes committed against African American men who practice "the work" of hoodoo. And although Papa La Bas is not a character in *Yellow Back Radio Broke-Down*, the hero of the text is a practitioner of "the work" of hoodoo, through whom Reed exposes the racism of the American frontier myth and infuses the American West with cultural diversity. The work of hoodoo is the work of multiculturalism. And this work is brought to the American frontier by the Loop Garoo Kid.

The hero of *Yellow Back Radio Broke-Down*, the Loop Garoo Kid is a trickster figure Reed first imagined in his poem "I Am a Cowboy in the Boat of Ra": "I am a cowboy in the boat of Ra. Lord of the lash, / the Loup Garou Kid."[31] The Loop Garoo Kid travels with the American Hoodoo Church performing lariat tricks, and it is after he joins the troupe that "their fame spread throughout the frontier and bouquets of flowers greeted them in every town," showing them to be adept performers and masters of the various frontier skills. Loop is certainly a notable figure, in no small part because of his race. As Maurice O. Wallace has argued: "The high profile of race in the West has created out of the black male body a walking palimpsest of the fears and fascinations possessing our cultural imagination."[32] Loop is also a stunt rider of "killer broncos" and an adept horseman.[33]

In fact, Loop's heroics are recounted at the start of the narrative, and Reed introduces him to the reader by means of a satiric play on the traditional western "tall tale," a genre that wildly overstated the positive attributes of the masculine western hero: the sharpshooter who could never miss, the pioneer who could tame the land by sheer will alone, or the pugilist who never lost a fight. Reed "signifies" on—or humorously works with and challenges—this tradition for two reasons. First, he shows that such heroic descriptions can belong to nontraditional (read, African American, hoodoo) heroes. And just as importantly, such "signifyin(g)" exposes the traditional "tall tale" as another means of establishing white (read, Euro-American) culture on the frontier. The Loop Garoo Kid is himself an African American, and so not the traditional hero of "tall tales." His introduction to the reader reflects his multicultural heritage, demonstrating that the frontier is certainly big enough for multiple traditions to coexist. Loop's physical presence on the frontier also helps to dislodge the notion that white cowboys represent our shared vision of the frontier. As Richard Dyer has noted: "There is no more powerful position than that of being 'just' human. The claim to power is the claim to speak for the commonality of humanity. . . . The point of seeing the racing of whites is to dislodge them/us from the position of power."[34] In addition to explicitly addressing race, Reed constructs Loop's character in such a way to suggest that his presence is common; he is "just folks."

The Loop Garoo Kid's description begins with an appeal to "Folks," common readers like those who would have read the dime novels and "yellow backs" that recounted cowboy tales to a popular audience (9).[35] Loop's heroic attributes start with a reference to "the work" of hoodoo: "A cowboy so bad he made a working posse of spells phone in sick." Reed here blends the attributes of hoodoo with the language of the frontier, "a working posse of spells." He was also "so ornery he made the Pope cry and the most powerful of cattlemen shed his head to the Executioner's swine." Loop is shown to be familiar with the leader of the Catholic Church—in fact, the end of the narrative shows them to be long-standing acquaintances—but at the same time Loop makes clear that western European religion does not satisfy him.

And just as he counters the religious sensibilities of Euro-Americans, he is also a thorn in the side of Western capitalism. The pope and the "most powerful of cattlemen" represent two of the major forces employed by Euro-Americans in their efforts to oppress African Americans as well as establish dominance over the frontier: religion and economics. Though the Loop Garoo Kid actively works against both oppressive systems, "he wasn't always bad, trump over hearts diamonds and clubs. Once a wild joker he cut the fool before bemused Egyptians" (9). Not a heart, diamond, or club, Loop is a spade. And to avoid the negative connotations of that word as slang for African Americans, Reed tells his readers that Loop is not a spade, but rather the trump, the suit that beats all others for the duration of the hand. In the card game played out in *Yellow Back Radio Broke-Down* (picture cowboys sitting to table in a dusty saloon), the Loop Garoo Kid controls the action. In other words, despite all of the indignities and attempts on his life that he must suffer, Reed here tells his readers that Loop will come out on top.

And just as importantly, he has "trumped" before, having entertained Egyptians before joining the American Hoodoo Church, showing Loop to be a world traveler, a multicultural hero who is not locked into the rigid racist mythology of the American West that he will later encounter. And as the hero of this western "tall tale," Loop is faced with two enemies; each enemy represents different facets of Euro-American culture, and so Loop must deal with each differently. The bulk of the narrative is devoted to Loop's conflict with Drag Gibson,[36] the "most powerful of cattlemen," who owns the most land and who manages his affairs through acts of violence directed toward all of the nonwhite characters in the work. But framing this conflict are Loop's experiences with the kids of the town of Yellow Back Radio, who may very well represent one of Reed's most subtle—and most damning—condemnations of white America.

Yellow Back Radio—a reference to the dime novels and later radio shows that helped popularize the mythology of the American West—is at best a fluid chronotopic space, or what Brian McHale would call a "heterotopian zone."[37] It exists on no map and, as we will see later, is populated with characters from different time periods. The town is an idealized space, a figurative Everywhere, and seemingly unreal in its operations.[38] For instance, at the start of the narrative, the town of Yellow Back Radio is run by its children, who have overthrown the authority of their parents. Early on, the text critiques traditional order by means of a younger generation. As one child explains: "We were tired of them ordering us around. They worked us day and night in the mines, made us herd animals harvest the crops and for three hours a day we went to school to hear teachers praise the old. Made us learn facts by rote. Lies really bent upon making us behave (16)."[39] The children represent many of the complaints against Euro-American culture that permeate a number of Reed's nonfiction works. Here, the new generation of white children—those who will presumably grow up to become cultural leaders—show a lack of respect for history. Euro-Americans, in Reed's estimation, are far too concerned with the new, with technological advancement, and as a result are ignorant of their own past.[40]

The children later in the novel forsake their past for a chance to find the Seven Cities of Cibola, a "magnificent legendary paradise where tranquilized and smiling machines gladly did all the work so that man could be free to dream," a city that can be discovered only by "those of innocent motives" (24).[41] Although the children do find Cibola, and thus prove that they do indeed have innocent motives, they are not above criticism. Their very innocence comes at a price, for they lose what culture they may have had for the chance to live a life of gratifying consumerism. Returning to Yellow Back Radio at the end of the narrative, the children drive in on a "white Chicken Delight truck" and reveal to the "common folk . . . a really garish smaltzy super technological anarcho-paradise," replete with "blue kidney-shaped swimming pools, the White Castle restaurants, the drive-in bonanza markets, the computerized buses and free airplanes, the free anything one desired" (170). The future of Euro-America, Reed suggests, is a world of chain restaurants and mass transit, a world where people no longer work, but also no longer have a culture for which to work. Reed here implies that the American dream of progress and consumption that began on the frontier will eventually lead to a world of instant gratification, devoid of cultural value; the myth of the American frontier will ultimately fail.

The Loop Garoo Kid's main nemesis is Drag Gibson, the richest cattleman around, who uses his influence to add Yellow Back Radio to his own holdings. It is later discovered that Drag hired the American Hoodoo Church to entertain the kids of Yellow Back Radio in an effort to distract them, giving Drag—and the displaced adults of the town—the chance to reassert their power. And though the kids leave for Cibola, Drag finds he must defeat the Loop Garoo Kid before he can assimilate Yellow Back Radio into his holdings. As a landowner, Drag Gibson represents for Reed the epitome of the Euro-American drive for property, introducing Drag "at his usual hobby, embracing his property" (19). Manifest Destiny is here reduced to a simple fetish for ownership, and is clearly sexualized. In fact, the reader learns that Drag does not develop, or in any way improve, his property holdings. His only interest is in ownership, and the parallel benefit of driving others away. Drag's primary impulse is control. And in his quest for control, he represents the Euro-American drive that resulted in the attempted genocide of the Native Americans and the related enslavement and mistreatment of ethnic minorities and oppression of women. By alluding to the performative aspect of gender in naming this character, one could generously argue that Reed recognizes Judith Butler's claim that "gender ought not to be construed as a stable identity of locus of agency from which various acts follow."[42] However, we must remember that Drag is the villain, who represents the (traditional masculine) desire for power and authority associated with Manifest Destiny. While drag the performance can often be "subversive," in this case it represents the "very regimes of power that [Reed] opposes."[43]

Ishmael Reed often argues that ethnic minorities (in particular, African American men) are forced into undesirable roles in American society. With respect to the war in Vietnam, Reed claims that African American men were unfairly relied upon for the worst of the fighting, asserting that "Black men made up three percent of the American population and fifty percent of the infantry in Vietnam. They did all the dirty work, the shit work. So they're condemned at home by the right and the left, and then they're sent off to protect the homefolks. They're supposed to save everybody's asses."[44] Even though Reed highlights the comparative number of African American men who served, it is just as important to him that African Americans are condemned by both ends of the political spectrum. In other words, African Americans are ostracized by the very people they protected, for having performed a duty imposed upon them (by the draft) by that very same group (white America). This conflict characterizes the core of race relations for Reed: African Americans are continually denied the means of political self-determination, and are treated unfairly by the political system that excludes themfrom participation and yet forces them to serve. This is not unlike Baker's understanding of history, where African Americans were not participants on the frontier, but were instead driven by that frontier like slaves.

Reed also recognizes that such treatment is not without precedent in America. In *God Made Alaska for the Indians*, a collection devoted in part to exploring the similarities between Native American and African American cultural extermination, Reed connects the attempted genocide of Native Americans to the war in Vietnam: "The superior technology in the hands of whites may not mean that much. Vietnam proved that heavy equipment doesn't necessarily mean victory. You can pound the hell out of the people and they'll still resist."[45] This comment—following a discussion of racial tensions in South Africa, African American consciousness of such tensions, and the concerns raised by political activism on college campuses—appears to be a clear indictment of white American technological advancement as a means of conquering the racial other. And although this particular essay does not specifically address Native Americans, its inclusion in this volume implies that such technological attempts at genocide are equally applicable to the American government's treatment of indigenous peoples. This argument reappears throughout his fiction, particularly in *Yellow Back Radio Broke-Down*.

Introduced as "the only surviving injun," Chief Showcase represents the loss of Native American culture on the American frontier as well as the fact that in modern America, Native American culture is often presented in the form of showpieces; fetishes have come to replace actual artifacts and the cultures that produced them (21). Royal Flush Gooseman, "aging unscrupulous fur trapper," is thankful for his pictures of the Native Americans "crawling across the plains like that with their hands clasped to their necks," which he can now sell to the Smithsonian. Here Reed alludes to Edward S. Curtis (1868–1952), whose photographs of Native Americans (many of which were staged and/or flush with inaccuracies) provided the popular visual image of Native Americans as well as life on the frontier. Euro-Americans are not interested, Reed implies, in Native American culture except for its value as a commodity. Chief Showcase is the only remaining Native American, as Drag points out, because of such technological advancements as Gooseman's "brand new revolving cylinder. It has eight chambers. A murderer's dream with a rapid firing breech-loading firearm." Just as technological advancement enslaved the children of Yellow Back Radio, leaving them devoid of culture, here technology is used to destroy the culture of others, as Drag explains that gun-makers, "sold them injuns those defected flintlocks allowing us to wipe them out" (23).

Showcase appears in the narrative first as Drag's employee, reporting to him about the developments in Yellow Back Radio. However, he appears later to be working for Field Marshall Theda Blackwell, a representative of the U.S. Army and the government's desire to regulate the western territories, which includes incorporating Drag's holdings and removing him from authority. Chief Showcase turns out to be working both sides, assisting in the preparations for Drag's assault on the town and also helping the Field Marshall to prepare for his attack on Drag's property. Chief Showcase—who manages to leave Yellow Back Radio without becoming directly involved in the final violence between the children, Drag, and the U.S. government—is revealed to be the mastermind behind the very battle that wipes out Drag's property holdings and exposes the U.S. government to be a mere throwback to British rule and the foppery of the British courts. Before riding out of town, Showcase witnesses the Field Marshall, dressed like a "doll" whose "wig had been curled and pressed" and whose gaudy clothing includes "evening pumps," arresting Drag "in the name of the Queen," in essence undercutting the masculine implications of the frontier mythology by having Drag arrested by a feminized figure of authority (171–72). Frontier masculinity, in other words, is little more than a stage performance.[46] Drag's actions throughout the narrative amount to an unconvincing performance of masculinity that, ultimately, leads to naught. As Judith Halberstam reminds us, "masculinity . . . has been reserved for people with male bodies," even though Reed here suggests that having a male body is not sufficient for properly performing masculinity.[47]

Chief Showcase is able to mastermind such a battle because both Drag and the Field Marshall considered him a harmless loner, with no support for the causes he raised in his militant social poetry. Drag's men could not see Showcase as anything more than a showpiece to be looked at but not understood or feared. Even Mustache Sal, who was sympathetic to Showcase, could not understand him. Sal, Drag's mail-order bride and the Loop Garoo Kid's ex-girlfriend, enjoyed Showcase's company but only for the purposes of sexual pleasure and the chance to smoke good tobacco. She is so ignorant of Native American culture that she "thought Indians were afraid of the dark" (108).[48] The only character who does understand Chief Showcase and can see through his manipulations is the Loop Garoo Kid. Early on, Chief Showcase explains to Loop that "Indians and black people have been roaming the plains of America together for hundreds of years. Why one of the chiefs of my tribe, the Crow, was James P. Beckwith, and Dick Gregory represented our Washington tribes in their treaty fights. Knappy hair rises like grass from the tracks through the Mandans and the Arikaras made by Sgt. York. And the Seminole fought invasion after invasion against the Fiend to protect black fugitive slaves" (42). Just as he will later imply in his collection *God Made Alaska for the Indians*, Reed here shows how Native Americans and African Americans both suffered at the hands of Euro-American oppression—including military force of arms—and worked together, helping to establish a multicultural heritage for America. Reed is here arguing that it was on the American frontier, a landscape on which white America attempted to erase the physical and cultural presence of ethnic minorities, that American multicultural cooperation was developed, in spite of the frontier mythology.

Although Chief Showcase turns out to be at the heart of the violence that ends the narrative, I argue that he is not to be read as the hero of this western. Chief Showcase's acts are not without cause, given his tribe's extermination at the hands of the forces he set against each other. Certainly, Showcase's actions constitute a major part of this work, and his exploits expose the racism and cultural single-mindedness of the Euro-Americans on the frontier. However, this is still the tale of the Loop Garoo Kid, the heroic black cowboy who brings hoodoo to the West and, by extension, into America. If the frontier mythology of western expansion is at the heart of Euro-American culture, then introducing hoodoo into the American frontier allows for a more multicultural approach to the frontier, and to America in general. As such, Reed is determined to demonstrate how hoodoo could have been a formative part of the mythology of the American frontier.

The Loop Garoo Kid is the representative of the signifying monkey, derived from the African figure of Esu-Elegbara, a role later filled in

Reed's works by Papa La Bas. Loop, as the central hoodoo character of the work (the other performers for the American Hoodoo Church are killed early on), comes to represent the antithesis of traditional, Euro-American frontier values. This is made explicit even before the start of the narrative. Two of the three epigraphs to the work explicitly reference hoodoo. In the third, Reed provides a stanza from "The Rustler," an American cowboy song:

> Oh, the hoodoos have chased me and still I am not broke,
> I'm going to the mountains and think I'm doing well;
> I am going to the mountains some cattle for to sell,
> And I hope to see the hoodoos dead and damn them all in hell. (7)

The "hoodoos" are clearly the enemies of the cowboy, and are one of the many obstacles he must overcome to succeed on the American frontier. Specifically, as Reed demonstrates by the conflict between Loop and Drag, the "hoodoos" stand in the way of economic advancement and individual self-sufficiency. The American frontier myth thus opposes "hoodoos," or those of African American descent who do not successfully shed their African heritage and adopt white, Euro-American values. Johnson makes this clear in his analysis of Nat Love's life and work: "Love's success as a cowboy, his overcoming of racial barriers, is represented as an erasure of racial marking." In his writing as well as in his life, Love had to "drop textual references to his race or skin color after journeying west."[49] Unlike Nat Love, the Loop Garoo Kid does not merely beat them at their own game; he changes—or signifies on—the traditional frontier mythology in order to succeed as both a western cowboy and a hoodoo practitioner. The Loop Garoo Kid, in other words, alludes to the failure of the traditional (read, white) frontiersman by embodying the positive values of figures such as Boone.

Loop is successful in ways that Drag is not because Loop represents those community values Reed celebrates. Where Drag is looking to increase his holdings and better his individual standard of living at the expense of his men, the Native Americans, and his Chinese servant, Loop finds ways that multiple people from various cultural traditions can live and work together harmoniously. This is seen in the passage where Showcase explains how Native Americans and African Americans have always worked together, as well as in the spell that Loop casts against Drag. In reciting this spell, Loop calls on the help of "*Legba master of the crossroads . . . Cousin Zaka . . . Judas Iscariot . . . Jack Johnson . . . Doc John*" and the "*Black Hawk American Indian houngan,*" among others (63–64). In calling upon important figures from various cultural traditions—African, Christian, African American, and Native American, respectively—Loop recognizes that power comes from community effort, particularly from multicultural community effort. Each tradition has its own power and its own importance, and the key to success is learning how to work with them all, as opposed to selecting one to the exclusion of others.

This brings us back to the second of the three opening epigraphs, which specifically mentions hoodoo as a multicultural force. Reed quotes Henry Allen: "America . . . is just like a turkey. It's got white meat and it's got dark meat. They is different, but they is both important to the turkey. I figure the turkey has more white meat than dark meat, but that don't make any difference. Both have nerves running through 'em. I guess Hoo-Doo is a sort of nerve that runs mostly in the dark meat, but sometimes gets into the white meat, too" (5). Hoodoo is a force that may run more strongly in African American culture, but that should not suggest it does not exist in Euro-American culture. In other words, although the traditional mythology of the American frontier has worked to exclude African Americans, the hoodoo response is not similarly exclusionary. Hoodoo, in other words, provides a corrective to the failure of the mythology of the American frontier.

Although Chief Showcase is the most obvious example of such work, Loop does employ two cattlemen in an effort to help bring hoodoo values to the West. These cattlemen, unable to resist the temptation of consumerism, sell Loop out for "10 dollars and a bottle of wine plus two tickets to the East on the Black Swan Stagecoach" (155). These two cowboys could be read as examples of the bleached African Americans who sold out their African heritage to participate in the Euro-American West (not unlike Deadwood Dick). Neil Schmitz points out that the Loop Garoo Kid is sold out by these African American cowboys "for the same dubious rewards that prompted Apache scouts to lead the cavalry to Geronimo."[50] The acquisition of money, not unlike the acquisition of land, proves to be too tempting, forcing them to sell out their own people as well as to allow their actions to be mediated by the cultural formulations of the oppressor.

By the novel's close, the town of Yellow Back Radio is ruined—"broke down"—precisely because it was unable to embrace the multiculturalism that hoodoo, through the Loop Garoo Kid, represented. The kids of Yellow Back Radio, having found Cibola, return to share their paradise of instant consumer gratification. Excited about the "exploitative possibilities" of becoming a "squillionaire" (171), Drag is first booed by the kids, then arrested by the Field Marshall. The resulting gunfight between Drag and the Field Marshall—the traditional ending of a western tall tale—leads to their mutual destruction. The kids, unable to rebuild the town and not particularly interested anyway—"the late late late show is about to begin on the boob toob [*sic*] and we can watch eating Pooped Out Soggies" (173)—return to Cibola, leaving Yellow Back Radio to its ruin. Like many other burned-out frontier towns, including E. L. Doctorow's Hard Times, Yellow Back Radio represents the failure of the American myth of the frontier. However, unlike Hard Times, Yellow Back Radio falls into disarray not because the frontier myth is just a myth; rather, Yellow Back Radio fails because of the monocultural failure of the frontier myth that actively works to exclude nonwhite races from participating, despite their physical presence and contributions to the mythology and American culture at large.

Although the narrative opens with a heroic description of the Loop Garoo Kid, and this is clearly a frontier romance celebrating him and his values, he is not a participant in the final gunfight as one might expect. Rather, the three groups of white participants—the kids, Drag and his men, and the Field Marshall with his troops—"all ignored the Loop Garoo Kid left standing on the scaffold and cheated out of his martyrdom" (174). In all the fuss over property and consumerism, the white characters simply forgot about Loop; in the end they are as ignorant of him as they were to the values he brought to the frontier. Further, despite his heroic exploits and talents—or maybe because of them—Loop is nonviolent, and spent much of the narrative trying to affect change through education, reason, and cultural inclusion. Finally, after watching the hogs consume the last of the cattlemen—symbolically showing how the product will come to consume the consumer—he simply rides "off into the distance" like many another masculine hero of the American frontier.

However, this is not to imply that *Yellow Back Radio Broke-Down* ends as a traditional western. Just as the narrative opens by "signifyin'" on the traditional "tall tale" with Loop's exploits, Reed similarly "signifies" on the traditional ending. In riding off into the distance, Loop is actually catching up with the Pope, who was called in by Drag to counter Loop's Hoodoo and reassert Euro-American values on the frontier. After trying to reason with him, the Pope realizes that "when you [Loop] have your mind made up on something, nothing can change it" (166). He then decides to leave Yellow Back Radio. Angered by Drag's desire for the Pope to kill Loop, the Pope replies: "You idiot slob, I didn't come here to kill the Loop Garoo Kid, I came to draw him out, to talk to him. If you think you can do away with him then you Americans are stupider meatheads than the rest of the world gives you credit" (167). In this interesting turn, Reed shows that it is not necessarily the Euro-American values that are at fault. Rather, it is the adoption of Euro-American values to the exclusion of others that fails the American frontier. America's foundational mythology—built as it is on celebrating white, European men and their exploits—is insufficient because it is not multicultural. It is also shown to be a bastardization of European values, not a continuation of them. If Turner could claim that America "finds [the American] a European in dress, industries, tools, modes of travel, and thought," Reed shows that this American has poorly appropriated the European's attributes, with disastrous results.[51]

Although Loop's decision to travel with the Pope may at first seem anticlimactic, even antithetical, with respect to the Loop Garoo Kid's function in the narrative as representative of hoodoo, this ending demonstrates Reed's larger point about hoodoo's desire to form a truly multicultural world where "every man is an artist and every artist a priest,"[52] and "Neo-HooDoos are Black Red . . . and occasionally White."[53] This world would have to include Europe. As the narrative closes, Reed's focus becomes clear: Euro-*American* values have failed America, not *Euro*-American values. European traditions are no more or less worthy of celebration than African ones, and Loop's choice to join the Pope as opposed to staying in America represents his desire to continue working with positive cultural values, instead of having to fight against such cheap bastardizations as he found in America. (The reader should remember that Loop is a world traveler.) Reed himself, however, has discussed a different reading of the ending, claiming that Loop and the Pope "return to art."[54] Although Reed is certainly manipulating and rewriting the western American "tall tale" in order to comment on the racist, monocultural implications of the American frontier mythology, he is just as clearly using his work to comment on the nature of art, particularly the nature of fiction.

Just as America needs, according to Reed, to embrace multiple cultural traditions in order to progress, America also needs to embrace multiple forms of art to help represent that progress. Reed's many avenues for publishing mutliethnic writers (such as the *Yardbird* journals, I. Reed publishing, and the Before Columbus Foundation) reflect his commitment to the idea that art and life are intimately connected. Who we are as a people, in other words, is determined by the kinds of art we create. And the more comprehensive the variety of that art, the more comprehensive we can become culturally. This is the basic impulse behind Loop's argument with Bo Shmo, white artist and musical thief, who made his career out of playing the music of Hoagy Carmichael, the early-twentieth-century songwriter famous for "Georgia on My Mind."[55] Bo, who understands art to be singular and is himself incapable of producing his own music, cannot understand Loop's claim that "No one says a novel has to be one thing. It can be anything it wants to be, a vaudeville show, the six o'clock news, the mumblings of wild men saddled by demons" (36). If Reed is using this work to comment on the state of art in the modern world and the necessity for artists—especially nonwhite artists interested in promoting multiculturalism—to "signify" on multiple traditions, it makes perfect sense for Reed to do so in the form of the western: "If, according to Afro-American folklore, spirits ride human hosts and are referred to as 'horsemen,' then I would naturally write a western, here again using the traditional styles of Afro-American folklore but enmeshing such styles with popular forms with which readers could identify."[56]

Reed, like Doctorow, "naturally" employs the western because it is a popular form on the American literary landscape, but also because it is the repository and transmitter of traditional American values as they were encoded on the frontier and passed down in the national mythology. And it is precisely because Reed is an African American living in the wake of unprecedented social and cultural reform that he is able to "signify" upon the myth of the American frontier.[57] If, as Tietchen and others have claimed, "the classic (or formula) Western embodies racial and imperialistic ideologies which have been repeatedly employed to justify U.S. military actions such as the Vietnam War," then Reed's "meditation on U.S. military aggression in Vietnam and the unrest it inspired at home" reclaims the western for a more racially diverse and internationally based audience.[58]

Reed is employing *Yellow Back Radio Broke-Down* to challenge his audience's assumptions about the American frontier mythology as it has developed in the wake of such figures as Daniel Boone and the popular figure of the cowboy. Although the myth may actively work to obscure African Americans, Reed shows his audience that African Americans could have succeeded by white standards on the American frontier and also could have worked to incorporate African traditions and values into this myth, in both instances overcoming the failure inherent in the racist mythology. Further, if we understand Reed's message about multiculturalism and art, we can see *Yellow Back Radio Broke-Down* as the western "tall tale" that should have been. Had America, Reed claims, understood the importance of multiculturalism and artistic variety, it may not have suffered the types of losses represented by the kids of Yellow Back Radio, Drag Gibson and his men, and the Field Marshall with his troops. Reed is showing his audience that African Americans are not on the outside of America's foundational mythology.

As Tietchen suggests, "it is quite possible that one out of every four cowboys employed during the cowboy's heyday (1860–1910) were Black (and many more were Mexican), but the American western has for the most part rendered the Black cowboy nonexistent."[59] Ishmael Reed works to correct this blatant historical oversight by peopling the West with African Americans. Just as importantly, however, African Americans of the twentieth century are no further removed from the frontier past of the American West than are Euro-Americans. Coming out of the civil rights movement and the negative responses to the war in Vietnam, Reed demonstrates to his audience that African Americans need to take proactive steps in reasserting their social, cultural, and artistic influence on America. One means by which African American artists can do this is by engaging with the traditional myths that have been employed by Euro-Americans and showing the ways by which these myths have ultimately failed America by refusing to embrace the inherent multiculturalism of America's diverse population.

Because Reed is "signifyin(g)" upon the traditional western in order to show how it has failed a contemporary audience, critics such as David Mogen can ask, somewhat insultingly, "Is Ishmael Reed [writing a western] when he writes a jive epic set in a Western Never-Neverland?"[60] That the events of Reed's work never happened is exactly the point. Reed, like E. L. Doctorow, John Barth, and Thomas Pynchon, is less interested in mimetic representation than he is with cultural commentary.[61] Critics who refuse to include Reed's work in the tradition of western frontier literature simply perpetuate the cultural problems inscribed into that tradition. Reed thus provides for his audience a model of the social, cultural, and artistic importance of "signifyin(g)" upon traditional Euro-American texts and myths in order to reassert the importance of African Americans as social, cultural, and artistic equals, thus taking an important step in eliminating Euro-American and African American distinctions that obscure what is more multiculturally "American," a point that is also addressed and further expanded upon, as we shall see in chapter 4, by Gerald Vizenor.

4 / Speaking for the Mixedblood Other: "Carefully Distorted" History in Gerald Vizenor's *The Heirs of Columbus*

One more thing—whites wrote the history of these and all the other conflicts that resulted from the coming together of the two races. Needless to say, this history has been carefully distorted throughout the years to justify the invasion and subjugation of the indigenous people.

—JAMES WELCH WITH PAUL STEKLER, *KILLING CUSTER: THE BATTLE OF THE LITTLE BIG HORN AND THE FATE OF THE PLAINS INDIANS*

Founded in 1968 by two members of the Minnesota Anishinaabe (Chippewa) tribe, Dennis Banks and George Mitchell, the American Indian Movement, or AIM, "was self-consciously patterned after the Black Panther Party's community self-defense model pioneered by Huey P. Newton and Bobby Seale two years previously in Oakland."[1] Chapters quickly appeared across the country, and the goals of AIM in short time moved from local (Minnesota) issues to more national concerns. AIM quickly entered the public spotlight due to its numerous acts of occupation, perhaps most famously at Alcatraz in 1969 and at the "Siege of Wounded Knee" in 1973.[2] This last event is particularly significant for two reasons. First, as I will address below, Gerald Vizenor was one of the few reporters on the scene, and the only Native American to cover the event. Even more importantly, the selection of Wounded Knee as a site for a Native American political protest—and the subsequent military action against AIM and its supporters—calls to mind the original massacre at Wounded Knee, where in 1890 nearly two hundred Native Americans were killed for participating in a peaceful religious event. This massacre is often read as the last in a long string of battles against "free" Native Americans, most of whom were afterward forced to live on reservations, under the paternalistic care of the federal government.[3]

Coincidentally, Frederick Jackson Turner—whose writings often characterize Native Americans as "hostile"—famously closed the American frontier in 1893 in his seminal essay "The Significance of the Frontier in American History." By staging an occupation of Wounded Knee and provoking a military response, AIM forced America to come to terms with its racist frontier mythology (a mythology that attempted to write Native peoples out of participation), to relive in the contemporary world the events of its hostile occupation of Native American lands. As such, AIM—and those writing in its wake—forced America to recognize the failure of the mythology of the American frontier in its refusal to address America's multicultural heritage.

In February 1973, members of AIM occupied the Pine Ridge Reservation as a statement of social and political resistance to the American government. As a local reporter for the *Minneapolis Tribune* who had previously reported on AIM specifically and Native American issues generally, Vizenor was one of the first reporters on the scene and the only Native American covering the event. The racial politics at play in his unique position as professional observer and implied racial conspirator are demonstrated in his recounting of the event and the subsequent reportage in his autobiography, *Interior Landscapes*:

> March 1, 1973, Wounded Knee, South Dakota: "Members of the American Indian Movement held ten people hostage Wednesday at this Pine Ridge Reservation town where more than 200 Indians were massacred by Cavalry troops in 1890. The hostages were being held after a takeover Tuesday night by about 200 AIM supporters." That first paragraph to a story on the front page of the *Minneapolis Tribune*, under my name, was written by a reporter for United Press International. The rest of the story was mine, but the editors had decided to enliven the first paragraph with hostages.
>
> My first paragraph indicated that there were no hostages; the owner of the store and the priest at Wounded Knee told me by telephone that there were no hostages. Leaders of the American Indian Movement were never charged with kidnapping or any other crime associated with the taking of hostages. I was close to the village, but the reporter for United Press International never moved from his hotel room.[4]

This episode parallels the means by which white America has made use of the frontier mythology to perpetuate racial stereotypes through textual transmission. Although Vizenor's story made no mention of hostages, his editors felt that the story needed "enlivening," or rather, romanticizing in order to appeal to an audience that expects Native Americans to be brutal savages. The injection of hostages into this story immediately follows the reference to the 1890 massacre, implying that the hostages were taken as a means of revenge, playing upon the vengeful savage motif common in the frontier mythology.[5] The editors confiscated Vizenor's story and appended text to it that expressed their own racial bias toward Native Americans.[6]

However, this does not mean that Vizenor was a supporter of AIM and its actions. In fact, given his later editorial pieces criticizing AIM and its founders, as well as his fictional characterization of them in his 1978 novel *Bearheart*, one could never claim that Vizenor was promoting an AIM agenda.[7] Rather, Vizenor was an outspoken critic of AIM's romanticizing racialism and their use of traditional stereotypes based on frontier imagery, such as the wearing of war paint and feathered bonnets to press conferences that AIM leaders attended on horseback, consciously adopting a traditionally masculine pose that only emphasized the "vengeful savage" motif familiar to readers of captivity narratives and viewers of classic westerns. Vizenor characterized the atmosphere in Minnesota in 1973, resulting from AIM pressures, as follows: "The militants were never at peace, the press conferences were mordant, and white people were terrified."[8] AIM was militant—both stubborn and armed, a combination not supported by Vizenor and his trickster aesthetic celebrating unity and playful discourse—and their press conferences were sarcastic and painful, again working against Vizenor's texts, which employ humor and satire to effect political change. The end result is fear, not cooperation, distrust rather than the coming together of two cultures, or supporting the dominant idea of the frontier as a "zone of [violent] contact" rather than dialogic cooperation.[9]

I would like here to suggest that *The Heirs of Columbus* dialogically engages with the discursive tradition of the Columbus mythology in order to project a specific image of our national community.[10] More specifically, just as Bakhtin demonstrates that language is by its very nature polyvocal—and earlier writers in this study have highlighted the complex nature of all texts that engage with the mythology of the American frontier—America is inherently mixedblood. Just as Bakhtin seeks to understand "the social atmosphere of the word, the atmosphere that surrounds the object," so too should we seek to understand the social atmosphere of the text, and the cultural dialogues with which it engages.[11]

However, as David L. Moore reminds us in his discussion on dialogic readings and colonial dialectics, "it is difficult, if not impossible, in the discourse of this not yet postcolonial world to attain, much less sustain, a dialogical stance."[12] Although certain Native American texts—Moore uses Vizenor's *The Heirs of Columbus* as his example—may frustrate "dualistic opposition," we must not forget the dangers of "naively assuming that [we] can cross from the colonial self to a full understanding of the colonized or the postcolonial other."[13] However, if we are all mixed-blood Americans, as I argue Vizenor's text suggests, then the dualistic colonizer/colonized construction needs to be rethought. And a dialogic engagement (between a novel and a discursive tradition, or between two cultures on opposing sides of the frontier line) is the best way to begin. Further, although Moore also notes that "the term 'frontier' does not by historical definition offer a dynamic beyond oppositional paradigms," suggesting that by its very nature the frontier is a dialectic rather than a dialogic space, it is just such claims as this that Vizenor works to refute.[14]

To call Vizenor's work "mixedblood" is to invoke the work of Louis Owens, whose now-classic study *Mixedblood Messages* characterizes Vizenor's contribution to the development of critical approaches to mixedblood culture as coming "from the frontier zone of the Native trickster."[15] Owens adopts "frontier" here not as a reference to the physical frontier, but rather as a reference to a position of cultural power, very much like Anthony Paul Farley's articulation of "colorlined space." Admittedly indebted to Mary Louise Pratt for his understanding of the frontier as "a space of extreme contestation," Owens nevertheless moves beyond a focus on "contact" to one on "play" in his definition of the frontier as "the zone of the trickster."[16] Further, where contact can bring to mind violent imagery, Owens adopts James Clifton's definition of the frontier as "a culturally defined place where peoples with different culturally expressed identities meet and deal with one another."[17] Though this definition may soften the violence that has often resulted from two different cultures "meeting" and "dealing with" each other, it should also remind the reader that the "frontier zone" can be a space for positive cultural development. Rather than characterizing Native Americans as the violently hunted "other" of the American frontier, Owens demonstrates that "frontier" is an adaptable term that represents a space of power resulting from the bringing together of two separate cultures. The "frontier zone of the Native trickster" is thus the space upon which the trickster—a figure who represents the crossing of boundaries/frontiers physical, spiritual, and social—plays.

More significantly, Owens argues that a frontier is a necessary cultural space, the power of which can come to reside in an individual who belongs to both cultures:

> Cultures can and indeed cannot do otherwise than come together and deal with one another, not only within the transcultural

> regions of frontiers or borders but also within the hybridized individual, Vizenor's "crossblood," who internalizes those frontier or border spaces. As conceived by Vizenor, and by Native American authors generally, however, the mixedblood is not a cultural broker but a cultural breaker, break-dancing trickster-fashion through all signs, fracturing the self-reflexive mirror of the dominant center, deconstructing rigid borders, slipping between the seams, embodying contradictions, and contradancing across every boundary. The Indian has appropriated and occupied the frontier, reimagining it against all odds. A century after Frederick Jackson Turner's famous pronouncement, the frontier appears to be moving once again, but this time it is a multidirectional zone of resistance.[18]

There is much here to be unpacked. First, Owens demonstrates that "frontier" is a slippery term, one that has been used to separate "border spaces" between cultures, but which is more appropriately employed positively as a space to "come together." Further, given the impossibility of strict zones of cultural separation on the American frontier—interracial marriages and offspring were not at all uncommon, despite literary expressions of the frontier that suggested otherwise—the frontier-as-unification ideal is represented by the mixedblood Native Americans who can trace their heritage to both sides of the cultural divide. It is in this sense that the mixedblood is a "cultural breaker," one who challenges and ultimately fractures the "self-reflexive mirror of the dominant center," showing it to be not the center at all, and "deconstructing rigid borders" that have previously separated what should more honestly be considered fluid and dialogic. Finally, a century after Turner's limited and racially unsympathetic discussion, Native Americans are asserting their cultural claims to the frontier, resisting the one-sided mythology that has unfairly excluded them from positive associations and dishonestly represented history.

Writing in the wake of the rise of AIM, Gerald Vizenor has explored the inheritance of the mythology of the American frontier, as well as the means of challenging that inheritance and the positive values associated with it. (Further, as a mixedblood Native American, Vizenor can himself be read—following Louis Owens—as having internalized the frontier topos in the very fact of his existence.) Not unlike Doctorow, Barth, Pynchon, and Reed, Vizenor explores and ultimately challenges the mythology of the American frontier by means of engaging with the American Historical Frontier Romance tradition. By creatively reimagining the history of Columbus's "discovery" of America, and inventing a fictional space through which he can explore border issues and the contemporary inheritance of the mythology of the American frontier, Vizenor joins his contemporaries in highlighting the dual failure of that mythology.

Like Ishmael Reed, Vizenor highlights the racism underpinning the mythology and alludes to the failure of the figure of the frontiersman; however, rather than invest a mixedblood figure with positive frontier values (as does Reed), Vizenor instead reimagines one of the earliest such frontiersmen (he who "discovered" America) as a mixedblood pioneer whose cultural heritage we have misunderstood all along. This is in keeping with a running theme in his works, many of which constitute a self-conscious exploration of his mixedblood heritage, embodying a unique perspective that situates him on both sides of the frontier line as it has been delineated by the mythology. Ultimately, such a situating move highlights the arbitrary nature of the "frontier" as a means for the objective separation of cultures.[19] For Vizenor, the frontier is a space where cultures can come together productively, a space where cultures and peoples can and do interact in nonviolent ways. It is for this reason that in *The Heirs of Columbus* Vizenor explores the possibilities of a recognition that America is inherently "mixedblood." America is not, therefore, a space defined by the frontier as a border, but rather by a frontier space that ignores the limitations of borders by means of dialogic cultural communication.[20]

Appearing in 1991—in what Arnold Krupat has called "a sort of preemptive strike against the anticipated excesses of the Columbian quincentennary"—*The Heirs of Columbus* was published to coincide with the celebration of Columbus's voyage to "the New World."[21] Timed to be in print on the anniversary of the year Columbus sailed, rather than the year he "discovered" America, Vizenor's work reminds his readers of the contentious story that has become part of America's founding mythology: that Columbus discovered the Americas and helped introduce the means by which European civilization was later able to conquer the savagery of Native America. Vizenor uses *The Heirs of Columbus* to directly challenge and creatively revise the mythology of the American frontier that has led to the social, political, and linguistic abuses discussed above. Not unlike *Welcome to Hard Times* and *The Sot-Weed Factor*, works that include fictional texts of dubious historical value, *The Heirs of Columbus* provides a counterhistory, one to be explored alongside the more familiar narrative of the frontier. In such a way, Vizenor is demonstrating the need for a more dialogic approach to the mythology that has come to define the interactions between Native and Euro-Americans. And by going back to Christopher Columbus, Vizenor is exploring the need for dialogic communication between the cultures at their earliest point of contact.

In *Heirs*, Vizenor creates a new cultural heritage for Christopher Columbus, claiming that "Columbus was Mayan."[22] Columbus, as *Heirs* explores, is thus not discovering America as a "New World" but rather returning to the old world of his forefathers, turning on its head the traditional civilized (explorers)/savage (indigenous) dichotomy that has characterized much of the discourse on America's founding by Europeans and showing the point of contact between cultures to be a much richer, more complex cultural space. Further, by introducing the descendants of Columbus as mixedblood Americans, Vizenor is suggesting the necessity for understanding America's cultural heritage as mixedblood like his own, as an intermarriage of disparate cultural traditions that have worked in an uneasy but potentially productive relationship with one another.

In other words, Vizenor is challenging the traditional mythology of the American frontier—inaugurated with Columbus's "discovery" of America and the subsequent westward expansion of Europeans and Euro-Americans over the American continent embodied by such figures as Daniel Boone—as an application of "civilized" European values on the "savage" American landscape. Vizenor is similarly, though much more subtly, addressing the gender dichotomy found in America's founding mythology. Through such figures as "Samana, the golden healer" (10) and Lappet Tulip Browne, a "wild founder of panic parks and their primal shout" (153), Vizenor attempts to give women a role in reevaluating our national mythology, consistent with his desire to ensure that all possible voices are given equal weight.

As Vizenor makes clear in numerous works,[23] Native American stories are often erased from the larger American cultural memory, and a full understanding of the complexity of American culture—especially a multicultural or mixedblood American culture—can only be had by exploring all of the stories, not just the official ones. However, Vizenor also tells the stories that have never been told, perhaps have never existed, as a means of exploring the racist implications and inheritances of the American frontier mythology. Like Doctorow and Barth before him, Vizenor grapples with the textual tradition of this mythology, here focusing on the Columbus legend, and introduces alternative texts—including invented texts—into the conversation. As such, Vizenor is liberating all of the stories—actual and fictional, historical and possible, textual and oral—to more critically explore the Columbus figure in American mythology, playing with what Larry McCaffery and Tom Marshall have called "the fissures and gaps that exist in even the most meticulously recorded historical event."[24]

Although Vizenor may appear to be concocting an implausible story, one that seems too fantastic to transmit any real social or political message, he reminds us elsewhere that "Columbus has been invented in many faces and historical scenes over the past five hundred years."[25] As a figure in a developing mythology as well as an actual historical person, Columbus is a "deverbative trickster, the one who landed in two pronouns, the he and you.[26] That is, Columbus exists no longer as merely an individual, but rather as a locus of dialogic communication, a construct around which writers and readers understand the transmission of the national mythology. In one respect, Columbus is "a simulation of the long gaze of colonialism."[27] However, as *Heirs* explores, he may also be the means to America's deconstruction of the racism implicit in the mythology his colonizing efforts triggered.

That Vizenor is playing with the textual tradition of the Columbus mythology is clear from his opening lines. In the very first sentence, Vizenor quotes Columbus's journal, commenting of the "blue light in the west" that "'it was such an uncertain thing,' he wrote in his journal to the crown, 'that I did not feel it was adequate proof of land'" (3), Throughout *Heirs*, Vizenor will repeatedly return to Columbus's journals and letters. This serves two purposes. First, like Barth, Vizenor shows himself to be familiar with the tradition he is writing both in and against. Second, Vizenor is allowing Columbus to retain his own position as one commentator on his own tradition. Although Vizenor may find fault with the traditional Columbus story and seek to provide creative alternatives, he does not do so at the expense of silencing Columbus, or removing him from the discussion. If, as Kimberly M. Blaeser argues, "those who control the land, have controlled the story . . . of the land and its people," then any attempt on Vizenor's part to control the story by silencing Columbus would work to establish his own control over history.[28]

This "control" over history, derived from a mastery over the documentary evidence (as we saw in chapter 1), is the position from which "historians" write, "who examine only the documents, the political and physical evidence of a cultural trial, and write out of dominance."[29] Speaking here of *Heirs*, Vizenor clearly wishes to upset the work of "historians" as well as the cultural prominence given to documents that serve to establish a myth of dominance over those whose stories were not included, whose voices have not been heard. As *Heirs* develops, Vizenor takes great pains to demonstrate that controlling history is not possible, particularly control through the manipulation of textual traditions. Or, in short, Vizenor refuses to commit the same crime committed against him at Wounded Knee.

Given Vizenor's insistence on including disparate voices, especially those voices which can provide personal testimony, Columbus himself is thus a key participant in his discussion. Or, as Kimberly M. Blaeser argues elsewhere: "For Vizenor, merely rejecting the errors of the historical accounts and relegating Columbus to the past would be both too simple and too unsatisfying, an absolution without the benefit of new revelation and without the pleasure of humor."[30] Vizenor's use of both the Columbus mythology and the figure of Columbus himself is complex and humorous, and recognizes that this mythology is still part of American culture today. Further, Vizenor's attacks on the mythology are with the inherited tradition, and not Columbus himself, whom Vizenor attempts to sympathetically associate with Mayan (indigenous) culture.

This is an important point to keep in mind because, in his suggestion that Columbus was Mayan, Vizenor is making his first claim in the text that America is an inherently mixedblood nation. Columbus did not bring European culture to America; he brought European culture *back to* America, giving birth to a mixedblood nation and a complex mythological inheritance. It is equally important to note that the Heirs of Columbus descend from Columbus and Samana, described as "an island in the ocean sea that would be imagined but never possessed in the culture of death." In fact, it is Samana and not Columbus who is thus imagined to have taken agency of their relationship, when she "swam out to touch the man from heaven that first night in the New World and here we are on radio." Stone Columbus is here explaining to his radio audience that it was actually Samana who "discovered the incredible truth that the great explorer was tribal and he carried our stories in his blood" (4). I do not think it is a stretch to say that Vizenor here is equating Samana with Columbus, both of whom "discovered" that which was already there, and which has been wildly misunderstood by succeeding generations. The reader is here presented with a counterhistory, one that suggests that Columbus's importance lies not in his actions, but in Samana's realizations.[31]

Although Vizenor addresses this complex textual tradition throughout *Heirs*, the "Storm Puppets" chapter is his most sustained exploration.

This chapter opens with a reminder to the reader that Vizenor is challenging the traditional westward expansion of cultural influence: "The Mayan shamans and hand talkers landed unused in the Old World and declared their heritable radiance in the shadows and spiritual causes of Jesus Christ, Christopher Columbus, and Sephardic Jews" (28). Also, as Arnold Krupat reminds us in his reading of *Heirs*, "not only was Columbus Mayan, but so, too, we are informed, was Jesus Christ—who, like Columbus, also had a Jewish mother, and therefore was himself a crossblood."[32] Vizenor here is taking pains to demonstrate that European pretensions to a monocultural tradition founded in history or religion—and in particular those traditions that consciously promote a gendered dichotomy—are a lie. Vizenor immediately suggests that Native American culture influenced European culture, and not the other way around. Though they may have been "unused" or, like the Sephardic Jews, banished, Mayan shamans left their influence, or their "heritable radiance," the "stories in the blood" that Vizenor discusses throughout his work.[33] The rest of the chapter explores how Columbus "would survive the culture of death, the wicked histories of his time" by providing for the reader histories both of Columbus's own life and the textual tradition that has developed, allowing the reader to discover along with the "stubborn mariner" both "the New World and the stories in his blood" (28, 32).

Intermixing autobiographical anecdotes about Columbus with quoted material from various texts (as well as allusions to other related literary traditions)[34] Vizenor is demonstrating to the reader that all knowledge of Columbus is mediated through the texts that have contributed to the Columbus mythology. Vizenor's own contribution to this mythology, then, serves as a critically self-reflective aspect of the mythology. Vizenor is not, as Kimberly M. Blaeser reminds us, asking his readers to substitute his Columbus narrative for the others, but rather to consider the ways they can all work together to further multicultural dialogue in America: "His goal obviously is not to replace one historical account of Columbus with another, not to 're-possess' history, but to place the realm of history beyond the reach of what he calls "'the striven western gaze,' 'the colonial gaze.'" History, he believes, should not be possessed but imagined. History should be, not an emblem or a tool of social and political power, but a vehicle of personal and communal empowerment. History should not enslave but liberate."[35] History, or in this case the mythological tradition that serves as the vehicle for historical knowledge, should not be the means by which peoples are culturally separated from one another, nor should it be the means for cultural dominance. "History," as with the "frontier," should be the means by which cultures come together. The "colonial gaze"—or the means by which Europeans looked upon America as a cultural frontier—has for too long dominated the American imagination, with drastic results for the colonized. Vizenor's multipart, dialogic discussion between texts that all participate in the continuance of the Columbus mythology, then, is an act of liberation, a freeing of voices. Vizenor is also here reclaiming Columbus for a larger, specifically mixedblood, cultural community, by assuming a position of authority over the discussion at large.

This mixedblood reclamation is also evident in the ways that Vizenor carefully selects not only the texts he references but also the specific passages he provides. One such example is taken from Samuel Eliot Morison's *The Great Explorers*: "Not since the birth of Christ has there been a light so full of meaning for the human race" [36] Referencing the blue light that Columbus saw when approaching the American continent, Morison here connects Columbus to Christianity, allowing his readers to make the connection that Columbus brought to America what Christ brought to Christians: moral guidance and a purpose for being, or more broadly, a culture. Just as Christ saved Christians from the horrors of Hell and damnation, Columbus "saved" the American continent.

However, remembering that Vizenor opens this chapter with the claim that Mayan culture influenced "the spiritual causes of Jesus Christ [and] Christopher Columbus," we can see how Columbus's arrival in America is a returning full circle of cultural influence (28). Further, if Mayans were an influence over Christ, then the whole of European Christianity is as indebted to Mayan culture as the "New World" is indebted to the "Old World." Vizenor is here suggesting that the birth of Christ and the discovery of America are not European celebrations, but rather global, multicultural—or mixedblood—celebrations. Vizenor's "mixedblood text" (a text constructed out of parts from various sources, as well as a text written by a mixedblood American about a multicultural national mythology) is thus a reflection of Columbus's mixedblood heritage as well as the mixedblood nature of the discursive tradition.

Vizenor ends this chapter with a discussion of a letter that Columbus wrote and discarded, to which he refers in his journal: "I sealed the parchment in a waxed cloth, tied it very securely, took a large wooden barrel, and placed the parchment in the barrel, without anyone knowing what it was . . . and had it thrown into the sea." This letter, lost at sea, holds for the Heirs of Columbus a special meaning, and Binn Columbus (one of the Heirs) claims to have "heard the stories in his letter." The Heirs of Columbus (like *The Heirs of Columbus*) know that Columbus was a more complex figure than his mythology generally allows him to be read as, and work to further a cross-cultural understanding of both the man and the textual tradition he began. This discarded letter, then, represents a side of Columbus—both the man himself and the textual tradition—that has been lost, and which both the Heirs and *The Heirs* seek to reclaim. The birth of the reclamation project is further symbolized in the birth of Samana, daughter of Christopher Columbus and Samana the hand-talker, conceived on "that blue night on the beach at Bahia de Bariay in Oriente Province" (44). Here are born both the first child of Christopher Columbus, a Native American from whom the Heirs of Columbus will descend, as well as the first story about Columbus's connection with Native American culture, from which *The Heirs of Columbus* will descend.

At issue, then, in this connection between Native American culture and European culture explored by Vizenor's creative textual and genealogical play with the Columbus narrative is the frontier, the mixedblood space uniting these two cultures, and the "colorline" that Vizenor is attempting to blur. Physically, the Heirs of Columbus reside on multiple frontiers simultaneously. While operating the *Santa María Casino*, the Heirs and their floating casinos are "limited sovereign states at sea, the first maritime reservations in international waters" (7–8). The casinos operate between the United States and Canada, physically situated between two distinct political entities. Stone Columbus, owner of the *Santa María Casino*, is arrested for violating federal (United States) gambling laws. Given their location in international waters, Stone is eventually set free, "anchored once more to his stories at the border" (7). These "stories at the border" represent the competing claims between tribes and federal governments over issues of sovereignty as well as the larger discourse on American colonialism, as all frontier tales—and thus the mythology of the American frontier—are created from "stories at the border." It is important to note that the stories must be addressed in the plural, allowing for as many to speak as possible because, historically, the oppression of ethnic minorities has always included a silencing of their voices. However, this is not merely a tool of racial oppression.

After the casino sinks, the Heirs work to establish Point Assinika, "declared a sovereign nation on October 12, 1992" (119). As a move of political and cultural reclamation for Native Americans, Point Assinika stands as a testament to cultural survivance[37] despite five hundred years of cultural assimilation and genocide.[38] Point Assinika is established to remind people "of that great explorer who landed in the New World five hundred years ago today" to represent the inability of the frontier mythology to incorporate mixedbloods (123). In other words, the frontier mythology is ill-equipped to work with figures who come from both cultural traditions, and rather upholds an increasingly unstable boundary between the "savage" and the "civilized."

As Vizenor reminds his readers elsewhere, "entire cultures have been terminated in the cause of nationalism."[39] As Hastings Donnan and Thomas M. Wilson have noted, "border wars have been a long-standing if not necessary component to the process of nation- and state-building in the post-imperial age, and have not only inspired their protagonists to greater nationalist endeavors but have fired the imaginations of people everywhere who sympathise with the rights of minority nations and small states to rule themselves."[40] By establishing a sovereign state whose purpose is inclusion, and whose borders are not policed, the Heirs of Columbus are trying to "fire the imaginations of people everywhere" without instigating military action. Vizenor is here exploring what nation building might look like if we could skip the unnecessary border wars. And for the Heirs, the first step is cultural inclusion. The Heirs of Columbus, then, must establish a sovereign nation that will accept all peoples, without regard for either cultural or political identity, so as to avoid potential political strife. And as Bradley John Monsma points out, "the heirs even offer mixedblood status to all," reminding us of Vizenor's point that we are all inheritors of Columbus through the foundational nature of the mythology, so all Americans are mixedbloods who need only recognize their multicultural heritage.[41]

Vizenor situates Point Assinika on the border between the United States and Canada, selecting a chronotopic situation that alludes to the contemporary situation of several tribal populations.[42] While Point Assinika may be fictional, but for a different mythological inheritance it need not be. Point Assinika allows for people to pass through its borders without passports, to the chagrin of both governments: "Bingo gamblers could enter the bright, enormous tandem pavilions and leave from either nation, as there were no inspections at the tribal border; indeed, the heirs honored tribal identities but no political boundaries on the earth" (131). As such, Point Assinika works to deconstruct arbitrary political frontiers. Further, even the tribal politicians dislike the Heirs, and "were determined to remove the crossblood heirs as members of the reservation" (120). Here, Vizenor demonstrates that his political and cultural motives are specifically mixedblood, and not necessarily Native American, showing him to be more interested in the exploration of where cultures work together, than where they separate from one another.[43]

Stone Columbus's goal for the Heirs is to eliminate arbitrary means of identification, which in America have been established and upheld by the mythology of the American frontier: whites are civilized, Native Americans are savage, and mixedbloods simply don't exist in any meaningful sense. Or, as Chaine Riel Doumet—named for the famous Métis revolutionary—explains in his report on the Heirs to the tribal president: "His point is to make the world tribal, a universal identity, and return to other values as measures of human worth, such as the dedication to heal rather than steal tribal cultures" (152). This "dedication to heal" is explored in the genetic experiments that the Heirs are involved in, bringing in scientists from around the globe to explore the "Columbus gene" and its healing properties. By exploring the healing properties of the genetic factor that ties together all of the Heirs of Columbus, as well as both the "Old World" and the "New World," Vizenor demonstrates that the biological factors uniting disparate peoples are far more important than the cultural factors separating them. That Columbus unites Europe and the Americas genetically as well as culturally shows how science as well as the arts should strive to bring together cultures and traditions rather than separate them.

In other words, where Bo Schöler has claimed that "to Gerald Vizenor, *all* Native Americans are essential[ly] mixedbloods," I would claim that for Vizenor, all *Americans*—regardless of cultural identities—are "essential[ly] mixedbloods."[44] Point Assinika, then, is that "frontier zone," that place where, in the words of Louis Owens, "cultures can . . . come together and deal with one another." It is also the "zone of contact" that does not result in violence, but rather in cross-cultural understanding. And Stone Columbus is, as Owens claimed of Vizenor, "the hybridized individual . . . who internalizes those frontier or border spaces," those spaces where the "colorline" begins to disappear.[45] As such, the American frontier is both a theme and a metaphor in *Heirs*, and Vizenor works to expose the "frontier-as-theme" as inherently racist, while simultaneously reclaiming the "frontier-as-metaphor" for mixedblood Americans. Vizenor does not here wish to deconstruct the frontier, or revise it out of the discursive tradition. However, he does wish for us to reimagine it, to transfer it (remembering that metaphor, from the Greek *metaphora*, means transfer) out of its negative associations and into its more positive ones. And such a transfer must come both from without and from within:

the discursive tradition must be critically reevaluated, as must our own notions of identity. This, of course, is exactly the work of the romance tradition, in particular the American Historical Frontier Romance; Vizenor participates in this tradition specifically to explore a counterhistory that, in effect, would create a very different counterpresent.

In his clearest engagement with gender relations in the novel, Vizenor has Lappet Tulip Browne, member of the Browne family that Vizenor often writes about in his fiction,[46] testify during the trial of Felipa Flowers, who was charged with the theft of the remains of Christopher Columbus. She stole these remains from Doric Michéd, Native American dealer in cultural relics and a force of tribal assimilation, in what could be read as a reclamation of Columbus's legacy for Native American women. "Felipa," we learn, "was a trickster poacher. . . . She had repatriated hundreds of sacred tribal pouches, masks, creatures, ceremonial feathers, bones, and she has liberated the stories of the shamans from museums and colonial dioramas" (50). In this regard, she is the vehicle for storytelling that Samana was not, perhaps suggesting that the contemporary world does a better (though far from perfect) job of recognizing the work done by women with respect to cultural preservation. Similarly, although Lappet Tulip Browne was only hired as "second private investigator" because "feminists insisted that the behavior of the heirs be reported by a woman," she was also "the best investigator" (79). That she is a woman is not incidental, if following Lush we accept that "the sexualized human body [is] central to generating the language of its representation."[47]

The testimony of the trial, through which Felipa is cleared of all charges for her part in reclaiming cultural artifacts for the Heirs, often digresses from the subject at hand—the theft of Columbus's remains—and deals instead with the politics surrounding ownership of tribal artifacts and larger questions of Native American cultural history.[48] During the course of her testimony, Lappet is asked to explain her ideas regarding "an individual separated from culture, lost and lonesome in a wilderness." Her answer addresses the idea of wilderness: "The colonists brought wilderness with them and planted their fears in the woodland, and once here their tragic virtues were unloaded with shame, the unnatural consequences of the loss of personal visions on a landscape of primal realities, cruelties of individualism in the church, and the loneliness of civilization" (80–81). Wilderness is here defined as a construct, as an idea that is not inherent in the landscape but rather a means of reading one's surroundings, not unlike what the titular characters of Pynchon's *Mason & Dixon* discover.

Further, this construct is one that did not exist until the "colonists"—the Europeans who viewed America as a frontier to be conquered—brought it with them. As such, Vizenor is again reversing the traditional dichotomy of civilized/savage, showing the savagery of the American wilderness to be a European construct, which was "planted" and then allowed to remain and continually grow. Further, civilization—at least as defined by Europeans—is shown to be lonely as well as unnatural, opposed to the inclusive communities that Europeans found in America but largely ignored, and that Stone seeks to re-create with Point Assinika. Although Point Assinika is a fictional space, Vizenor has identified it with Point Roberts, in Washington State, in part because "I've had my eye on it for about twenty years because it's a perfect place to seize and declare a tribal sovereign nation."[49] Vizenor has also claimed that at least part of the impetus for writing *Heirs* came from his "idea for a novel of revolution, something describing the creation of a new nation," not entirely dissimilar to some of the stated goals of AIM.[50] However, as *The Heirs of Columbus* demonstrates to its readers, we should begin with a reinvestigation of an old nation, and then make it new.

The remains of Columbus at issue in the trial are a reminder of the faulty understanding of civilization and wilderness inherent in European thinking. Instead, as the rest of the testimony suggests—and is given legal standing by the court's decision, thus writing it into the law books, another form of documentary evidence that has been used to oppress ethnic minorities—Columbus's remains should be celebrated as a means of bringing cultures together. That such an idea is given the backing of the courts and still not ascribed to by monoculturalists such as Doric Michéd testifies to the difficulty in changing long-standing cultural assumptions and modes of understanding, even after five hundred years. Five centuries into America's development, Columbus and his legacy remain a potent locus of intellectual controversy. The problems that exist in the idea of colonialism, represented by the legal fight over the remains of Columbus (and later Pocahontas) are humorously addressed near the end of the work, where Stone Columbus explains his plans for annexing the United States.

Writing to the president of the United States, Stone claims the support of "precedent in international courts" for "the tithe of our namesake":

> King Ferdinand and Queen Isabella signed seven documents and granted to "Don Christóbal de Colón in some satisfaction for what he hath discovered in the ocean sea," a tenth of the gold, and

> other precious metals, spices, pearls, gems, and other merchandise obtained in commerce and free of all taxes.
>
> These rights and capitulations have never been abrogated by treaties, conquest, or purchase; therefore, since we are the legal heirs of the unpaid tithe on this continent, be so advised, that unless your government pays the inheritance due, we shall annex, as satisfaction of the tithe, the United States of America. (160)

Of course, Stone and the Heirs are incapable of carrying out this threat. That they are outnumbered, outgunned, and ill-positioned for such an undertaking is clear. However, the humor inherent in such an idea is, Vizenor seems to be suggesting, true of any colonial project. Both the Heirs and the original European colonists have the support of legal documents from those in positions of power, and both are capable of manipulating legal language to support their imperialist causes (much as Henry Burlingame was in *The Sot-Weed Factor*). Further, both can appeal to the power implicit in Columbus's name, as well as his authority as central figure in the national mythology. However, just as the Heirs would be unsuccessful in their efforts, so have the European colonists been similarly unsuccessful. Europe may have come to colonize America, but Native American cultures continue to exist, and continue to exert influence through both cultural and legal venues.

This leads the reader to an ironic realization. If Columbus was a Mayan returning home in 1491, then the European colonization of the Americas was actually a return to cultural roots. If Stone Columbus were to annex the United States, he would be returning lands that once belonged to mixedblood Americans (Columbus and his heirs) back to mixedblood Americans (the Heirs of Columbus), and in fact taking them from both Native American and Euro-American peoples (themselves the dichotomous sides of the mixedblood culture). Stone's annexation of the United States would thus work to emphasize America's mixedblood heritage and deconstruct the traditional "colorline" between Native American and Euro-American, between savage and civilized. In other words, America would become the "frontier zone" that Vizenor already knows it to be, a bloodless "zone of contact." In the process, Vizenor's larger goal for the reader is the realization that we are all responsible for the direction of the national mythology, the stories we tell ourselves that give meaning to our shared experiences and define our national character.

This realization, I would argue, is the purpose behind his "Epilogue" to *The Heirs of Columbus*.[51] In this "Epilogue," Vizenor gives a short narrative of his research, interspersed with cultural and political context. It is an invitation for the reader to continue reading the discursive tradition to which Vizenor is contributing, demonstrating that just as he does not have the first word on the matter, neither should he have the last. In fact, the last words are given back to Columbus, whom Vizenor quotes to conclude the work. The reader will recall that Vizenor also opened his novel with a quotation from Columbus's journal. As such, Vizenor is demonstrating for his readers the communal nature of the creation and transmission of the national mythology. Rather than simply accepting the stories as they have been transmitted, Vizenor creatively and productively engages them, and in so doing challenges their fundamental premises and opens up new directions for continued multicultural exploration.

Further, he has not been working alone to achieve these ends; the reader has been working with him the whole time. For as he claims elsewhere, the "readers become the trickster," by which he means that readers contribute to the "communal signification that cannot be separated or understood in isolation."[52] For Vizenor, reading is never a passive act, especially in trickster fiction; or, in keeping with the language of this study, in the tradition of the American Historical Frontier Romance.[53] The "readers become the trickster" because "the trickster is real in those who imagine the narrative."[54] This is ultimately an act of great social importance, because "in the trickster narratives the . . . readers imagine their freedom."[55] In the case of *Heirs*, the readers imagine their freedom from the oppressive racist national mythology. And it is through such reimagining that readers also come to understand the dual failure of the mythology of the American frontier: the heroic frontiersman (here, Columbus) is not the embodiment of European culture the mythology imagined him to be, and the frontier itself is not the "contact zone" where civilized whites fight off "savage Indians."

Recalling the challenges to documentary evidence that John Barth made with *The Sot-Weed Factor*, Gerald Vizenor includes in *The Heirs of Columbus* an annotated bibliography of the Columbus mythology.[56] Though delivered as a metanarrative—as a story about a story about Columbus—Vizenor here provides his reading list, and invites the reader to explore this textual tradition further, rather than simply accept his contribution as the new authority. In addition to the various academic studies and biographies that he consulted, Vizenor also researched "colonial discourse" more generally, as well as multiple translations of Columbus's journal. Vizenor is using his work on the Columbus myth to challenge both the larger idea of colonial discourse as a means of controlling the conversation about Columbus, and the possibility that any one representation of Columbus's own testimony is sufficient (much as Barth did with the various fictional accounts of Smith's adventures). And as Stephen D. Osborne points out, "Vizenor revises the defining cultural narrative of heroic discovery and conquest symbolized by Columbus *but also* the tragic 'oppositional' narrative spun by more recent liberal historians."[57] In such discursive play, we see Vizenor challenging the Columbus mythology itself as well as the notion that one textual tradition—from any one political or cultural point of view—can fully represent the complexities of monumental historical events and their subsequent mythological traditions.

Finally, Vizenor includes in his critical bibliography such seemingly disparate works as Milan Kundera's *The Art of the Novel*, Albert Hyamson's *The Sephardim of England*, Hartward Bosfield's *Louis Riel: The Rebel and the Hero*, and Jack Matthews's *Collecting Rare Books*. The inclusion of these works highlights Vizenor's claim that the story of Columbus is more complex than the traditional narrative allows for. Columbus's own cultural heritage, including the influence of Sephardic Judaism, is explored by Vizenor to challenge any claim that there was a clear "European culture" that can be opposed to a similarly narrowly defined "Native American culture." Further, by including discussions of the Métis revolutionary Louis Riel, Vizenor connects Columbus to Native American—particularly mixedblood or, as the Métis define themselves, "Half-Breeds"—efforts to gain political and cultural sovereignty.[58] Columbus and his textual tradition thus stand as only one part of a larger cultural dialogue. Finally, by including texts that reference narrative artistry and textual history, Vizenor reminds his readers that he is dealing with stories, with narrative chances at approximating the past, and not with strict historical verisimilitude. Again, this is the work at the core of the American Historical Frontier Romance tradition.

By the end of *Heirs*, Vizenor has challenged the traditional inheritance of the mythology of the American frontier, exposing it as a racist means of understanding the development of American culture. By setting up the "frontier" as a zone between two opposing poles, writers and scholars of frontier literature and culture have established a false cultural dichotomy while erasing people with a mixed cultural heritage. In Vizenor's work, such people deconstruct the traditional inheritance of the frontier mythology and embody a more progressive understanding of the possibilities of "the zone of trickster" (as Owens would have us think of the frontier), where cultures can—as in the example of Point Assinika—come together in mutual understanding to explore the variety of stories that can build progressive understandings of cultural unity: "Stone and the heirs nurture the view that stories are in bones, stones, trees, water, bears, air, everywhere, and stories have a natural right to be heard and liberated" (78).[59]

Vizenor may himself be carefully distorting history, but his purpose is not to justify the invasion and subjugation of Native Americans, as Welch and Stekler comment in this chapter's epigraph regarding the common history of Europe's conflict with Native America. Rather, Vizenor tells healing stories, stories intended to bring disparate peoples together. One such story is that of Columbus and his heirs, and their work to explore America's mixedblood heritage and the progressive cultural possibilities of the frontier space. Point Assinika exists in the novel to promote a "dedication to heal," making the frontier a space for wounds to close and cultures to interact, in stark contrast to the dominant understanding of the frontier as a zone of conflict, to which we will return in the final chapter of this study.[60]

5 / "The World Which He Inherits Bears Him False Witness": A Reading of Cormac McCarthy's *Blood Meridian* and Border Trilogy

Even in this world more things exist without your knowledge than with it and the order in creation which you see is that which you have put there, like a string in a maze, so that you shall not lose your way.

—CORMAC MCCARTHY, *BLOOD MERIDIAN, OR THE EVENING REDNESS IN THE WEST*

With these words, Judge Holden seeks to instruct his marauding followers—those western "bad men" who have aligned themselves with the judge's evil pursuits—about the nature of the world. The world, the judge argues, is chaotic and inherently without order; whatever order it appears to have is an order we bring to it, a story of our own composition. In other words, a mythology of our own creation. The stories we tell—the myths we develop and pass down to succeeding generations—are complicated yet fragile inventions, like a string pulled around the twists and turns of a maze the depths of which we can never hope to explore. Mythmaking, in other words, is an act of imposing a temporary order on a permanently disorganized world. And without that order, self-imposed and often traced back behind corners we can no longer see around, into a darkness hiding tracks we can barely recall, man would surely be lost.

In his American Historical Frontier Romances *Blood Meridian, Or the Evening Redness in the West*; *All the Pretty Horses*; *The Crossing*; and *Cities of the Plain*, Cormac McCarthy explores the enduring mythology of the American frontier as it has developed from such pioneering figures as Daniel Boone, demonstrating the ways it has failed to achieve its promises of social and political advancement that were the anticipated result of those masculine efforts at conquering the savage frontier by taming the wild lands and hostile peoples who inhabit them. However, as Roger Horrocks has noted, "patriarchal law and order is just another form of savagery, no better or worse (just more hypocritical) than the savagery of the outlaw."[1] As we will see, the order that McCarthy's cowboys—embodiments of white frontier masculinity—bring to the world is no less savage than the disorder those cowboys find. Or, extending Sara L. Spurgeon's comments on *Blood Meridian* to all of McCarthy's works under discussion, McCarthy exposes the "revelation of the profound disorder at the heart of our myths."[2] McCarthy unravels the complex mythology that has come to define America's dominant model of cultural interaction and, like his contemporaries discussed above, demonstrates the dual failure of the mythology of the American frontier.

Writing in the latter half of the twentieth century, McCarthy shares many concerns with his contemporaries E. L. Doctorow, John Barth, Thomas Pynchon, Ishmael Reed, and Gerald Vizenor. In this chapter, I will provide readings of his frontier works that often clash with established readings, particularly in my assertion that McCarthy's works engage contemporary politics in ways not unlike his contemporaries. Although not generally read as a political writer, nonetheless McCarthy has produced fiction that engages in the same critiques as the writers explored above.[3] I will demonstrate how McCarthy's works make similar challenges to authority political and textual, expose the problems inherent in the arbitrary yet painfully realized borders between the "savage" and the "civilized," and call for Americans to recognize and embrace their multicultural heritage, for which our national mythology should have prepared us.

As such, it is clear that McCarthy's texts participate in the American Historical Frontier Romance tradition by means of their selection of a specific frontier chronotope and the exploration of a counterhistory designed to expose the failure of the national mythology. Although one could fruitfully explore these ideas in all of McCarthy's fiction, I am here focusing on those works that I identify as most clearly working with the tradition of the American Historical Frontier Romance, as well as those most directly engaged with the frontier mythology.[4] It is in these four works—structured so as to comprise, I would like to suggest, a tetralogy—that McCarthy works most closely with his contemporaries to reevaluate the misguided and ultimately failed inheritance of the frontier mythology.

Unlike his contemporaries, McCarthy does not produce nonfiction works attesting to his political beliefs and ideological positioning. That said, however, I am not using this chapter to make a claim about McCarthy's personal political beliefs. Rather, in this chapter I will explore how McCarthy's fiction engages the same concerns as those of his contemporaries. With this chapter, in fact, I hope to show the ways that McCarthy's fiction challenges the mythology of the frontier that his works also (on the surface, at least) would appear to lament. Identifying McCarthy's own politics is beside the point, and likely as difficult to pin down as is his place in literary history. As Dana Phillips has argued, "McCarthy's work seems designed to elude interpretation."[5] Phillips divides McCarthy's readers into two camps, those who read him as a southern writer and those who read him as a western writer; the former seek "something redemptive or regenerative" in his work, while the latter read his work as "addressing not just the Wild West but Western culture as a whole." Phillips argues against this binary logic by claiming that the "provenance of *Blood Meridian* is still difficult to specify; fittingly for a work set in a borderland, it seems curiously suspended, not just between regions and geographies, but within literary history. It is a difficult text to periodize."[6]

While I agree with Phillips that McCarthy's work is difficult to classify, this is (at least in part) due to the falling out of favor of the romance as a genre category employed by literary critics. Quoting McCarthy himself saying of his work that "the ugly fact is that books are made out of books. The novel depends for its life on the novels that have been written," Phillips almost seems to acknowledge that McCarthy should be read within the discursive traditions that he actively engages, and this would include the textual tradition engaging the mythology of the American frontier. Just as we saw that Vizenor explicitly engages that textual history, and Barth invents a textual history to mock and satirize, so too does McCarthy (albeit much more subtly) engage with the frontier mythology and, as a result, critiques it alongside his postwar contemporaries.[7]

McCarthy is no less affected by and responding to the sociopolitical situation facing America after the 1960s than are his contemporaries, and his works participate no less than his peers' with their contemporary moment. We can read his work as commentary on both the frontier mythology as well as contemporary America. The responses to the war in Vietnam, the civil rights movement, and the American Indian Movement are no less apparent for their being less directly engaged. Further, scholars commonly note that *Blood Meridian* is challenging our notions of the frontier. The critical industry has concerned itself with new ways of describing *Blood Meridian* as a western, variously employing such phrases as "revisionary western," "dark western," "apocalyptic western," and "postmodern western" to characterize *Blood Meridian*, not to mention the seemingly necessary focus on violence to justify such descriptions of the work.[8]

That *Blood Meridian* reevaluates the mythology of the American frontier is clearly noted by the critical community. However, McCarthy's reasons for making such a challenge, or the sociopolitical factors to which his work is responding, remain largely unaddressed.[9] Although we may be improperly prepared to discuss McCarthy's own personal politics, his romances are indeed allies of the revisionist movement of the latter half of the twentieth century coming to terms with the sociopolitical impact of the various social movements that characterize the period. And like many of his contemporaries, McCarthy explores very particular frontier chronotopes (exploring four discrete moments on the America/Mexico border from 1850 to 1952, a geographical space that Gloria Anzaldúa has described as "where the Third World grates against the first and bleeds")[10] in order to engage the destructive persistence of the frontier mythology in America.[11]

Speaking cryptically to the kid at the end of the text, shortly before brutally killing him, Judge Holden remarks that "men's memories are uncertain and the past that was differs little from the past that was not,"[12] reminding the readers of the importance of "the past that was not." I take this passage to mean not that our knowledge of the past differs little from the actual history, but rather that we can no longer tell the difference between the two. In other words, similar to what we explored in Barth's *The Sot-Weed Factor*, we see here that the myths that have been handed down to succeeding generations have so clouded general understanding that any reckoning of "the past that was" is forever lost and can only be based on the myths we have inherited. Of all the characters in *Blood Meridian*, the judge knows best that man may be manipulated in his understandings. From his baseless charges against a preacher at the start of the work to his final conversation with the kid at the end, the judge manipulates every man with whom he comes into contact. The judge, in many ways self-authoring his own myth and forcing others to actively engage with that myth as reality, can be read as the central character with respect to McCarthy's investigations of the failure of the frontier mythology.

Much like Mason and Dixon in Pynchon's romance, Judge Holden is based on an actual historical figure. His existence, however, is only known through Samuel Chamberlain's personal narrative *My Confession*, an account of Chamberlain's 1846–48 adventures in Mexico and the American Southwest.[13] And like Barth before him, McCarthy works with a specific textual source; however, McCarthy does not acknowledge this source text in his narrative. Such an omission works to deauthorize the importance of the source text as a means for transmitting historical information. Instead, McCarthy is emphasizing the mythic aspects of the judge's character. Further, some aspects of the judge's character may be drawn from Chamberlain himself, who illustrated his memoirs, not unlike how the judge illustrates his own journal. But more importantly, even Chamberlain's source text is not generally considered historically accurate. As Roger Butterfield notes in his introduction, "Some of his more serious errors and outright fictional passages have been omitted from this book. Others have been corrected in the text, or through the use of footnotes. Still others, of a minor nature, have been allowed to stand."[14] McCarthy is deemphasizing the importance of a source text whose historical accuracy is already in doubt, demonstrating to the reader just how far we are from the facts of history or, conversely, just how important mythmaking is to the construction of history. Because of this unreliable account, Judge Holden is the perfect figure in McCarthy's narrative to undercut the inheritance of the frontier myth more generally.

One of the ways that the judge negates this inheritance is by challenging textual authority. Though the judge himself keeps a book—a very detailed record of everything he encounters—his purpose differs greatly from that of Blue in *Welcome to Hard Times* or Henry Burlingame in *The Sot-Weed Factor*. Where Blue and Burlingame try—and fail—to keep accurate records of their frontier experiences, eventually exploring the failures of the frontier mythology, the judge keeps his ledger to control—and ultimately destroy—that which he records. Sitting in camp by the ruins of a frontier town, a town not terribly different from Hard Times, the judge records in his ledger book the dimensions, the characteristics, and even the impressions of various artifacts he finds. And immediately after recording such artifacts, he "gathered up the other artifacts and cast them also into the fire. . . . Then he sat with his hands cupped in his lap and he seemed much satisfied with the world, as if his counsel had been sought at its creation" (140). The judge destroys what is written into his book. By destroying these artifacts, he is able to conquer them, to own them, and to disseminate them (or not) at his will. By subjecting everything to his ledger book, the judge is asserting his authority textually. Although this may appear to simply highlight the authority of texts, his destruction of the artifacts marks textual authority—or, rather, authority based in textuality—as a negative, destructive authority. This is why Webster will not allow the judge to draw him into the ledger book; inclusion in the judge's destructive "textual enterprise" is a death sentence.[15]

Further, as with the textual authority upon which the American frontier mythology has been based, the judge's "textual enterprise" is selective. Just as Captain John Smith's journal was exposed by Henry Burlingame's personal account to be a biased history, allowing for a selective mythological inheritance, the judge's ledger book contains only that which he chooses to inscribe for posterity. Near the town of El Paso, the gang discovers "ancient paintings," the judge recording only "the ones he required." However, after copying them into his ledger book, "he rose and with a piece of broken chert he scrappled away one of the designs, leaving no trace of it only a raw place on the stone where it had been. Then he put up his book and returned to the camp" (173). As with mythmaking more generally, the judge here selects only those paintings that he deems worthy of transmission. And even though some of the paintings are clearly recent ("some bright yet with color")—not unlike historical moments in the recent past that eventually get swallowed up by the mythmaking process—all are equally fodder for the judge's destructive "textual enterprise." The history of these paintings, or their relation to each other, matters not to the judge, just as the facts of history matter not to the process of mythmaking. That the judge selects what he will and will not include is no different, then, from what the mythmakers select and transmit.

We also see that the judge's process of selection is carefully thought out. The judge works with "assurance," and knows what is "required." And after completing his selections, he steps away from the paintings to carefully consider his work, studying them with the objectivity gained by separating himself from the paintings. Then after careful deliberation, he scrapes away one of the designs, puts up his book, and returns to camp. If we are to read the judge's actions as a critique of the process of mythmaking, whose destructive enterprise mirrors the inherent destruction promoted by the American frontier mythology, here we see that the process of mythmaking is neither without careful deliberation nor devoid of purpose, even if—in a similar situation as the rest of the judge's gang—such purpose is never revealed to us. The narratives that the frontier mythology has excluded—as addressed by Ishmael Reed and Gerald Vizenor as well as E. L. Doctorow and John Barth—are not ignored by accident, but by design. In many cases, those narratives were "scrappled away" intentionally.

However, this should not suggest that the judge places value in the "textual enterprise" for its own sake. The judge is merely using his text as a means to an end, as a tool of destruction and domination. As he states early on, "Books lie" (116). And he makes no exception for his own ledger book, which unlike other books seems to have no audience but the author himself. The connection between the judge's "textual enterprise" and his acts of destruction is made by Tobin, the ex-priest and as such the metaphysician of the gang. At the end of a story told to the kid recalling the judge's foul creation of gunpowder that saved them from Native Americans—a narrative punctuated with references to the judge's book—Tobin explains that the judge "had the pistols stuck in his belt at the back and drew them one in each hand and he is as eitherhanded as a spider, he can write with both hands at a time and I've seen him do it, and he commenced to kill Indians" (134). The judge's ambidexterity thus marks the connection between writing and destruction, writing and gunfire both being successful tools in the erasure of Native Americans from the historical and cultural records. Just as the judge states that "it was his intention to expunge them [his "notes and sketches"] from the memory of man," the mythology of the American frontier works to "expunge . . . from the memory of man" those cultural and historical artifacts that challenge its authority (140). Mythology can also become record keeping, not as a reminder of the past but as an active means of destroying it.

Just as the judge is the record keeper of the gang, he is also one of its most engaging and inventive storytellers, whose capacity to hold an audience is never surpassed. Even on the plains when he is hunting the kid but unable to locate him, his words—and the stories he tells the kid to lure him out of hiding—always find their intended audience. However, after repeating the tale of the harnessmaker and his murder of a helpful traveler, other members of the gang voice their objections, correcting the judge's tale "with every kind of disclaimer":

> He was no harnessmaker he was a shoemaker and he was cleared of them charges, called one.
>
> And another: He never lived in no wilderness place, he had a shop dead in the center of Cumberland Maryland.
>
> They never knew where them bones come from. The old woman was crazy, known to be so.
>
> That was my brother in the casket and he was a minstrel dancer out of Cincinnati Ohio was shot to death over a woman. (145)

Just as Barth demonstrated that various documents will often not agree on the details of the history from which the mythology springs, the details of the judge's story are disputed by a variety of kinds of witness.

Neither the place nor the people involved can be agreed upon. Nor can the other facts of the story, given the questionable sanity of one of the tale's earliest tellers, the old woman whose son was murdered and who first tells the tale.

Though they do not change the lesson of the story for the audience—that the frontier is a dangerous place and those who live upon it do so at their own peril—the details are often not important, and are themselves mutable pieces of the story. Even if one of those who correct the tale claims to be personally involved—claiming a privileged form of knowledge that could possibly trump the judge's secondhand account—such objections finally amount to nothing. The tale will continue to exist as the judge has told it, hinted at by its inclusion in the text of the narrative as well as the later revelation that the judge alone among Glanton's gang survives to continue telling his various tales.

Even if the events of this tale indeed occurred "in no wilderness place," the implication is clear that the frontier mentality and values survive the actual frontier itself. Just as Vizenor reminds us that "wilderness" was a concept brought to America by Europe, so too can "the frontier" and its cultural baggage be brought to any region. And just as importantly, a version of this tale may well exist in Cumberland, Maryland, adding a local place-name to provide regional color. This would only further our understanding of the power of the frontier mythology to provide meaning to events even after the frontier itself has closed. In this respect, McCarthy is here demonstrating what his narratives assume at the outset: that the American frontier mythology is the defining narrative in American life and letters. Further, if there are multiple versions of this tale—a very minor tale with respect to the collection of such stories that comprise the narrative backbone of the frontier mythology—then the facts of history will be forever lost. The telling of tales—and the transmission of the mythology for McCarthy and others writing in the latter half of the twentieth century—obscures rather than preserves the facts of history, a negative transmission we are reminded of every time the judge destroys what he records.

Although the judge may be the teller of the tale and the sole survivor of the gang, even he with his ledger book and destructive "textual enterprise" cannot silence the multiple voices, each providing their own unique contribution to the frontier mythology. In fact, given the judge's ability to speak and write in multiple languages as well as his detailed understanding of various cultures—particularly the various Native American peoples who also inhabit the "contact zone" that he travels—I would argue that the judge himself represents the very multiplicity that his "textual enterprise" attempts to eliminate. In other words, just as the judge seeks to impose his own singular narrative upon the world, he cannot do so without a detailed understanding of the multiple cultures with which he comes in contact and from which he inevitably learns. Although the frontier mythology itself attempted to erased from its record the traces of a multicultural presence in America, the frontier was indeed populated by nonwhite peoples who did not conveniently fit into the frontier stereotype of savage "other," as Ishmael Reed demonstrated. And just as the writers discussed in previous chapters challenged the traditional frontier stereotypes regarding African and Native Americans by exploring the possibilities of a multicultural frontier, so too does McCarthy hint at the necessity of an American frontier mythology that recognizes America's complex cultural heritage, albeit through the reluctant figure of the judge. In this way the judge, too, is a failed frontiersman, but with a twist: he's not a failure by virtue of his skill set or the successful completion of his goals (remembering that he is the last man standing at the end of the narrative), although he does fail to recognize his diverse education and the possibility of the frontier as a space for progressive cultural and political values.

Although the gang's violence against both Native Americans and Mexicans can be read as an example of the violence of Anglo-American cultural domination, Captain Glanton's band is the most multiethnic community in the entire text, comprised of "crossbreeds some, free niggers, an Indian or two" in addition to the white members (20). Glanton employs Delaware scouts and African American gunmen, two displaced peoples who have been violently "scrappled away" from both the physical frontier as well as the subsequent mythology. Writing about male bonding during the Vietnam War, Susan Jeffords reminds us "of the American mythography of masculine bonding in wartime that disregards such barriers as class, race, and demography."[16] On the surface, at least, war (and Glanton's gang can be said to be engaging in an undeclared war) brings men together under a common cause. And for all his efforts at slaughtering Native Americans and Mexicans, the judge is equally pleased with hunting and killing Tobin and the kid. The pleasure comes from the act of killing itself, and not the race of the victim. Although certainly far darker in comparison, *Blood Meridian* in one respect gestures toward the multicultural communities that were formed on and existed upon the "contact zone" that such works as *Yellow Back Radio Broke-Down* and *The Heirs of Columbus* similarly reconstruct.

That said, I am hesitant to claim that Glanton's gang represents a progressive model of community; paid to bring in the scalps of Native Americans to help protect the towns on the Mexican-American borderlands, Glanton's group certainly excelled in their work. For all that it may appear to be a multicultural unit, the truth is that such units are at best temporary, and at worst a mockery of progressive social politics. As we saw after the troops returned from Vietnam, race relations did not become less strained because of the interracial male bonding among the soldiers. And while racial tensions appear to have been nonexistent in Glanton's gang, we should keep in mind that the gang was no model of cooperative decision making, nor did it engage in anything resembling progressive social advancement. In a similar fashion, we should also note that the gang is a thoroughly masculine social institution; in addition to the gang of cowboys who embody (largely negative) masculine attributes, we also find a judge, an ex-soldier, and an ex-priest, three roles that were denied to women in this particular time and place in American history. Although McCarthy rarely comments explicitly on gender roles in *Blood Meridian*, we can certainly read this grouping of masculine figures of authority as a subtle nod toward the destruction that traditional masculinity has wreaked upon the American frontier.

The judge himself is arguably the figure who most embodies multiculturalism in the text, ironically so perhaps because he is also clearly the most violent. The judge is fluent in multiple languages, conversing as easily in Dutch, German, and Spanish as he can in English. (The name of his gun—*et in arcadia ego*[17]—as well as his demonstrated study in law, suggests his fluency in Latin as well.) However, for all his learning, the judge does not speak any of the Native American languages that were spoken on the borderlands between America and Mexico. When he speaks to Native Americans, he does so in Spanish.[18] Whether or not this represents a desire to speak to the "savages" from the position of cultural (and linguistic) oppressor is not made clear in the text. However, given the judge's proficiency with languages and the time he has spent on the frontier, it is unlikely that the judge is either unable to learn the languages or has not had the time to do so. Rather, I read his inability to speak with Native Americans in their own languages as a conscious choice. Though *Blood Meridian* does explore the multicultural nature of the American frontier by means of Glanton's gang, it stops short at providing a progressive model for interracial social understanding, such as those provided by Reed and Vizenor, from which a contemporary audience frustrated by the racial tensions of the late twentieth century can extract a positive inheritance. The gang's inability to provide such a model can be read as a microcosm of the racial problems that exist on the Mexican-American border.

Before becoming a member of Captain Glanton's gang, the kid signs on with Captain White, whose title more accurately reflects his position in the U.S. military than does Glanton's, while his name suggests the racist intentions of his government. Captain White explains to the kid that the U.S. government is in the process of "forming in Washington a commission to come out here and draw up the boundary lines between our country and Mexico." Not unlike Pynchon's Mason and Dixon, Captain White's men are to act as "the instruments of liberation in a dark and troubled land" (34).[19] They are here instructed to protect the interests of the American government until such time that the indigenous inhabitants of the area can be driven out (or killed) so that the United States can increase its land holdings and exert more political influence in the region.

Captain White suggests this when he tells the kid that "I dont think there's any question that ultimately Sonora will become a United States territory. Guaymas a U S port. Americans will be able to get to California without having to pass through our benighted sister republic and our citizens will be protected at last from the notorious packs of cutthroats presently infesting the routes which they are obliged to travel" (34).[20] Here, the Mexican-American borderland is characterized as a den of thieves, from which Americans—by implication, peaceful whites—need protection. Characterized as animals traveling in packs, the "cutthroats" are not even given a nationality, which would seem to be the easiest countercharacterization to "Americans." Finally, in an amazingly subtle understatement, Captain White refers to the California gold rush (1848–55)—which resulted in the trampling of both the environment as well as the Native Americans who stood in the path of "progress"—as simply "get[ting] to California," suggesting that the move west and the procession of Manifest Destiny was a peaceful endeavor, keeping in mind that those traveling west needed protection from the Mexican "cut-throats."

Much as the Mexican-American border may exist as a political entity, however, McCarthy does suggest in *Blood Meridian*, as Pynchon did in *Mason & Dixon*, that such arbitrary political borders are relatively meaningless. Even if Captain Glanton refuses to cross into Texas, "soil where Glanton was subject to arrest," no hint is ever given that such an arrest would or could be made, given the violent nature and military successes of Glanton's gang (172). Further, even if such men as Captain White believe that the border is a discrete location that exists on the landscape as clearly as it does on maps, those who reside on the other side of the politically sanctioned "colorline" are under no obligation to adhere to such a belief. After being accepted as heroes by the City of Chihuahua for the protection from Apaches they provide, Glanton's gang show themselves to be ignorant of the history and culture of the country in which they operate, and whose cities and peoples alike they are intent on wiping out.

At a banquet held by the local governor, Angel Trias—a man who "had been sent abroad for his education and was widely read in the classics and was a student of languages" as well as "a man among men" who enjoys the company of "rough warriors" (168)—we learn that "patriotic toasts were drunk, the governor's aides raising their glasses to Washington and Franklin and the Americans responding with yet more of their own country's heroes, ignorant alike of diplomacy and any name at all from the pantheon of their sister republic" (169). A man of learning and action alike, the governor is the closest thing to an equal that Judge Holden is likely to find on the frontier. However, instead of a display of learning and culture, we are shown the comparative ignorance of the Americans next to the Mexicans, highlighting the judge's failure as noted above. Familiar with the political and cultural history of their "sister republic," the Mexicans are hardly the savage "cut-throats" that Captain White (and the government he represents) believes them to be. In fact, given the rampant destruction and debauchery committed during their stay in Chihuahua, Glanton's gang would be more rightly characterized as the savages.

McCarthy here suggests that some Mexicans were more educated and cultured than the American frontier mythology would have us believe, going so far as to note that America and Mexico are "sister republics," or political equals. And the hospitality given to and squandered by Glanton's gang suggests that Mexicans are far more cultured than Americans regarding the treatment of foreign citizens. Cultural influence is not inhibited by the arbitrary political borderline that separates Mexico from America, as some Mexicans seem to be both well traveled and educated outside of Mexico. Just as Vizenor suggests that Anglo-America needs to learn from the cultures inhabiting the other side of the "frontier zone," McCarthy suggests that America has much to learn from Mexico. He develops this idea more clearly in *All the Pretty Horses,* which, as Mark A. Eaton reminds us, "continues the examination of national identity in the borderlands one hundred years later, after a century of US efforts to contain the region's ethnic diversity."[21] Among other things, the Border Trilogy explores the failure to develop a successful separation and containment of the racial "other."

In many ways, *Blood Meridian* can be read as the prelude to the Border Trilogy. Ending just before the actions of John Grady Cole and Billy Parham that are recounted in *All the Pretty Horses* and *The Crossing*, *Blood Meridian* also explores the Mexican-American borderlands that are the main concern of the Border Trilogy as a whole. And although one of the first actions of the kid that we witness is that "he wanders west," his wanderings—once he teams up with Glanton's gang—move south (4). Although the frontier is both popularly and critically imagined as "the West," McCarthy reminds us that the same concerns with the "savage/civilized" dichotomy, the annihilation of the racial "other" as a move toward positive cultural progression, and the construction of a heroic mythology based on the exploits of white men, all existed on America's southern border as well, suggesting that the frontier mythology became America's means to understand its relationships with other cultures.

Dueña Alfonsa, grandaunt and godmother to Alejandra, John Grady Cole's love interest, tells Cole: "We weep over the might have been, but there is no might have been. There never was."[22] These words remind the reader of *All the Pretty Horses* about the dangers associated with reading the world through the imperfect lens of mythology. In a narrative through which she relates her personal history as well as Mexican political history to the hero of the text, who finds himself living and working in a country in whose social and political history he is far less fluent than in the language, Alfonsa attempts to teach many lessons to Cole, the most important lesson of which is that those who read the social and cultural history of Mexico through the faulty understanding provided by mythology are doomed to die due to their ignorance. Recalling Judge Holden's understanding of mythology as a string in a maze, Alfonsa's view of mythology is similarly bleak. At the end of her narrative, she reminds Cole of the story of the "myopic coiner at his press, taking the blind slugs one by one from his tray, all of us bent so jealously at our work, determined that not even chaos be outside of our own making" (241). Having previously told the story of this coiner, whose actions at his mint led to further actions that he was unable to foresee, Alfonsa now sounds very much like Judge Holden, arguing that our efforts to ascribe meaning—and mythology is just one such effort—are merely an attempt to render orderly the inescapable disorder of the world.

If in *Blood Meridian* we saw a group of hypermasculine frontiersmen wreak havoc upon the borderlands, in *All the Pretty Horses* we see a woman of no small means lecturing a young, enthusiastic, but ultimately ignorant man about the reality of the "contact zone," a space he only understands through the rose-colored glasses provided by the mythology of the American frontier. A woman of social standing, personal wealth, and a formal education , the Dueña Alfonsa holds a position of power that John Grady Cole—despite the privilege he carries with him as a white American man—will never possess, no matter how successful his endeavors on the frontier. (One should note that, having lost two of her fingers in a shooting accident, Alfonsa is also no stranger to the violence of the frontier.) In language akin to what one finds in Betty Friedan's *The Feminine Mystique*, Alfonsa notes, "I knew that as a woman the world would be largely denied me," though her persistence led her to her studies, "and no one ever took a book from my hands" (235).[23] One reading allows us to see this action as a sign of her strength, a strength that she is clearly using to try and intimidate Cole (and one backed by her social standing). However, one could also read this comment as a subtle admission (one that Cole does not pick up on) that she is familiar with the textual tradition into which Cole is attempting to write himself, the romance of the American frontier that would find him as the hero, one to whom is due the rewards, including a happily-ever-after love story.

One of the text's only pragmatic characters (the other being Cole's friend and partner Lacey Rawlins, who often balances Cole's idealized view of the world), Alfonsa tries to explain to Cole why he cannot romantically pursue Alejandra, and why he should not pursue a life in Mexico. She is not opposed to her grandniece marrying a man of no education, or from another country. Rather, given the state of affairs in Mexico, Alfonsa wishes her grandniece to abandon the idealism that attracts her to Cole, a cowboy, a figure cut from the same heroic cloth as such western legends as Owen Wister's Virginian, a modern-day Daniel Boone, a figure who no longer belongs in the world.[24] As she explains to Cole, "I dont know what sort of world she will live in and I have no fixed opinions concerning how she should live in it. I only know that if she does not come to value what is true above what is useful, it will make little difference whether she lives at all. And by true I do not mean what is righteous but merely what is so" (240). In attempting to get Cole to see "what is so," Alfonsa is effectively discouraging him from understanding the world as what it is not: the mythologized space of the frontier dream where the white, male hero will tame the savage other and find true love at the end of his adventures.

All the Pretty Horses, the first installment of McCarthy's Border Trilogy, is in one respect a narrative of the adventures of John Grady Cole and his best friend Lacey Rawlins as they travel to Mexico to live the idealized life of the cowboy: working on a horse ranch, riding the open plains, and testing their frontier skills against an often hostile landscape. However, their adventures are frustrated by the addition of a young horse thief to their party, whose actions land Cole and Rawlins in jail, where they are nearly killed, as well as Cole's failed attempts at a romantic relationship with Alejandra. Leaving home upon the death of his grandfather after having been abandoned by his mother into the sole custody of a father who seems unable to properly care for him (there are hints that he drinks and gambles too much), Cole rides to Mexico with Rawlins. Although there are certainly jobs to be found for Cole and Rawlins in the United States, they travel to Mexico to find work and to live a life they believe no longer exists in America, searching for the frontier of myth and legend. In this respect, their view of Mexico is already—as Alfonsa would later suggest to Cole—romanticized, intentionally ignoring the complex reality of Mexican social and political life in favor of an understanding of the romanticized "other" provided by the frontier mythology.[25]

Soon after crossing into Mexico, Blevins—the horse thief who attaches himself to Cole and Rawlins—comments that "Back in the old days . . . this'd be just the place where Commanches'd lay for you and bushwhack you." Rawlins, the realist of the gang, asks Blevins, "What in the putrefied dogshit would you know about the old days?" (57). Blevins, the youngest of the three, is here attempting to read their circumstances through the past, and particularly a violent past involving the possible murder at the hands of "savage" Indians. Cole's lack of comment in this exchange—failing to choose either the past or the present as a means of understanding their place—suggests that Cole himself has not yet decided to fully accept the frontier mythology and all it entails. However, it is his decision to go to Mexico, suggesting that Cole's impulse is to attempt to live in the mythic past, a past that in his mind "might have been," but as he soon discovers "never was." Allowing Blevins to join their company—at the vehement objections of Rawlins—suggests that Cole shares Blevins's understanding of the world, which Rawlins refuses to accept.

However Cole and Blevins may view the move into Mexico, McCarthy renders the crossing of the border itself without any ceremony, or any change in either their characters or their circumstances. After crossing a river, Rawlins notes, "Goddamn . . . You know where we're at?" They then quietly ride on to "the dry scrublands of Coahuila" (46).[26] Like the crew in Pynchon's *Mason & Dixon* who invest much meaning in the crossing of the equator, they invest the border between America and Mexico with much meaning (Cole and Rawlins look to lead the life of the cowboy, and Blevins is escaping from the law),[27] meaning that is not inherent in the landscape itself. In fact, much as Mason and Dixon discovered, Cole and Rawlins demonstrate that the man-made borders lack any inherent meaning, save what others may choose to invest in them, "crossing the old Mark Fury ranch in the night" by temporarily disabling a wire fence (30). The man-made border between private and public property is here rendered meaningless as it fails to keep Cole and Rawlins off of the land. McCarthy furthers this point by having Rawlins ask Cole, "How the hell do they expect a man to ride a horse in this country?," suggesting that such man-made borders are unnatural, as the natural work of the cowboy involves the ability to ride uninhibited. "They dont," Cole replies, suggesting that man-made borders violate not only the realistic ranching practices to which Rawlins refers, but also the frontier mythology through which Cole understands the world (31).

The border between public and private property, no less than the border between Mexico and America, exists only on a map, with no natural markers to reinforce man's ideas of boundaries. Both borders are easily crossed by all who wish to do so. For Susan E. Hawkins, this concern with arbitrary borders helped to determine the selection of this particular chronotope, the post–World War II American Southwest, a time in which the United States was involved with the Cold War and with the arbitrary borders it established and invested much symbolic meaning in, and a space that witnessed (as we will see below) the testing of atomic weaponry: "Multiple and invisible borders define America's relationship to itself and to others: The Iron Curtain, The Bamboo Curtain, The Cold War, the 38th parallel in Korea, the global separation between the West and the East."[28] However, as Pynchon adroitly demonstrated, America has long been defined by "multiple and invisible borders."

Perhaps McCarthy, like Pynchon and Vizenor, is suggesting that America's insistence on arbitrary boundaries as a means of sociopolitical separation is also part of the human condition, which can be disturbingly read in America's involvement with Vietnam. He may also be suggesting that America only understands other cultures in terms of its own national mythology, hinted at by his claim that "there isn't a place in the world you can go where they don't know about cowboys and Indians and the myth of the west."[29] Further, just as Pynchon suggests that political borders play no role in the separating of cultures by showing the problems of slavery that exist on multiple continents—a point reinforced by Vizenor's fictional Point Assinika—McCarthy demonstrates that cultures can and do intermix despite those political markers. The clearest example in *All the Pretty Horses* is Cole's fluency in Spanish.

Cole's first conversation in the text demonstrates this fluency. Speaking first in English to the Mexican woman who works for his grandfather, he then switches to Spanish. Throughout the Border Trilogy as a whole, the protagonists are fluent in Spanish and converse at length (especially in *The Crossing*) in Spanish with various Mexicans. Cole often acts as interpreter for Rawlins, who does not speak any Spanish. This suggests that, while the crossing of cultural borders is possible in the "frontier zone," it is not true that all who live on the frontier are equipped to do so, or even care to do so. Rawlins's inability to speak Spanish is never explained, even though he inhabits the same cultural and chronotopic space as Cole. I would argue that Cole, and only Cole, speaks Spanish to suggest that although his idealized understanding of the world will eventually fail him, this does not mean that the frontier mythology is completely devoid of progressive value. Cole is able to travel in the world of the foreign "other" in large part because of his ability to speak the language. However, this ability to travel among the "others" is severely limited, as fluency in the language does not equal fluency in the cultural language, nor does it guarantee acceptance (if anything, it highlights his failure in that regard). Cole is taught this lesson both by Alfonsa and by his own experiences, especially in the Mexican prison where he is beaten and fails to learn how to survive beyond the exercise of his own brute strength in the knife fight that nearly kills him.

Though Cole will eventually die, and the traditional frontier mythology with him, McCarthy, like Reed and Vizenor, suggests that those who live lives informed by the spirit of multiculturalism may be those who represent the only progressive inheritance of the American frontier mythology. Or, as Gloria Anzaldúa phrased it: "To survive the Borderlands / you must live *sin fronteras* / be a crossroads."[30] That Cole, not Rawlins, survives to the third book of the trilogy suggests that Cole may be one such character. Cole's reminder to Rawlins that "Blood's blood. It dont know where it come from," after Rawlins is given "over a litre" of Mexican blood and fears being "almost a halfbreed," further suggests that Cole is more accepting of cultural diversity (211). However, that

Cole eventually dies in the third book may suggest that he ultimately failed to understand Mexican culture, and refused to completely abandon the heroic frontier mythology as his means of trying to find his place in the world. As such, his death will mark both ways that the mythology of the American frontier has failed: first, he has failed as a frontiersman, in that he does not fulfill the traditional role of the heroic frontiersman; second, his death marks the failure of the mythology itself as a means to understand the world. In short, he was doomed from the start, and it would appear that only the Dueña Alfonsa—a woman who was aware of the mythology but who avoided being led astray by its ideological failures—could see the truth.

Ultimately, *All the Pretty Horses* demonstrates that the borders between Mexico and America—political, cultural, linguistic—are inherently arbitrary, as they are easily crossed and unreflective of the "savage/civilized" dichotomy that is applied to them as a result of the American frontier mythology (and as we saw them developed in *Blood Meridian*). Although Cole and Rawlins are able to find the kind of work that they originally sought, their arrest—having been turned over to the authorities by the very man who employed them—suggests that any attempts to lead a life lived in the past as defined by the frontier mythology will be short-lived at best. Or, as Robert C. Sickles and Marc Oxoby suggest, Cole "has been beyond the frontier and back again, finding not a further frontier but more of the same."[31] The lifestyle promised by the mythology of the American frontier does not exist in Mexico any more than it exists in America, if it ever did exist. Further, where their experiences in the Mexican prison may reinforce the "savage/civilized" dichotomy between Mexicans and Americans, they are freed by the means of the Dueña Alfonsa, the matriarch of a wealthy, educated, and aristocratic Mexican family, subtly suggesting that where masculine endeavors will lead to no good, the frontiersmen need a strong woman to save their skins. The "savage/civilized" dichotomy as applied to the Mexican-American borderlands that McCarthy begins to deconstruct in *Blood Meridian* is thus further dismantled in *All the Pretty Horses*.

In imagery that recalls Judge Holden's understanding of the nature of the universe, the narrator of *The Crossing* suggests that if there is an order to find in the world, it can only be discovered in the world's destruction: "In that wild high country he'd lie in the cold and the dark and listen to the wind and watch the last few embers of his fire at their dying and the red crazings in the woodcoals where they broke along their unguessed guidelines. As if in the trying of the wood were elicited hidden geometries and their orders which could only stand fully revealed, such is the way of the world, in darkness and ashes."[32] Just as the judge destroys that which he records in his journal, suggesting that understanding is inextricably tied to destruction, Billy Parham here can only see the "hidden geometries and their orders" of the coals while they burn. If the mythology of the American frontier is one such method of establishing order, then I would posit that in *The Crossing* McCarthy demonstrates that any attempts to understand the mythology of the American frontier will come only by means of destroying that mythology.

More than simply portraying the negative inheritance of the American frontier mythology for the twentieth century, McCarthy effectively works to unravel that mythology, furthering the project begun by Doctorow and Barth more than three decades earlier. And it is in *The Crossing*, the middle book of the Border Trilogy and as such a transitional text, where McCarthy moves from exploring the negative implications of the mythology of the American frontier to actively dismantling it. If mythology is, as the judge suggests, a string leading us back into the darkness, that string is now being pulled apart by its threads.

The Crossing follows the adventures of Billy Parham, who first crosses into Mexico to return a captured wolf to the mountains, rather than allowing it to be killed. For the remainder of the story, Billy travels through Mexico—both alone and with his younger brother Boyd—crossing and recrossing the Mexican-American border. His ability to cross unimpeded, much like John Grady Cole's in *All the Pretty Horses*, suggests the relative insignificance of the political border. Further, like Cole, Billy speaks fluent Spanish, allowing him to cross both the political and the linguistic borders with relative ease. And finally, like John Grady Cole, Billy Parham embodies all the traits of the iconic American cowboy. In *The Crossing*, McCarthy suggests that such figures as Cole are not unique on the Mexican-American border; the cultural influences did not stop at the political boundary, but rather bled into one another, showing that lines on a map do not meaningfully exist on the landscape. Like Vizenor, McCarthy demonstrates that the "frontier zone" is far more complex and diverse than any map could indicate.

The failure of maps to accurately reflect the world, a central idea in Pynchon's *Mason & Dixon*, is similarly addressed in *The Crossing*. Maps, as manifestations of an idea of order, do more harm than good to the traveler, as an old Mexican explains to Billy and Boyd. Commenting upon a map in the dirt drawn for Billy and Boyd by a local Mexican, which he asserts is "un fantasma," the old Mexican traveler asserts that all maps are fantasies, and that "a bad map is worse than no map at all for it engendered in the traveler a false confidence and might easily cause him to set aside these instincts which would otherwise guide him if he would but place himself in their care. He said that to follow a false map was to invite disaster. He gestured at the sketching in the dirt. As if to invite them to behold its futility. The second man on the bench nodded his agreement in this and said that the map in question was a folly and that the dogs in the street would piss upon it" (185). Maps allow men to set aside their natural instincts—an understanding of and reaction to a world based on their own experiences—and assume a confidence in their travels that their experiences, especially on the frontier, will often shatter.

Further, the act of drawing a map for another implies a degree of mastery, that he who draws the map can confidently relay enough information to provide the traveler an accurate description for passage. However, as the old Mexican traveler points out, a map "was after all not really so much a map as a picture of a voyage. And what voyage was that? And when?" (185). Maps, as we saw in *Mason & Dixon*, are documents that reflect more about the writer than about the subject depicted. And not unlike the false documents that Doctorow and Barth construct in *Welcome to Hard Times* and *The Sot-Weed Factor*, maps reflect not the objective understanding that they promise but rather the subjective realities that constructed them. Just as Blue and Captain John Smith highlight certain aspects of their narratives at the expense of other details—which turn out to be important to those who read their incomplete narratives—every mapmaker will include only those details that were important to him on his own journey, making his map a reflection of his perceptions more than anything else.

However, even as subjective accounts, maps still fail. As the gerente Quijada explains to Billy: "The world has no name, he said. The names of the ceros and the sierras and the deserts exist only on maps. We name them that we do not lose our way. Yet it was because the way was lost to us already that we have made those names. The world cannot be lost. We are the ones. And it is because these names and these coordinates are of our own naming that they cannot save us. That they cannot find for us the way again" (387). Maps are a failed attempt to construct an order out of complexity, and not a reminder of an order that once existed. If the way was lost to us before the creation of the map, Quijada asks, how can our construction of a map help us to find our way again? If maps, like myths, are strings that run back into the darkness to situate us, they are strings that were laid by the blind, who could not see even before the darkness fell.

Like his contemporary American Historical Frontier Romancers, McCarthy distrusts documents that attempt to provide a sense of order over a chaotic landscape, and the underlying assumption of mastery that informs all such "false documents." Billy is also taught the insignificance of documents as a means of order and ownership when his "papers" assigning ownership of his Tom horse are ignored, and he loses his horse despite them, "seein [*sic*] what papers are worth in this country" (246).[33] If official documents fail because they are the creations of man and as such subjective understandings rather than objective truths, then perhaps all such efforts at order are so flawed, including the mythologies built upon those documents that we create to give meaning to our world.

Suggesting that maps are "false documents" that fail to provide order, McCarthy is further hinting at the inherent meaninglessness of borders more generally. Like Pynchon, McCarthy explores not only the relative ease by which one may transgress borders, but also the destructive implications of imposing such borders in the first place. Similar to Cole, with whom he works and travels in the final book of the Border Trilogy, Billy can slip in and out of Mexico by means of his fluency in Spanish. However, unlike Cole, Billy does not descend from wealth (Cole's family is no longer wealthy, but they do employ a Mexican servant).[34] Rather, Billy himself is part Mexican, whose cultural memory is kept alive by the Spanish songs he sings as well as the memory of his dead sister, named Margarita after their grandmother. In this respect, Billy is more representative than Cole of the multicultural crossings that take place in the "frontier zone" and akin to the Heirs of Columbus whose existence troubles the frontier-as-"colorline." Billy occupies those positions that Josiah McC. Heyman notes "can mediate, translate and negotiate such relations [on the border]" and is one who possesses "hybrid backgrounds and skills."[35] This may be what separates him from Cole, what keeps him alive after Cole is killed.

Billy's fluency is demonstrated repeatedly throughout the text, and there is more Spanish text in *The Crossing* than in both *All the Pretty Horses* and *Cities of the Plain* combined. This disparity may suggest Billy's "mixedblood" heritage, separating his fluency in Spanish as a family language from Cole's mastery of Spanish learned from a household servant. Billy engages in more extended conversations in Spanish than does Cole, and the Spanish-language scenes—many of which start in Spanish and then move to English (presumably for the benefit of the English-language reader)—appear regularly in *The Crossing*. And it is at this point that I would like to return to Owens, who suggests that the use of Spanish in the Border Trilogy is limited "to authenticat[ing] his locale," no more or less significant than "the ever-present tortillas and eggs."[36] Such a reading ignores the complex "mixedblood" work of both the Border Trilogy as a whole, and Billy Parham in particular, suggesting that his complex familial history and unique position on the "frontier zone" serve little more purpose than decoration. I would further suggest that such a reading is built in no small part on the inherent racism of the American frontier mythology, which insists that its heroes be of unmixed cultural lineage (like Cole, for instance, on whom Owens focuses in his discussion of the Border Trilogy, or Deadwood Dick, the whitewashed cowboy discussed in chapter 3) and that any hints of "crossblood" tainting be explained away or used as the means to banish the hero from civilized society.[37]

A far more progressive reading of the bilingual nature of McCarthy's text is that provided by Isabel Soto, who reads Parham's fluency in Spanish as a linguistic manifestation of McCarthy's critique of borders: "Thus the unfamiliar or defamiliarized Spanish articulated in *The Crossing* is generated by crossing or transgressing various thresholds, linguistic and/or rhetorical. . . . Its singular quality draws attention to itself, as does the fact that the monolingual Anglophone reader is frequently unable to infer meaning from the surrounding English. For pages at a time, the Spanish in the text contests and displaces the English as the primary discourse, even as it absorbs it into itself."[38] McCarthy's use of Spanish in *The Crossing* "draws attention" to the linguistic border that separates Americans and Mexicans, while also providing a model for the transgression of that border. By including long passages and entire conversations of untranslated Spanish, McCarthy is not merely decorating his text with local color, but demonstrating to his readers the possibility of transgressing what is often perceived as a marker of cultural difference. Billy, not fully "white" yet not exactly "Mexican" either—a true "mixedblood," to borrow from Vizenor—demonstrates through his actions that all borders arbitrarily assigned on the "frontier zone" are bound to be crossed, given their inherent meaninglessness.

The fact, admitted at the start of the narrative, that one "could ride clear to Mexico and not strike a crossfence" (3) is evidence of this meaninglessness, as is the fact that the wolf—as well as "ever [*sic*] other damn thing"—can cross without impediment (60). Even though he is hassled by the Mexican authorities on the border for not having the proper "documentos," including a "pasaporte," Billy is not impeded from entering Mexico (95). Rather, his lack of official papers is used as a means to take the wolf from him, which is subsequently sold to a fair. Billy eventually rescues the wolf, but must kill her in the process. He manages to bury only the wolf's skin in the country where he intended to set her free.

More than merely a reason for Billy to cross the border into Mexico, the wolf also highlights the arbitrariness and unnaturalness of man-made borders. The sociopolitical boundaries that man has constructed and continues to recognize as separating the United States from Mexico are not natural, for we know that "the wolf knew nothing of boundaries" (119). That Billy similarly enjoys such freedom of movement suggests that he, and perhaps all "mixedblood" figures, are the natural inhabitants of the frontier, models of a progressive acceptance of cultural diversity. Although the wolf dies, she does so in the company of "all nations of the possible world ordained by God of which she was one among and not separate from" (127). Those figures like the wolf—and, I would argue, Billy—who are able to understand the world as it was "ordained by God" as opposed to parceled out and subjected to the management of man, live in harmony with all nations of the possible, if not the actual, world. In other words, how such figures live and operate represents the world as it should be as opposed to the world as it actually is, a world not understood through the lens of a failed mythology. It is for this reason that Billy learns from a priest that "the boundaries of the world are those of God's devising" (134). The "boundaries of the world" that man devises are inherently meaningless, working against the world as it was created. Here McCarthy teaches the same lessons learned from Reed and Vizenor: sociopolitical borders that were constructed in accordance to the savage/civilized dichotomy of the American frontier mythology impede the development of the progressive America the frontier should promote.

Of course, like those described by Reed and Vizenor, McCarthy's "mixedblood" frontier heroes find life on the frontier difficult, frustrated especially by those who uphold the man-made boundaries and cultural assumptions that ineffectively separate Mexico from the United States; they are failures not necessarily in their actions and achievements but in their refusal to abandon the failed mythology. One such difficulty is the hassle Billy receives when trying to cross the Mexican border with the wolf. As punishment for not having the proper papers—papers that would be meaningless anyway—Billy loses the wolf to the authorities.

Those who attempt to circumvent the man-made laws that govern the arbitrary boundaries between nations are penalized by those authorities established to uphold them. Vizenor demonstrated the humorous extreme to which such punishment can lead in the court battles that Stone Columbus and Point Assinika face in *The Heirs of Columbus.*

But legal repercussions are only one means of punishing such "mixedblood" heroes. Billy also finds himself unwelcome in the company of those traditional frontiersmen who embrace the imposition of the arbitrary borders and who live in accordance with the racist frontier mythology. After speaking to the sheriff about his parents' murder, his missing horses, and his time in Mexico, Billy is described as an "outlandish figure" in whom the townspeople "beheld what they envied most and what they reviled most. If their hearts went out to him it was yet true that for very small cause they might also have killed him" (170). Though the townspeople feel sorry for Billy's loss, they cannot accept his choice to leave the confines of the town for a life on the "frontier zone." This life challenges their understanding of man's place in his society, even if they envy the freedom that accompanies such a life. The free-roving, rugged individual who can travel in both Mexico and the United States—and as such not accept the racist attitudes of his countrymen—is not wholly welcome in either community.[39]

That the townspeople feel sorry for him in their hearts—if not in their minds and certainly not in their actions—reminds the reader that man's "heart" may be the real concern of the narrative. The reader should recall the warning Billy received earlier from an old Mexican, a warning to stay out of Yaqui country in his travels: "the world could only be known as it existed in men's hearts. For while it seemed a place which contained men it was in reality a place contained within them and therefore to know it one must look there and come to know those hearts and to do this one must live with men and not simply pass among them" (134). Paradoxically, although the world that man has made—a world of arbitrary borders described by useless maps in accordance with a failed mythology—is faulty and naturally inconsistent (as well as inconsistent with the world God intended, as Billy learns from the Mexicans), it is the only world that one can ever come to know. This world, faulty though it may be, is the only world we have.

Cities of the Plain, the third volume of the Border Trilogy, may perhaps be McCarthy's clearest political statement based on his characterization of the United States government and the war. In the words of Billy Parham: "Anyway this country aint the same. Nor anything in it. The war changed everything. I dont think people even know it yet."[40] In *The Crossing*, we saw a young Billy Parham attempt to enlist, in order to join the fighting in Europe and support American involvement in World War II. Barred by multiple doctors because of his bad heart, Billy returned to the only life he knew, working on a ranch. In *Cities of the Plain*, we see Parham and John Grady Cole working together as ranch hands in New Mexico. Specifically, McCarthy selected a chronotope that places his characters on a ranch near Alamogordo, the site of the first nuclear explosion in 1945 of the 20-kiloton Trinity series. This location is significant, as is the complaint early on in the text that, "We'll all be goin [*sic*] somewhere when the army takes this spread over" (50). Further, near the end of the book, Billy daydreams, thinking of himself "as if he were a young lord. As if he were never to be disinherited by war and war's machinery" (204). In other words, his displacement from the ranch, from the chance to live on the American frontier, is inevitable, and comes at the hand of war and its attendant machinations.

Although the novel is set in 1952, seven years after the success of the Allied forces in Europe and two years into the war in Korea, I argue that McCarthy's antiwar sentiments are at least in part informed by the larger antiwar movement following the 1950s and 1960s, especially concerning the fear that nuclear weapons will forever change the people and the landscape of those who use them as well as those against whom they are used. This fear is shared by the Vietnam-era antiwar protesters, many of whom feared that the United States would use such weapons to end a conflict in which an increasing number of lives were being lost.[41] Aside from these references to the eventual loss of the ranch to the United States government, *Cities of the Plain* is devoid of political commentary. However, such brief passages serve to demonstrate to the reader that war and its machinations are incompatible with a progressive frontier mythology.

Cities of the Plain follows the adventures of two different embodiments of the frontier hero in the figures of John Grady Cole and Billy Parham.[42] Both characters, as was demonstrated in *All the Pretty Horses* and *The Crossing*, can be read as traditional frontier heroes: both are Boone-like rugged individualists, capable of survival on the harsh frontier landscape, and who have survived seemingly impossible scrapes with the "savage" Mexicans. Both characters are also outcasts, much in the same model of frontier masculinity established by Cooper with Natty Bumppo; and both left their homes and families to follow their desire to live a life apart from society. Additionally, both found that life on the frontier is not the romantic life they had believed it to be. Cole nearly dies in a Mexican prison for crimes he did not commit, losing both his friends along the way, while Parham fails to return the wolf to her homeland and loses his brother during their travels (after having lost both his parents to murder). Their personal losses only serve to further remove them from the "civilized" communities of which they were once part. Finally, both characters are bilingual, which emerges as the only likely basis for their ability to survive on the "frontier zone."

And although Cole and Parham are similar in many respects, it is perhaps their differences that are important with respect to reading *Cities of the Plain* as a commentary on the American frontier mythology. While Parham is a "crossblood" who can trace part of his ancestry back to a Mexican grandmother, Cole is not; he learned his Spanish from a household servant. Cole's comparative inexperience with Mexican culture may also be read through his desire to marry a Mexican prostitute, to save Magdalena from her profession and provide her a life on the frontier, in a house on the edge of the ranch that Cole is fixing up while courting her. Even though Cole and Magdalena do not live to see this happy ending, such a simplistic turn is uncharacteristic of McCarthy's reevaluation of this mythology. Rather, Magdalena serves to highlight Cole's inexperience, as well as his ignorant positive thinking. Cole, whom Parham repeatedly calls "The Great American Cowboy," is incapable of recognizing the danger of his endeavors, despite repeated warnings.

If Cole is the failed frontier hero unable to abandon traditional frontier values, his death—and as such the death of the traditional American frontier mythology—is not an easy affair. In what is often read as the narrative's climax, Cole fights with Eduardo, Magdalena's pimp-turned-murderer. For much of the fight, Cole is slowly cut up by the much faster and more experienced Eduardo, in what can be read as the slow dismantling of the American frontier mythology and its values by an engagement with a real Mexican, as opposed to fantasy-based, racially motivated stereotypes (even they are engaged in another frontier stereotype, a battle between a hero and a villain over the fate of a woman). However, in a moment of reckless abandon, Cole advances on Eduardo and accepts the wounds that eventually kill him in order to close the distance enough to kill Eduardo in the process.

If Cole does, in fact, represent the traditional American frontier mythology, then perhaps the fact that "he made no effort to step or to parry" in response to Eduardo's killing strike reflects McCarthy's belief that the American frontier mythology cannot help but ultimately fail (254). This could be what Eduardo suggests when he explains to Cole: "That is what has brought you here and what will always bring you here. Your kind cannot bear that the world be ordinary. That it contain nothing save what stands before one. But the Mexican world is a world of adornment only and underneath it is very plain indeed. While your world—he passed the blade back and forth like a shuttle through a loom—your world totters upon an unspoken labyrinth of questions. And we will devour you, my friend. You and all your pale empire" (253). Eduardo is a realist while Cole is a romantic, and their violent collision will put an end to the romanticized frontier mythology that underwrites Cole's understanding of the world. Further, that this romanticism is a phenomenon of white America—as opposed to ethnic minorities and "mixedbloods"—is hinted at in Eduardo's reference to Cole's "pale empire," which has traditionally employed the frontier mythology as a means to erase other races from the landscape.[43]

Further, McCarthy's description of Eduardo's handling of the blade, passing it "back and forth like a shuttle through a loom," as well as Eduardo's description of Cole's world as a "labyrinth of questions," recalls Judge Holden's characterization of the apparent order in the world as a "string in a maze." Just as the judge believes order to be a myth, proposed and perpetuated by those who are lost in the world, Eduardo believes Cole's understanding of the world—that is, the order which Cole believes exists in the world—to be just such a maze; Eduardo will cut the string that Cole has used to situate himself by cutting into Cole, demonstrating that his romantic notions as informed by the American frontier mythology are a false means of understanding the world.[44]

Parham, on the other hand, seems to know from the start that the frontier as he had imagined it as a boy and tried to find with his crossings into Mexico does not exist, and perhaps never did. Early on, when he tries to explain to Cole that "the war changed everything," Cole asks him in reply, "How did the war change it?" Parham's cryptic answer—"It just did. It aint the same no more. It never will be"—can now be read as his acknowledgment that if there was a world as it had been imagined by the American frontier mythology, that world is forever lost to us. The dreams that Parham once had about a life on the frontier have been abandoned, in part because such dreams are for children who have no experience in the world: "When you're a kid you have these notions about how things are goin to be, Billy said. You get a little older and you pull back some on that. I think you wind up just tryin to minimize the pain" (78). Parham was able to minimize his pain by recognizing the failure of the American frontier mythology; Cole's inability to recognize that failure led to his very painful death.

However, if McCarthy is setting Parham up to be the hero of the American frontier mythology we deserve as well as the embodiment of progressive frontier values, the epilogue to *Cities of the Plain* shows this characterization to be at the very least ironic. Parham leaves the ranch after Cole's death, riding off into the sunset like many frontiersmen before him: "He rode out in the dark long before daylight and he rode the sun up and he rode it down again" (264). We are told that Parham looked for work as a ranch hand but no such work was to be found. His ability to live any semblance of a frontier life is permanently denied him, and we pick up his life again fifty years later, where he is working as an extra in a movie. Parham ends his career—for he holds no job after this one—as a representation, as a character in a fiction. McCarthy may be suggesting here that Parham's life up to this point has similarly been a fiction, and Parham little more than a representation himself. All the progressive values he has come to embody are but a part of this larger fiction.

Further, as he is an extra in the movie—a minor character around whom the plot does not revolve, and the details of whose life are not important to the story—Parham may have at best been a minor character in the fiction that was the American frontier mythology. Even the best of such characters, McCarthy may be suggesting, play such a small role in the larger mythology that they are almost not worthy of notice. If this is the case, then even the small measure of diversity that Parham represented—salvation and success on the frontier by means of an acceptance of the multiculturalism that the "frontier zone" embodies—is relatively meaningless. Such a negative reading is not out of line with McCarthy's works in general, many of which end on scenes of violence.

Where Parham earlier in his life recognized that the world was changing and that he had to abandon his boyhood dreams, he now realizes that "in everything that he'd ever thought about the world and about his life in it he'd been wrong" (266). Evicted from his room after his movie work ended, Parham is left with nothing, and we are told that "he'd long since sold his saddle," the last physical possession that tied him to the frontier life he tried to lead in his youth (265). However, the narrative does not end here. First, Parham happens upon a homeless old Mexican, "another such as he"—also a refugee from the American frontier mythology as the acculturated but ultimately undesirable "savage" other—with whom he speaks in both English and Spanish at some length (266). McCarthy may be suggesting that those stranded on the frontier zone, bilingual figures who can operate in both communities, will never be fully accepted by either. Both are homeless, without a country, permanent residents of the "frontier zone" between savagery and civilization, even if that "frontier zone" no longer occupies a physical space, has no chronotopic reality.

After his encounter with the old Mexican, Parham again travels, and is eventually taken in by a family just outside of Portales, New Mexico. The family owns a colt, and Parham shows the children how to "work the colt with rope and halter," though such instruction is largely superfluous for what is in fact a domesticated animal, a small horse stabled in a shed in the family's backyard. Parham's life's work as a ranch hand on the frontier has thus been boiled down to simple lessons taught to children who do not need them to survive as Parham once did. To further highlight Parham's separation from his former life, we learn that one night he dreams of his brother Boyd, "but he would not speak for all that he called out to him" (290). Boyd, who may represent Parham's past life and adventures on the frontier as well as the family that he lost many years ago, is nothing more than a dream; Parham's life on the American frontier and all that it represented for him is also such a dream, and in no fashion affects his current situation. I would suggest that this dream, in addition to the other incidents described in the epilogue, signals McCarthy's suggestion that the mythology of the American frontier is as dead as the frontier itself, a dream of old men with no place in the world, used up and ultimately abandoned by the mythology that informed their lives. Or, in the words of Dianne C. Luce: "From the title of *All the Pretty Horses* to the dedication of *Cities of the Plain*, the trilogy is a lullaby singing to sleep the vanishing cowboy."[45] And Billy Parham, restless in his sleep but weary nonetheless, may be the cowboy to whom McCarthy's trilogy sings.

Even such figures as Billy Parham, figures who never abandoned their grounding in reality for the romanticized notions of the American frontier mythology, and who embodied the progressive values that unite people rather than the negative stereotypes that separate them, are ultimately destroyed by that mythology. Unlike many of his contemporaries, McCarthy demonstrates to his readers that the mythology of the American frontier has no progressive inheritance for Americans in the latter half of the twentieth century; further, keeping in mind that the epilogue is set in "the spring of the second year of the new millennium," McCarthy may be suggesting that the new age will be born out of the failure of the American frontier mythology (264). If the old mythology of the American frontier has ultimately failed to provide for Americans a progressive cultural model, then perhaps it is time to claim for the frontier mythology what the superintendent of the 1890 Census pronounced for the frontier: "In the discussion of its extent, its westward movement, etc., it can not, therefore, any longer have a place in the . . . reports."[46] But until such a time comes, there is still much work to be done in reevaluating the mythology of the American frontier, recovering old voices, giving shape to new discussions, and further understanding our rich national heritage.

Coda: New Directions for the Mythology of the American Frontier

Myths are the agents of stability, fictions the agents of change. Myths call for absolute, fictions for conditional assent. Myths make sense in terms of a lost order of time, illud tempus *as Eliade calls it; fictions, if successful, make sense of the here and now,* hoc tempus.

—FRANK KERMODE, *THE SENSE OF AN ENDING*

The temptation to close, to limit, to set boundaries in time and space repeatedly reappears throughout the works examined in this study as a means of exerting control. Additionally, academic studies themselves are bound to set limits in the course of their work: What genre? What period? What area? What manifestation of the frontier? are all questions with which I have had to grapple. By defining the borders of a place, a period, or a genre, one attempts to exert mastery over the subject. However, as I have demonstrated above, such attempts at mastery by means of clearly defined boundaries often paradoxically expose one's inability to establish control. When in 1890 the superintendent of the Census pronounced that "there can hardly be said to be a frontier line," one could scarcely have expected the frontier impulse, and its attendant mythology, to simply halt in its progress.[1] As several writers have demonstrated, the "frontier line" was not merely westward-moving, but was used to mark various political and cultural barriers as well. The writers included in this study explore the means by which the "frontier line"—or, following Louis Owens, the "frontier zone"—has been applied to a variety of physical and cultural sites of difference. More than simply a geographical marker for use in official Census reports, the "frontier line" has been employed as a major means of physical and cultural separation, allowing for a dangerously dichotomous separation of peoples within the diverse American landscape.

Physical separation along such lines is common in American culture, from the north/south division dating back to the establishment of the Mason-Dixon Line, to the red state/blue state distinctions employed by political analysts in election years. Americans have become accustomed to making us/them distinctions, and representing those distinctions in various kinds of documents, from subjective narratives to seemingly objective maps. From E. L. Doctorow to Cormac McCarthy, the writers whose texts I have explored all challenge the authority with which we commonly invest such documents. Although narratives and maps may appear to provide the reader with a sense of authority, these documents are at the very least biased accounts, and at the very worst outright fictions. Engaging with such disparate texts as John Smith's self-congratulatory auto-hagiography to Judge Holden's destructive ledger book, American Historical Frontier Romancers writing in response to the challenges to traditional authority inspired by the political unrest of the latter half of the twentieth century have explored the humor, the destruction, and ultimately the unreliability of textual materials to exert any real control over the complex American physical and cultural landscape.

This desire to set limits, and particularly the desire to mark an ending, also characterizes academic scholarship. Periods, movements, and individual careers are often outlined by trajectories that have established starting and ending points, allowing us to study such trajectories as discrete entities. This is particularly the case in the study of the American Historical Romance, a genre that Michael Davitt Bell (borrowing from Henry James) identified as having already reached its endpoint. Bell defines the imaginative work of the romance in terms of its "sacrifice of relation" to its immediate sociopolitical reality, and then identifies Herman Melville's *The Confidence Man* as *the* work through which such a "sacrifice of relation has been fully and fatally realized."[2] Although I have fallen prey to the necessity of establishing a starting point, I hope to avoid the arrogance of identifying a conclusion to this rich, living tradition. Far from being "fully and fatally realized," the American Historical Romance is a discursive tradition to which writers continually turn in order to identify, develop, and ultimately reevaluate America's national mythology. From James Fenimore Cooper to Cormac McCarthy, the American Historical Frontier Romance (a subset of the American Historical Romance that Bell studies) remains a popular and engaging genre employed by a variety of authors who wish to critique America's foundational mythology.

Similarly, Bell's reading of the imaginative work of the American Historical Romance should not imply that the genre deals solely with fanciful flights of the imagination, and that the cord between the text and the world in which it is produced can ever be completely severed, even if for dramatic purposes he makes such a claim. Rather, such writers are always responding to and reacting against their immediate sociohistorical moments. Although the romancers writing in the wake of the various sociopolitical movements of the postwar period—including the response to the war in Vietnam, the civil rights movement, and the American Indian Movement—may have more clearly put into full relief their engagement with their immediate sociopolitical situation, they chose to work in this genre, I argue, precisely because the romance is a fit vehicle for developing imaginative sociopolitical critique. Because the mythology of the American frontier is not merely an abstract concept but demonstrates its influence in the everyday lives of contemporary Americans, those who grapple with the contentious terms and situations of the frontier mythology are bound to draw on their immediate circumstances for material.

Rather than separating imagination from "the real world," the romance brings the two together in richly imaginative and diverse ways. The romance explores the space, as Hawthorne has famously written, "where the Actual and the Imaginary may meet."[3] Hawthorne's description of the space where romance becomes imaginative commentary on the actual world metaphorically suggests the very "frontier zone" that I have explored in the previous chapters. Though not directly concerned with the physical space of the American frontier, Hawthorne's attempt at bridging the gap between the "Actual" and the "Imaginary" is framed by the very same dichotomous thinking that characterizes the mythology of the American frontier. In other words, where Perry Miller claims of American Historical Romancers that "all of them were basically concerned with . . . the continent, the heritage of America, the wilderness"[4]—in other words, the American frontier and its mythology—I would like to suggest that the American Historical Frontier Romance itself is a "frontier zone," a space where two seeming opposites meet and explore common ground: the "Actual" and the "Imaginary," the past and the present, the self and the other, the savage and the civilized, the known and the unknown. The romance is the fitting—if not inevitable—genre for writers working with the American frontier and its mythological inheritance, as well as those who wish to reevaluate that inheritance and explore its failings. Many writers working in the wake of the contentious 1960s have used their works to provide those "counterhistories" and "oppositional possibilities" that Peter Bellis identifies as the work of the romance.

What has traditionally been viewed as the mythology's positive influence on American culture—the forward march of economic and technological progress borne on the backs of white, male heroic figures, working to tame the wild land and its even wilder inhabitants—is now exposed as a destructive force in American culture. Just as the documents that have transmitted the mythology inevitably betray themselves as limited and faulty, the lessons learned from the traditional frontier mythology are revealed to be destructive. I believe that the best inheritance left us by the American frontier mythology is the exploration of the rich cultural diversity of the "frontier zone" itself, that border on which, following Louis Owens, two cultures can productively come together in mutual exploration, celebrating the mixedblood who is the "cultural breaker, break-dancing trickster-fashion through all signs, fracturing the self-reflexive mirror of the dominant center, deconstructing rigid borders, slipping between the seams, embodying contradictions, and contradancing across every boundary."[5]

The American Historical Frontier Romancers on whom this study focuses are a small but exemplary sampling of writers in the second half of the twentieth century who have explored America's diverse cultural heritage. These writers, and others too numerous to name here, have worked to explore America's contentious cultural history in no small part as a result of the widespread sociopolitical movements that characterized the 1960s and whose shockwaves are still felt today. The backlash against the war in Vietnam opened the floodgates for a variety of challenges to forms of authority. Additionally, the civil rights movement and American Indian Movement each worked to encourage African Americans and Native Americans to actively participate in their immediate sociopolitical situation, at times advocating violent action in response to years of cultural oppression, not the least of which was the continuing disenfranchisement from or negative characterizations within the dominant national mythology. And other movements such as the women's movement inspired many people to demand the freedom and equality under the law that all Americans should enjoy.

Resulting from these various national, and ultimately literary, movements was the understanding of the larger role that all Americans have played in the settlement of the West, in addition to exposing the frontier mythology as both sexist and racist by design. And although the protests against the war in Vietnam may not appear to be motivated by racism, Richard Slotkin reminds us that the rhetoric of the war was adapted wholesale from the frontier mythology's stock characterization of "cowboys and Indians," and Ishmael Reed reminds us that the war was fought by a disproportionately large number of disenfranchised African

American men. Further, all of the writers examined in this study suggest (albeit subtly in some cases) that this mythology is rooted in a gendered dichotomy that also does not serve contemporary America.

My study joins the growing number of popular and critical texts devoted to explorations of the American frontier mythology and its failed inheritance for a diverse American community. Nor is this work limited to the American Historical Frontier Romance, either. As McCarthy hints at the end of the Border Trilogy—noting that Billy Parham works as an extra for cowboy movies—the American film industry has similarly explored the failure of the frontier mythology to establish order over the complex American physical and cultural landscape. As Richard Slotkin has noted, "unemployed cowboys and hungry reservation Indians looked to regional and Hollywood movie companies for work, as once they had looked to the Wild West."[6] When the frontier itself had passed, its former inhabitants found refuge in America's growing fascination with the frontier mythology and Hollywood's demand for a constructed verisimilitude. If the frontier itself has died, it can be re-created with the help of actual frontiersmen.

My study thus returns full circle to Richard Slotkin, from whose work I developed my methodology. Slotkin's multivolume study of the development of the American frontier mythology ends with *Gunfighter Nation: The Myth of the Frontier in Twentieth-Century America*. Though beginning with an exploration of the impact of the historical work of Frederick Jackson Turner and Theodore Roosevelt, much of his study is devoted to the film industry's adoption of the "western" as a genre, and its development throughout the twentieth century. Slotkin identifies Edwin S. Porter's *The Great Train Robbery* (1903) as the first movie western, and claims that "by 1908 the genre was so well established that distributors' catalogues listed their products under the headings 'Drama,' 'Comic,' and 'Western.'"[7] And just as American Historical Frontier Romancers through the nineteenth and early twentieth centuries followed (to varying degrees) the formula established by James Fenimore Cooper (who himself adapted the formula he found in Sir Walter Scott's *Waverley* novels), so too did early-twentieth-century filmmakers "imitate Porter's work and repeat its success."[8] Just as dime novels and "yellow backs" were popular vehicles for the transmission of the American frontier mythology in the nineteenth century, film is a popular vehicle for the transmission of this aspect of our national mythology in the twentieth and twenty-first centuries. Hollywood westerns provided a form of sociopolitical commentary, demonstrating American popular culture's indebtedness to the frontier mythology.

As with American life in general, the film industry was changed by America's involvement in World War II: "Wartime rationing of resources limited the kind and number of productions Hollywood could mount. At the same time, the government's need for films to popularize the war effort and the audience's desire to learn about the war through the mass media reshaped the genre map of Hollywood production, creating new genres like the combat film and redirecting older genres like . . . the western to war-related themes and symbols."[9] The universality of the themes associated with the western—rugged individualism, personal and national fulfillment at the expense of a racial "other," and the various binaries associated with the "civilized/savage" dichotomy—were all easily adapted to combat films of the Second World War.

Rather than simply repeat Slotkin's work here, I would like to make two suggestions. First, there is still much work to be done in exploring the various media that have drawn their subject matter from the national mythology, including literature, film, television, and popular song. Second, as such recent critical and popular film successes as *Unforgiven* (1992) and *Brokeback Mountain* (2005) demonstrate (not to mention movie adaptations of three of Cormac McCarthy's most recent novels), the mythology of the American frontier has left contemporary America with a problematic inheritance that is still being evaluated. Clint Eastwood's *Unforgiven* nicely parallels McCarthy's *Blood Meridian* in its use of unredemptive violence and its noticeable lack of any clearly heroic character; the American frontier is a cold, harsh environment inhabited by people who, to various degrees and for various reasons, employ and even embrace violence. Ang Lee's *Brokeback Mountain*[10] forces its audience to rethink masculinity and how it was both formed and also challenged on the "frontier zone." The frontier was populated by a diverse range of characters, not simply the white heterosexual males on which the mythology has traditionally focused its attention.

For this reason, my study also gestures toward a range of writers from diverse ethnic backgrounds whose work engages with the mythology of the American frontier. In ending my study on McCarthy's Border Trilogy, I nod toward the necessity for studying Latino writers whose work engages with the national mythology and the construction of the borderlands. For instance, one could productively read the works of Yxta Maya Murray for their use of the frontier mythology and colonial history (especially *The King's Gold* and *The Conquest*) as a means of navigating contemporary Latina/o identity. Similarly, in *Caramelo*, Sandra Cisneros explores contemporary border politics through a multigenerational family narrative. Turning our attention north, contemporary narratives set on the U.S./Canadian border—particularly those that engage historical sources or provide historical revision, such as Thomas King's *Green Grass, Running Water*—are a rich field of potential study for the continued engagement with the frontier mythology. Looking west, Native American writers of the Southwest have long addressed the vexed inheritance of the frontier mythology as a means of defining savagery and civilization, as seen in the works of Leslie Marmon Silko (but perhaps most clearly in her often underappreciated historical novel *Gardens in the Dunes*).

Many contemporary novels that engage with history—even if they are not in the strictest sense historical novels—do so by alluding to the mythology of the American frontier. Toni Morrison's *Paradise*, to give but one example, incorporates historical narratives as a means of providing context for the tension between the all-black town of Ruby, Oklahoma, and the former convent, now inhabited by women of different racial identities. The inheritance of the frontier mythology is also central to Percival Everett's *Walk Me to the Distance*, *Watershed*, and *God's Country*. The first tells the story of David Larson, a (presumably) African American Vietnam veteran who settles in the former frontier town of Slut's Hole, Wyoming; the second explores the implications of U.S. treaties with reservation Indians over the use (and abuse) of water rights. The third most explicitly engages the frontier mythology by imagining the life of a free African American trying to survive on the American frontier.

And even if it's true that discussions of the American frontier tend to focus more on Latina/os, Native Americans, and African Americans, one cannot deny the value of reading the canon of Asian American literature in terms of the frontier mythology, remembering the reliance on Chinese labor to build the railroad, the technological marvel that helped collapse the distance between the civilized East and the frontier West. One could read Karen Tei Yamashita's novel *I Hotel*—a fictionalization of how the civil rights struggles of the 1960s played out in San Francisco—in terms of how the national mythology helped to establish many of the social codes that such struggles attempted to rethink. Certainly, a more nuanced understanding of the problematic inheritance of the frontier mythology would assist in reading contemporary narratives set on the very borders the frontier mythology helped to establish and codify.

Similarly, this study focused on male authors who grappled with the frontier mythology as embodied in the Daniel Boone tradition. As Annette Kolodny has demonstrated (particularly in *The Land Before Her: Fantasy and Experience of the American Frontiers, 1630–1860*), women had very different experiences on the American frontier. As such, their later engagement with their inheritance of the mythology would be a fruitful area of study. There is much more work to be done exploring the challenges and revisions to the frontier mythology with respect to gender construction and sexual identity. Looking at works outside of the tradition of the historical romance, Annie Proulx's work generally, but particularly *Close Range: Wyoming Stories,* would provide an excellent starting point for exploring the ways that the mythology of the American frontier manifests itself in the lives of contemporary men and women, living in the space formerly known as "the frontier." Additionally, Ang Lee's award-winning adaptation of *Brokeback Mountain* to film explored many of these issues more explicitly and in more depth.[11] While there has been much discussion of the movie's exploration of the relationship between Ennis and Jack, comparatively little has been written about their wives as inheritors of the frontier mythology.

It is for these various reasons that this final section is called a "coda" and not a "conclusion." To write a "conclusion" would imply that the work I have focused my attention on has been completed, that the reevaluation of the national mythology is complete. Although American Historical Frontier Romancers have performed this work for a half century, such works as *Brokeback Mountain* demonstrate that we have only just begun to extensively revisit the American frontier mythology. It is my hope that the present study will serve to inspire future critical investigations of America's most fascinating and influential mythology and the continuing usefulness of what for two centuries has been a consistently popular genre. As Sara L. Spurgeon reminds us: "Myths are what we wish history had been—a compressed, simplified, sometimes outright false vision of the past but a vision intended to serve a specific purpose in the present and, just as importantly, to bequeath a specific shape to the future."[12] We know the uses to which the American frontier mythology has been put, just as we also know the reasons it has been employed, adapted, and ultimately challenged. So now we must ask, how will we use these lessons to help shape our future?

Notes

Introduction

1. Throughout, I will use "the American frontier myth" as shorthand, though I do not mean to suggest that there was only one frontier mythology. For instance, as demonstrated by the literary theorist Annette Kolodny in *The Land Before Her: Fantasy and Experience of the American Frontiers, 1630–1860* and the historian Julie Roy Jeffrey in *Frontier Women: "Civilizing" the West? 1840–1880,* women experienced a very different frontier than did men, and as such their mythological inheritance differs from that of men. Though I do not have the space for such an exploration here, a study of the ways women in contemporary America respond to the inheritance of their frontier myth(s)—particularly in response to the feminist/womanist movement(s) of the late twentieth century—would certainly help to paint a larger, more complete picture of the period and the cultural inheritance of the frontier mytholog(ies).

2. Connell, "The History of Masculinity," 245.

3. As Rachel Borup succinctly noted, "In the national imagination, the West was closely tied to these lone white males' conquests." She further suggests that "the meaning of the West" lies in "the rhetorical competition between male adventure stories and female domestic narratives" ("Bankers in Buckskins," 230). This may be historically true, but the works under discussion in the chapters that follow will frustrate this distinction; Blue (*Welcome to Hard Times*) writes a very domestic narrative, for instance.

4. Silverman, *Male Subjectivity at the Margins,* 16.

5. Worden, *Masculine Style,* 2.

6. Ibid., 6.

7. For a history of "hegemonic masculinity," the reader is directed to R. W. Connell and James W. Messerschmidt, "Hegemonic Masculinity." Although they do not name any specific figures as exemplars of hegemonic masculinity, one can certainly see Daniel Boone—and the legion of frontiersmen constructed in his image—in their

explanation that "it embodied the currently most honored way of being a man, it required all other men to position themselves in relation to it, and it ideologically legitimated the global subordination of women to men" (832). From Daniel Boone to the Marlboro Man, the frontiersman has long been the standard against which masculinity has been measured. Further, for a critique of hegemonic masculinity—in particular an effort to move beyond "Connell's dualism between hegemonic masculinity and non-hegemonic masculinities"—see Demetrakis Z. Demetriou, "Connell's Concept of Hegemonic Masculinity: A Critique." Such a critique might be useful in constructions of masculinity built upon other models; this study is concerned with a very particular masculine figure that has long dominated the popular imagination.

8. Although the authors included in this study were not directly responding to the women's movement in their works, it is impossible to understand the full implications of their engagement with hegemonic masculinity without discussing how changes to women's rights and social roles affected constructions of masculinity. Further, many of the activists working toward civil rights generally were involved with multiple groups, organizations, and movements in the latter half of the twentieth century. As James Penner has recently noted: "The women's movement grew out of the New Left and the antiwar movement. Women, who were crucial to the civil rights and antiwar movements, began to resent the sexism of New Left men and women's second-class status within the movements. The key splintering point for many early feminists centered about the issue of whether gender could be disentangled from the class struggle and the broader aims of traditional left-wing politics (i.e., ending the Vietnam War, racism, and poverty)" (*Pinks, Pansies, and Punks*, 226). Although the writers in this study explicitly focused their attention on male figures and the construction of masculinity, their works certainly gesture toward the broader politics of gender construction. While the authors included in this study did not directly engage feminism in the works I have selected, more recent feminist criticism—particularly the contemporary work on gender and masculinity, as well as certain paradigmatic moments in the struggle for women's social and political equality—will help to illuminate the subtle ways these authors construct and critique classic American masculinity. See also Keith D. Miller and Kathleen Weinkauf, "Discovering the Erased Feminism of the Civil Rights Movement."

9. Slotkin, *Gunfighter Nation*, 10.

10. Roosevelt opens his history with a chapter titled "The Spread of the English-Speaking People," making his work almost epic in nature, and allowing him to understand American Manifest Destiny as an irrepressible force of nature. The "whites" succeed in no small part due to the "superior" technological advantage they hold over their "foes" (*The Winning of the West*, 34). The "West" was literally "won" as a result of violent warfare that is whitewashed to give it a heroic luster. Roosevelt's positive historical account is bolstered by such claims as "[the Indians] were never numerous in the land" (36), which demonstrates his desire to highlight Euro-American superiority; however, it may also reflect guilt in knowing that westward expansion came "*sometimes* at the expense of the natives" (34, my emphasis).

11. Dalton, "Failing to See," 15.

12. Lipsitz, *The Possessive Investment in Whiteness*, 3.

13. In this regard, the authors whose work I include are engaging with the same kind of protest we see in contemporary "rock artists Iggy Pop, David Bowie and Lou

Reed," who, Esther Zaplana argues, "depart at this time [the 1960s and 1970s] from dominant models of masculinity and subvert the limits of patriarchal representation." For Zaplana, "representations of the male body at this historically specific location destabilized hegemonic representations of masculinity, dovetailing with the radical politics of a younger generation that strove to break the molds of an alienating social and gendered order" ("Breaking the Mold," 64).

14. Admittedly, this is a very sympathetic reading of a series that also goes to great pains to distinguish between white and Indian "gifts." One should also note that this Bumppo figure—the white hero who comes to embody Native American values—is a cornerstone of the mythology of the American frontier, and perhaps is most recognizable in the film *Dances with Wolves* and its various thematic remakes (such as *The Last Samurai* and *Avatar*).

15. When specifically referring to the genre of the Historical Romance (or the American Historical Frontier Romance), I will capitalize the term. Otherwise, following convention, "romance" will be lowercased throughout.

16. P. Miller, "The Romance and the Novel," 252.

17. Bakhtin, "Form of Time and of the Chronotope in the Novel," 84. Bakhtin defines the "chronotope" as "the intrinsic connectedness of temporal and spatial relationships that are artistically expressed in literature."

18. Lukács, *The Historical Novel*, 60.

19. Ibid., 53.

20. Ibid., 63.

21. M. Wilson, "Saturnalia of the Blood," 131. Although the issues were different for African Americans (as we will see in the chapters below), it is safe to say that both Native Americans and African Americans occupied a precarious position in frontier fiction, whose presence was consciously and conspicuously erased from both the land and the literary representations. In his article "Playing Like a Man: Noncompetitive Manhood and Frontier Humor," Scott Romine suggests that humor is one mode by which authors can escape the quandary Wilson identifies; certainly Barth, Pynchon, Reed, and Vizenor employ humor (much like their predecessors Twain, George Washington Harris, and others).

22. Farley, "The Poetics of Colorlined Space," 98.

23. Ibid., 105.

24. As Michael Uebel reminds us, race and gender are culturally constructed, and as such would be renegotiated for each specific chronotope: "Around the central question 'How do men inhabit simultaneously their color and their gender?' others are elaborated: How is the imbrication of race and male subjectivity to be understood as a historically, culturally specific construct?" ("Men in Color," 2).

25. Connell, "The History of Masculinity," 251.

26. Reeser, *Masculinities in Theory*, 91.

27. In fact, Bumppo's nickname "Hawkeye" is given to him by a fallen Indian, whom Bumppo slew in self-defense. Even in his death and despite his attempts to kill Bumppo, the Indian recognized Bumppo's superior skills as a marksman. The dying Indian gives Bumppo his first sobriquet earned on the warpath: "Great warrior, soon—No, Deerslayer—Hawkeye—Hawkeye—Hawkeye—Shake hand" (Cooper, *The Deerslayer*, 124).

28. For a compelling reading of Cooper's use of the Historical Romance to explore the "Great American Desert," see Stephanie LeMenager's *Manifest and Other Destinies:*

Territorial Fictions of the Nineteenth-Century United States. As a work of postwestern literary criticism (postwestern studies will be discussed below), LeMenager's work engages in a reevaluation of (in this case) the Midwest and its function in popular literature, in that "the tensions that undermine the anti-referential privilege of the Romancer in *The Prairie* are also problems of imagination, and insofar as the inland deserts were projections of nationalist doubt they spelled out a world that *was* Romantic because it engaged in the possible rather than reifying a probable, already hegemonic understanding of North American space" (32). Cooper's work is a reminder that "the West" is not a stable location, given that whether he was hunting in New York State or trapping in the Great Plains, Natty Bumppo was always a figure of "the West."

29. Frye, *Anatomy of Criticism,* 305.

30. Ibid. It should be noted that, in addition to being a romancer, William Morris was also a social and political activist, whose affiliations would today likely align him with the political Left.

31. Ibid., 304.

32. Ibid., 33.

33. Clara Reeve, *The Progress of Poesy* (1785), cited in Thompson and Link, *Neutral Ground,* 81.

34. Frye, "The Four Forms of Fiction," 33.

35. Bellis, *Writing Revolution,* 12.

36. Ibid., 18, emphasis mine.

37. Cooper, *Wyandotté,* 3.

38. Thomas Philbrick and Marianne Philbrick, "Historical Introduction" to *Wyandotté,* by Cooper, xxv.

39. Robinson, *Marked Men,* 45. In a similar vein, John Wheeler noted that "the Vietnam veteran was the nigger of the 1970s" (qtd. in Wiegman, *American Anatomies,* 124). Moving beyond Wheeler's obvious misunderstanding of race relations in Vietnam (which Ishmael Reed will address in chapter 3), such a statement demonstrates a larger trend of conflating the issues raised by the three sociopolitical movements to which the writers discussed below are responding.

40. M. M. Bakhtin, "Epic and Novel," in Holquist, ed., *Dialogic,* 37.

41. Chase, *The American Novel,* 12, viii.

42. Baym, "Concepts of Romance in Hawthorne's America." 430.

43. Chase, *The American Novel,* 1.

44. Or, as Perry Miller so boldly asserted in "The Romance and the Novel": "The distinction between the two was as precise in the mind of an untutored Melville as that between, let us say, an epic and a sonnet, simply because it was equally present to every even semiliterate consciousness in the era" (242).

45. See the work of Emily Miller Budick for an excellent study of women's contributions to the romance tradition, discussed below.

46. James, *The Art of the Novel,* 33–34.

47. Bell, *The Development of American Romance,* 245.

48. Porte, *The Romance in America,* 215.

49. Thompson and Link, *Neutral Ground,* 151.

50. Ibid., 140.

51. Quoted in Thompson and Link, *Neutral Ground,* 151.

52. Budick, *Engendering Romance,* 1.

53. Ibid.

54. One may, at this point, ask why I have not included authors from other racial/ethnic backgrounds, such as Latino authors or Asian American authors. To this question I have two replies. First, given the social and political events to which this study is responding (Vietnam, civil rights, and AIM), I have chosen authors whose works directly address those events while working within the romance tradition. Second, no study can be exhaustive, and it is my hope that this work advances the discussion of the romance tradition in such a way that future scholarship may help advance, develop, or critique my efforts here. The present study is intended as a starting point, and not as the final word on the subject.

55. That is, it is one thing to note the sex of the authors, and quite another to note the gender, or the social construction of identity.

56. Ibid., 4.

57. P. Miller, "The Romance and the Novel," 252.

58. Hutcheon, *A Poetics of Postmodernism*, 40. One phrase I will absolutely avoid using, though some readers may perhaps be reading it between the lines, is "postmodern romance." The works I include can certainly all be considered examples of "historiographic metafiction." However, I wish to avoid the categorical slippage that ideas like "postmodern romance" tend to allow for, as one can see in Diane Elam's *Romancing the Postmodern*. Although I certainly agree with her claims that "in postmodernism, as in romance, the division between high and low culture, the study and the boudoir, becomes blurred" (1), I disagree with her claim that "romance is a signature of postmodernism" (2). As scholars like Budick (and others) have demonstrated, such claims are simply historically inaccurate; while it is true that postmodern writers have actively engaged the romance tradition, postmodernism engages multiple literary historical traditions, and the romance has been developed throughout American literary history. It is this kind of slippage that allows for the claim that "romance, by virtue of its troubled relation to both history and novelistic realism, has in a sense been postmodern all along" (3). It would appear that Elam is suggesting that postmodernism gives legitimacy to the romance, or at least that we can only understand the romance tradition with the advent of postmodernism, both of which undervalue the degree to which past romancers have highlighted our problematic relationship to historical fidelity. At the risk of piling on, I'd like to end my criticism of her work by noting that any line of reasoning that allows one to conclude that "[Sir Walter] Scott's romance is postmodern" fails to understand either postmodernism or romance, by ignoring literary history in favor of a bold—if oversimplified—reading. More properly understood, the romance has always been engaged with reevaluating our relationship with history. As such, it is the most fitting genre for those authors who, following the sociopolitical upheaval of the 1960s, wish to use their fiction to reevaluate our national mythology. This is a specific choice made on the part of the authors, and not the methodological inevitability that Elam would seem to suggest. In short, while I will in places simply take for granted that the authors in this study are "postmodern," I will spend much time exploring their engagement with the romance tradition; the two, in other words, are not coterminous and interchangeable. One could also argue that an overinvestment in the notion of "the postmodern" allows for too clean a break with the past. To give but one example of such a break, Caren Irr agues that "in the early twenty-first century, a revival of the political novel has begun in the US"

("Postmodernism in Reverse," 517), a claim that only makes sense if you ignore the development of the romance tradition throughout the twentieth century, particularly as it has been engaged by writers responding to the major sociopolitical movements of the mid- to late twentieth century. Hopefully, one side effect of the present study will be to help bring into relief the connections between late-twentieth- and early-twenty-first-century American fiction.

59. McHale, "Break, Period, Interregnum," 328–29. The present study can also productively be read alongside Mark McGurl's study of the second half of the twentieth century, as providing a more nuanced means of reading how "the literary cultural nationalisms of the sixties sought to liberate U.S. minority writers from the assimilative coercions of the American mainstream by symbolically affiliating them with decolonized peoples engaged in more literal acts of nation building" (*The Program Era*, 330–31). While this is an apt way of reading "minority" writers, it is also a useful way to read several of Thomas Pynchon's novels, especially *Mason & Dixon*. More importantly, there is no shortage of studies seeking to situate the fiction of the late twentieth century, from Mark McGurl's study of the influence of creative writing programs (and institutionalism more broadly), to Jay Clayton's argument that American fiction has moved beyond "the old Romantic notion of the masterpiece" in his study of the conversation taking place between literary fiction and critical theory (*The Pleasures of Babel*, 30), to Jeremy Green's formulation of "late postmodernism" and the ways writers at the tail end of the twentieth century respond to "anxieties about the irrelevance of literature" (*Late Postmodernism*, 11). It is for this reason that I tend to agree with David Perkins, who has noted that "literary history comes at a very high cost" because, once a work is read in terms of a literary history, that work "becomes a more complicated experience, aesthetically and intellectually" (*Is Literary History Possible?*, 184). Any literary history will help us to better understand the complexities of the individual works under discussion, and as such all attempts at historicizing works produced during a discrete period should be read as complementary rather than competing studies.

60. Hutcheon, *A Poetics of Postmodernism*, 55.

61. Ibid., 44.

62. Jameson, *Postmodernism*, 367.

63. Turner, "The Significance of the Frontier in American History," 38.

64. Quoted ibid., 1.

65. Senator John F. Kennedy, Address Accepting the Nomination for Presidency of the United States of America, July 15, 1960.

66. Slotkin, *Gunfighter*, 504.

67. Ibid., 513.

68. Slotkin develops this connection in much more detail, and the interested reader is directed to part 4 of *Gunfighter Nation*, "Democracy and Force: The Western and the Cold War, 1946–1960," for a fascinating discussion of how "the rise and fall of the Western mirrors the development of the Cold War and its sustaining ideological consensus from its seedtime in 1948–1954 to its fulfillment in the years of the liberal counteroffensive under Kennedy and Johnson, to its disruption by the failure of the war in Vietnam" (347), which is roughly the starting point for the present study.

69. Corkin, *Cowboys as Cold Warriors*, 2.

70. Ibid., 246.

71. Slotkin, *Regeneration*, 564.

72. Ibid., 565. Around the time that Slotkin was discussing the frontier inheritance in the war in Vietnam, many Native Americans were reading American involvement in Vietnam as a continuance of Manifest Destiny. See, for instance, William Meyer (*'yonv'ut'sisla*), an Eastern Cherokee artist and political activist, in his 1971 history of Native American social and political protests, *Native Americans*: "One wonders whether the war in Vietnam is not merely the western frontier extended to some warped, 'logical' conclusion, a 20th century form of Manifest Destiny. Also, in a Green Beret training manual designed as a comic book, there is a picture of a U.S. soldier killing a Vietcong soldier. The caption reads: 'That's one little Indian that won't talk anymore'" (75n).

73. H. White, "Droysen's *Historik*," 96.

74. Ibid., 91.

75. For more on this school of study, the reader is directed to such works as Patricia Nelson Limerick's *The Legacy of Conquest: The Unbroken Path of the American West*; Richard White's *Railroaded: The Transcontinentals and the Making of Modern America*; and Robert V. Hine and John Mack Faragher's, *The American West: A New Interpretive History*.

76. Limerick, *Legacy*, 54.

77. Ibid., 152.

78. Kollin, ed., *Postwestern Cultures*, x, xi. Kollin's collection is but one place to start, and the interested reader is directed to the Postwestern Horizons series at the University of Nebraska Press, as well as the Spring/Summer 2013 special double issue of *Western American Literature*, for further study.

79. Campbell, *The Rhizomatic West*, 1. It is worth noting that, while much of the work being done in postwestern studies engages with some aspect of the frontier mythology, Alex Young Trimble would remind us that "for many 'postwestern' critics (if they might so be called), representing the West as a region defined by the proliferation of competing *petit récits* rather than one shaped by a frontier metanarrative has been an essential part of a "western critical regionalism" ("Settler Sovereignty," 116). However, I would be remiss if I did not note that Trimble makes his point in an article consciously alluding to Frederick Jackson Turner and his essay "The Significance of the Frontier in American History."

80. Limerick, *Legacy*, 254.

81. Comer, "Introduction," 3, 5.

82. Pratt, *Imperial Eyes*, 4.

83. D. Johnson and Michaelson, "Border Secrets," 15.

84. Zinn, *A People's History of the United States*, 8.

85. Ibid., 10. Not surprisingly, given his desire to move away from the traditional kind of hero worship found in many works of history, Zinn spends little time recounting the actions of such famous frontiersmen as Davy Crockett (and no time on Daniel Boone). In fact, the frontier doesn't even warrant an entry in the index. That said, there are many ways to understand American history, and many myths that needed reevaluation in the latter half of the twentieth century.

86. Foucault, *The Archaeology of Knowledge*, 6.

87. Ibid., 7.

88. Ibid., 6.

1 / Rewriting the Historical Record

1. Filson's account appeared in numerous printed forms, published independently as well as in collected works, including translations into French and German. For a full account, see Slotkin, *Regeneration*, esp. chaps. 9–11.

2. Ibid., 517–18.

3. Slotkin is not the only historian to give Boone special treatment. Volume 1 of Theodore Roosevelt's *The Winning of the West* devotes two chapters to Daniel Boone: chapter 6, "Boon [*sic*] and the Longhunters; and Their Hunting in No-Man's Land, 1769–1774," and chapter 10, "Boon and the Settlement of Kentucky, 1775." Note that the title of chapter 6 characterizes the land occupied by Native Americans as "No-Man's Land."

4. Connell, "The History of Masculinity," 245.

5. Ibid., 247.

6. This phrase—and ones similar to it—have appeared in multiple interviews and addresses given by Doctorow. See Christopher D. Morris's introduction to Doctorow, *Conversations with E. L. Doctorow*; as well as Doctorow, "Author, Author," interview by James McInerney; and Doctorow, "10 Questions for E. L. Doctorow," interview by Lev Grossman, 6.

7. This is true for all of his works except for the disastrous futuristic novel *Big As Life* (1966), both a commercial and critical failure, and his most recent novel *Andrew's Brain* (2014). As of this writing, *Big As Life* is Doctorow's only out-of-print work.

8. Doctorow, "History and the Forms of Fiction," interview by Jared Lubarsky, 37–38.

9. Doctorow, "Mr. Ragtime," interview by Jonathan Yardley, 10–11. However, Doctorow also warned against the use of fiction for the political and moral instruction of the audience, claiming that "as a writer, you avoid bringing any calculated, thematic political or social intention to the book, because, if you do, you're in grave danger of becoming didactic" (Doctorow, "A Talk with E. L. Doctorow," interview by Liesl Schillinger, 108). Doctorow believes that political and social didacticism would kill the aesthetic intention of the work.

10. Doctorow, "*Ragtime* Revisited," 20.

11. Ibid., 42–43.

12. Doctorow, "A Spirit of Transgression," interview by Larry McCaffery, 85.

13. Ibid., 87. In this respect, the writer is somewhere between a trickster and a revolutionary, roles more clearly adopted by his contemporaries Ishmael Reed and Gerald Vizenor (see chapters 3 and 4).

14. Doctorow, "A Multiplicity of Witnesses," interview by Herwig Friedl and Dieter Schulz, 114–15.

15. Friedan, *The Feminine Mystique*, 16, ix.

16. Ibid., 383.

17. Zinn, *A People's History*, 494.

18. For more on this connection, see Slotkin, *The Fatal Environment* (part 7: "The Boy General, 1839–1876"); and *Gunfighter Nation* (chapter 11: "Studies in Red and White: Cavalry, Indians, and Cold War Ideology, 1946–1960").

19. Doctorow, "A Spirit of Transgression," interview by McCaffery, 85.

20. Doctorow, "A Multiplicity of Witnesses," interview by Friedl and Schulz, 114.

21. Ibid., 124.

22. Doctorow, "False Documents," 161.

23. H. White, "The Question of Narrative in Contemporary Historical Theory," 57, emphasis mine.

24. Doctorow, *Welcome to Hard Times*, 44; hereafter cited parenthetically.

25. Note also that Blue is consciously writing "across the red lines" in his ledger. As we will see in John Barth's *The Sot-Weed Factor*, Ebenezer Cooke similarly must write across the red lines of his ledger in order to record his *Marylandiad*. In both cases, the act of writing in these ledgers is marked as a somewhat violent use of their account books, as if in recognition that neither "account" is accurate.

26. Morris, *Misrepresentation*, 30.

27. Of course, I am here (and elsewhere) referring to the figure of Daniel Boone that comes from the mythology, and not the historical figure. As Robert Morgan has noted: "The hero is mostly a name to which the deeds and exploits, qualities of character, can be attached. The figure becomes a springboard for the folk imagination, for collective memory and a record of culture" (*Boone*, 300).

28. Ibid., 16.

29. Although Blue believes he is giving to Molly some measure of respect by introducing her as his wife, this action is better read as his attempt to imprison her in the "concentration camp that American women have walked into, *or have been talked into by others*" that Betty Friedan claims marriage to be (*The Feminine Mystique*, 308, emphasis mine). As soon as he unofficially "marries" Molly, Blue begins to lament that she does not act the proper wife. Where before, as prostitute, Molly was a self-possessed woman and member of the community, now, as a wife, Molly is essentially trapped in the "home" she shares with Blue and Fee. As such, Molly is little more than another prop Blue uses (like the gun) to assert his failed masculinity.

30. Gardiner, "Theorizing Age with Gender," 109.

31. Jeffords, *The Remasculinization of America*, 93. Although the United States would not officially enter the conflict until 1961, soldiers were already stationed and had fought a similar war in Korea. This is but one part of the "amplification by a later generation" Doctorow noted above.

32. Horrocks, *Male Myths and Icons*, 60.

33. Although John Bear is a minor character in this work, his presence should suggest to the reader the racial politics of the nineteenth-century American frontier. Deaf and cowardly, John Bear is initially a far cry from the "savage injun" figure often portrayed by the mythology of the American frontier. His cowardice is actually praised by Blue, who notes that "if he was dumb he wasn't too dumb" (15). However, at the end of the novel, Blue suggests that John Bear scalped Zar, the barkeeper, likely in retaliation for Zar's having hit him from behind earlier in the narrative. Although Doctorow does not give any significant time to exploring the racial politics of this frontier chronotope (and I will refrain from reading too deeply into his portrayal of an almost entirely white settlement), I would like to take note of John Bear's presence as the "vanishing Indian" as a prefiguring of what will be discussed in more detail in later chapters. In other words, in his 1960 Historical Frontier Romance, Doctorow makes a slight nod toward the critique of the frontier myth provided by writers in the wake of the American Indian Movement.

34. The problem of mapmaking as a means of constructing order on the American frontier will be addressed in chapter 2.

35. Jeffords, *The Remasculinization of America*, 14.

36. Doctorow, "The Writer as Independent Witness," interview by Paul Levine, 42.

37. Special mention should be made of Bernd Engler and Kurt Müller, eds., *Historiographic Metafiction in Modern American and Canadian Literature*. Several contributors to this collection include Doctorow in their overview of historiographic metafiction.

38. I borrow the term "fabulator" from Robert Scholes's study *The Fabulators*, which was one of the first attempts at a comprehensive study of what would later be termed "postmodern" novelists. Scholes discusses the inheritance of classical myth and fable in the works of such contemporary writers as Iris Murdoch, John Hawkes, Kurt Vonnegut, and John Barth. Scholes reclaims the term "fabulators"—which "dropped out of our language a few years ago" (6)—to refer to those writers who "return to a more verbal kind of fiction. It also means a return to a more fictional kind. By this I mean a less realistic and more artistic kind of narrative: more shapely, more evocative; more concerned with ideas and ideals, less concerned with things" (12). In other words, a "fabulator" is a romancer, as I have defined it in the introduction to this volume.

39. Doctorow, "*Ragtime* Revisited," 14.

40. Punday, "John Barth's Occasional Writing," 599.

41. Barth, "An Interview with John Barth," interview by Kevin Bezner, 7. Although this comment is made in an interview about his novel *LETTERS*, the context in which it is made could easily be applied to *The Sot-Weed Factor*, which similarly employs "false documents, falsified documents, forged and doctored letters, mislaid and misdirected letters and the like, in the history of History" ("Historical Fiction, Fictitious History, and Chesapeake Bay Blue Crabs, or, About Aboutness," 181).

42. Müller, "The Development toward Historiographic Metafiction in the American Novel," 43. Although Barth's novel was published, like Doctorow's, in 1960, both take part in the larger cultural discussion that would lead to the social and political movements of the 1960s, and as such should be read as part of the larger historical moment of the 1960s.

43. Barth, "The Literature of Replenishment," 200.

44. Barth, introduction to "A Poet to the Rescue," 91.

45. Barth, "Intelligent Despisal," 118.

46. Barth, introduction to "Intelligent Despisal," 110.

47. Barth, "Intelligent Despisal," 119.

48. "A Poet to the Rescue" was originally published in "Norman Cousins's short-lived *World* magazine" (introduction to "A Poet to the Rescue," 93).

49. Barth, "The Literature of Exhaustion," 75, emphasis mine.

50. Barth, "An Interview with John Barth," interview by Bezner, 8.

51. Müllenbrock, "John Barth's *The Sot-Weed Factor* as a Prototype of Historiographic Metafiction," 164.

52. Barth, "Historical Fiction, Fictitious History, and Chesapeake Bay Blue Crabs, or, About Aboutness," 188.

53. Barth, introduction to "The Literature of Exhaustion," 64.

54. Hutcheon, "Historiographic Metafiction: Parody and the Intertextuality of History," 4. And while I agree with Hutcheon that "postmodernism is less a period than a poetics or an ideology" (28), I must insist that this ideology, this poetics, is informed by its politics, and thus inseparable from the political/historical moment.

55. Gado, ed., *First Person*, 117.

56. Ibid., 118.

57. Barth, *The Sot-Weed Factor*, 25; hereafter cited parenthetically.

58. J. Smith, *Captain John Smith's America*, ed. Lankford, 48.

59. For a study on the importance of the Pocahontas myth and its development in American art, see Robert Tilton's *Pocahontas: The Evolution of an American Narrative*.

60. Although Barth has not published on the importance of the history of "the pill" in relation to his work, it is difficult to read his revision of the Pocahontas narrative without considering the changing perception of sex brought on by the release in 1960 of the birth control pill. This silence on the issue is certainly in keeping with what Elizabeth Siegel Watkins has noted as the general lack of discussion about the pill "in the pages of the popular press at this time"; what discussion was taking place centered on "the morality of oral contraception as a method of family planning" (*On the Pill*, 44). Sir Burlingame's disapproval of Pocahontas's sexual exploits (with multiple sexual partners) mirrors the "discussions of changing sexual morality" (55) taking place in the 1960s. As Watkins further points out, "[Vance] Packard's sweeping portrayal of American society in the 1960s [*The Sexual Wilderness*, published in 1968] found little that did not have to do with the changing male-female relationship" (59). Although a sexualizing of the "savage other" is not uncommon in the frontier mythology (which we will also see in chapter 3), this overt focus on vaginal penetration as both a physical and a moral issue certainly gestures toward the social upheaval brought on by "the pill."

61. Connell, "The History of Masculinity," 245.

62. Smith's *Secret Historie* explains how a competitor for the throne may use a proxy to sit at the table for him. Should this proxy win the contest, he rules jointly with the Ahatchwhoop who sponsored him. This could very well be another jab by Barth at authority: not only does the contest have nothing to do with political acumen or leadership qualities, but in this case there is no winner, as authority must be shared.

63. For a more thorough discussion of Barth's use of Captain Smith's *Generall Historie*, see Joseph Weixlmann, "The Use and Abuse of Smith's *Generall Historie*," 105–15.

64. Barth, "An Interview with John Barth," interview by Bezner, 8, emphasis mine.

65. Reuben Gold Thwaites, *Daniel Boone* (1902), qtd. in Morgan, *Boone*, 380.

66. Bergmann, "The Whys and Wherefores of 't,'" 22.

67. It is interesting to note here that, between his time in school and his service to Lord Baltimore, Cooke was apprenticed to a business firm, where he was to learn enough of such fields as accounting that he may run his father's sot-weed plantation. Cooke's inability to excel in this business is here alluded to in his inability to properly keep an accounting ledger.

68. In this regard, Barth provides somewhat more of a critique than did Doctorow of the racist underpinnings of the mythology of the American frontier, though his critique was not nearly as sustained as those provided by later authors. In this, as in other regards, Doctorow's and Barth's Historical Romances of 1960 set the stage for much more nuanced examples of reevaluatory texts.

69. Ebenezer Cooke's poem *The Sot-Weed Factor* is subtitled *or, A Voyage to Maryland: A Satyr* [satire]. For a discussion of how Barth uses Cooke's original poem as the basis for his fictional Cooke's adventures, see David Morrell, *John Barth*, 38–41.

70. Ziegler, *John Barth*, 31.

71. Rovit, "The Novel as Parody," 122.

72. Ibid., 116. The scare quotes for "interest" are employed by Rovit. Originally appearing in 1963, Rovit's essay suffers from the same shortsightedness shown by many early reviewers and critics with regard to an emphasis only on formal experimentation and abuse of historical data.

73. Barth, "Historical Fiction," 180.

74. Ibid., 191, emphasis mine.

75. Barth, "The Literature of Exhaustion," 72.

76. Barth, "Historical Fiction," 190.

77. In "The Custom-House," Nathaniel Hawthorne defines the nature of romance as "a neutral territory, somewhere between the real world and the fairy-land, where the Actual and the Imaginary may meet, and each imbue itself with the nature of the other" (35).

78. Hutcheon, "Historiographic Metafiction," 4.

2 / "Crimes of Demarcation"

1. "Black humorism" as a critical category has survived at least until 1988, with Elaine B. Safer's *The Contemporary American Comic Epic: The Novels of Barth, Pynchon, Gaddis, and Kesey*. This is very similar to Robert A. Hipkiss's "literature of the Absurd," discussed in his study *The American Absurd: Pynchon, Vonnegut, and Barth*. Brian McHale has also noted that Pynchon "is generally regarded, I think justifiably, as [postmodernism's] paradigmatic figure," whose magisterial *Gravity's Rainbow* "coincides with other indicators of the major phase's onset around the years 1972–74" ("Break, Period, Interregnum," 331).

2. See the introduction to this volume.

3. Fludernik, "History and Metafiction," 94.

4. Gary Thompson, "Pynchonian Pastiche," 165. In his article, Thompson discusses how both Pynchon and Barth "adopt the mode of pastiche," which is "not read as if an actual text of the period, but incorporates signs that it is not in fact of the past," and whose work is to comment metatextually on the written documents that have formed our knowledge of the past (165).

5. Cowart, *Thomas Pynchon & the Dark Passages of History*, 152.

6. Elias, *Sublime Desire*, ix.

7. Ibid., 223.

8. Subsequent chapters will discuss how "the facts of history" have often excluded African American and Native American accounts of and participation in the American frontier myth, including the incorporation of oral narratives into the official (i.e., written) historical narrative.

9. Although there is no collection of Pynchon's nonfiction pieces available, numerous websites have devoted space to reprinting what little exists in the form of editorials, essays, and remarks. The most comprehensive of such websites is *Spermatikos Logos*, found at www.themodernword.com/pynchon.

10. Hite, *Ideas of Order in the Novels of Thomas Pynchon*, ix.

11. Mattessich, *Lines of Flight*, 1.

12. S. Moore, foreword, *The Letters of Wanda Tinasky*, ix.

13. Ibid.

14. Mattessich, *Lines of Flight*, 43.

15. Ibid., 4.

16. Patell, *Negative Liberties*, 168.

17. Cowart, "Pynchon and the Sixties," 5.

18. Patell discusses the ways that Pynchon's texts respond to the "residue of slavery . . . and the continuing power of the myth of the rugged individual" (*Negative Liberties*, 29). Mattessich suggests that Pynchon's "novels can be historicized in relation to a discrete period, the 1960s, and discrete social and political imperatives" (*Lines of Flight*, 40).

19. Pynchon, "Is It O.K. to Be a Luddite?," 40.

20. Ibid., 41, emphasis mine.

21. Patell, *Negative Liberties*, 83.

22. Mattessich, *Lines of Flight*, 14.

23. Pynchon, "Is It O.K. to Be a Luddite?," 40.

24. Cowart also reads *Mason & Dixon* as "an expansion of sentiments previously articulated in Pynchon's 1984 article 'Is It O.K. to Be a Luddite?'" For Cowart, Pynchon "characterizes America as a crossroads for the energies of the eighteenth century, and here the Mason-Dixon Line becomes a powerful symbol of rationalism's putting its mark on a land once consecrated to multiple perspectives" (*Thomas Pynchon & the Dark Passages of History*, 139). Similarly, as we will see below, Pynchon's nonfiction work on race helps us to understand the full scope of *Mason & Dixon*'s critique of enlightenment rationalism.

25. Pynchon, introduction to *Slow Learner*, 8, emphasis mine.

26. Pynchon, "A Journey into the Mind of Watts," 78.

27. Ibid., 80.

28. Pynchon, *Mason & Dixon*, 6; hereafter cited parenthetically.

29. Another connection to Barth's *The Sot-Weed Factor* can be made here, as it is the Calvert family (Lord Baltimore) that is behind the political intrigues in colonial Maryland that Cooke and Burlingame explore. Further, one should note that all of the major players on this stage are, predictably, male; they also all, to one degree or another, serve as models for masculinity, as political/military leaders, accomplished academics, and successful frontiersmen. And as we will see at the end of this chapter, Mason's two sons accept the model of masculinity his story presents and express their desire to one day uphold those values.

30. That this story—a rousing romantic adventure about conquest that includes the exploitation of slaves and oppression of women—is told by a reverend may also be a subtle suggestion on the part of Pynchon. As Nancy MacLean reminds us of the 1960s and 1970s, "social conservatives also began to find a new base of popular support in the churches" (*The American Women's Movement, 1945–2000*, 34). The fact that "Catholic sisters were among the founders of NOW in 1966" (ibid., 36n) only emphasizes the polarization between men and women in many of the social movements of the 1960s. As such, Revd Cherrycoke can be read as the vessel through which white patriarchal authority is transmitted to succeeding generations, and given the authority of the religious establishment.

31. Memmi, *The Colonizer and the Colonized*, 3.

32. I would argue that *Mason & Dixon* shows how Europeans treated all native peoples similarly. For this reason, I feel I can discuss reactions to native Africans and

Native Americans as representative of the general European reaction to dark-skinned peoples, later suggested by his reference "another kind of Nigger" with respect to "the Africans, Hindoos, and other Dark peoples they [Europeans] enslave" (572).

33. It should be noted that both the Scottish Highlanders and the Native Americans are here viewed as savage remnants of an earlier age.

34. Pitt and Pliny, the two male twins who, along with their older sister Tenebrae listen to their Uncle Wicks Cherrycoke's narrative, bear names that suggest war. Pitt recalls William Pitt (1708–1778), the British officer for whom Fort Duquesne was later renamed when the English assumed control in 1758. Fort Duquesne was established near the junction of the Allegheny and Monongahela Rivers, near what is now Pittsburgh, Pennsylvania. Pliny recalls Pliny the Elder (23–79), who served in the Germanic Wars and later wrote the twenty-volume *History of the German Wars*. One could read both children as representing large-scale, colonial wars for multinational empires (England and Rome), which were in part characterized by the confrontation of the civilized state with a savage frontier. By naming the two youngest children—twins, no less—after such figures, Pynchon is calling attention to the similarities between these colonial enterprises. And given the eventual fall of the Roman Empire due, in part, to the insurrection of the "savage" Germanic peoples, Pynchon may also be suggesting the potential downfall of the American "empire" at the hands of its racist sociocultural relations with ethnic minorities, who have been characterized as "savage" throughout American history. I am indebted to Joshua Eyler for drawing my attention to the names of the twins.

35. van Houtum, "Remapping Borders," 416.

36. Greiner, "Thomas Pynchon and the Fault Lines of America," 75. Note specifically that Greiner here specifies that these are "bonded *males*."

37. Greiner reads a further connection between Pynchon and Cooper in Pynchon's overt references to Braddock's defeat in the French and Indian War, the setting for *The Last of the Mohicans*. One should also keep in mind here Pynchon's subtle reference to William Pitt (see note 34 above).

38. This is but one of the reasons Russ Castronovo gives for including the Mason-Dixon Line in discussion of border theory, a scholarly conversation originally concerned with the U.S./Mexico borderlands. As he notes, "An inquiry into the cultural history of the Mason-Dixon line, however, can be useful for reframing the critical narratives that describe the outcome of contact of border zones" ("Compromised Narratives along the Border,"197). As the rest of my chapter makes clear, such "contact of the border zones" also allows us to read the Mason-Dixon Line as a frontier space; obviously, there is much overlap in the scholarly discussions about the frontier and borderlands.

39. As Elizabeth Jane Wall Hinds points out, "the Line" was only one manifestation in *Mason & Dixon* that was employed for such purposes: "But like the Mason-Dixon line, dictionary making and calendar reform served the symbolic purpose of clarifying old maps, of signifying a scientifically 'modern' understanding of space and time, finally of physically recording a culture intent on redesigning the natural world in light of intellectual categories" ("Sari, Sorry, and the Vortex of History," 188).

40. Certainly far less mean-spirited than those pranks played on Ebenezer Cooke in *The Sot-Weed Factor*.

41. As Stacey Olster argues, the Mason-Dixon Line has political implications far beyond that with which it is generally associated, or that Pynchon seeks to expose: "We

forget that the Land Ordinance of 1785 that was meant to survey and auction off public lands in order to pay the national debt took as its starting point the Mason-Dixon line . . . [;] we forget how fundamental to westward expansion the Mason-Dixon line was, even though evidence of all those right-angled boundaries that are superimposed upon the landscape today—framing Colorado, Wyoming, Utah, Arizona, and New Mexico—reminds us of how lasting the legacy of that eighteenth-century line is" ("A 'Patch of England, as a Three-Thousand-Mile Offset'?," 298).

42. Friedan, *The Feminine Mystique*, 33. Although Pynchon does not explore this in detail, he is certainly alluding to the work done by the women's movement, which, as we have seen, worked in tandem with other civil rights movements of the late twentieth century.

43. Saltzman, "Cranks of Ev'ry Radius," 64.

44. Olster, "A 'Patch of England, as a Three-Thousand-Mile Offset'?," 292.

45. Ibid., 297.

46. Pynchon may here by having fun at Washington's expense. Although there is much money to be made in land speculation, Washington himself lost money in his ventures.

47. Patell, *Negative Liberties*, 29.

48. Ibid., 5.

49. Note here that one use for slaves is sexual gratification, again subtly linking the oppression of slaves to the oppression of women.

50. Remember Ebenezer Cooke's stereotyping of the Native Americans, discussed in chapter 1.

51. Thompson, "Pynchonian Pastiche," 162.

52. Cohen, "*Mason & Dixon* and the Ampersand," 282.

53. K. Smith, "Serving Interests Invisible," 193. For a discussion of Pynchon's treatment of postcoloniality throughout his fiction, see Michael Harris, "Pynchon's Postcoloniality." His connections to Pynchon's other texts demonstrate Pynchon's continued interest in postcoloniality and representations of the Third World.

54. Ibid., 195.

3 / The Signifyin' Cowboy

1. Turner, "The Significance of the Frontier in American History," 3–4.

2. Baker, *Long Black Song*, 2.

3. I do not mean to suggest that Baker's work is without merit. On the contrary, it is one of the formative statements about the development of African American literature. I only mean to suggest that his position on the influence of the frontier mythology on African Americans is shortsighted, and that such recent work as that done by Michael K. Johnson goes a long way to correcting that position. Further, although Baker claims that "only when the frontier had closed . . . did the black American begin to make his presence felt" (ibid., 5), and that white America "den[ied] the black American the frontier" (6), he employs the frontier as a trope in his discussion of the development of African American literature. The trickster figure of the John Cycle is compared positively to Pecos Bill (26); and Baker speaks generally of a "new frontier" opening up for Americans and "the quest for frontier" to rhetorically position himself in his discussion of David Walker and Frederick Douglass, both of whom he reads as "pioneers" in African American literature (58). I would argue that such references

demonstrate the influence of the American frontier mythology on the development of African American literature, which Baker himself appears to actively argue against. It should also be noted that *Long Black Song*, which first appeared in 1972, was composed during the rise of the Black Panther Party and grew out of the revolutionary social work that Baker witnessed as part of the civil rights movement, to which Baker attests in his introduction to the 1990 reissue, and which demonstrates that the civil rights movement actively engaged the racist inheritance of the American frontier mythology.

4. Although Edward Wheeler's fictionalized character is white, his description reflects the African American on whom he was based. Johnson suggests that the "tight-fitting black (buck-)skin" always worn by Deadwood Dick refers specifically "to a black cowboy, whose true racial identity must be both overtly referred to (he is black from head to toe) and hidden away (even his hands are covered by gloves)" (M. Johnson, *Black Masculinity and the Frontier Myth,* 113). That Deadwood Dick appears in thirty-three novels published between 1877 and 1884 further suggests his persistence in the popular imagination. As Daniel Worden has recently noted, the "masculine style" of the dime novels "connotes whiteness," and that "while masculinity can be performed across class and sex in dime novels, the same cannot be said for racial difference" (*Masculine Style*, 33). For a thorough discussion, see chapter 1, "Masculinity for the Millions: Gender in Dime-Novel Westerns," 17–34.

5. M. Johnson, *Black Masculinity and the Frontier Myth,* 32.

6. Ibid., 248.

7. As Reeser has noted, "The cowboy's popularity as American cultural icon means that he represents an ideal of masculinity that appeals to so many boys that it effectively becomes an American myth" (*Masculinities in Theory,* 23).

8. Though not in the scope of the present study, William Gardner Smith's *The Stone Face* has been described as "an effort in the 1960s to reformulate the frontier myth in a context informed by both black activism in America and nationalist independence movements in Africa" (M. Johnson, *Black Masculinity and the Frontier Myth,* 32). In constructing a character who can internalize and apply the frontier mythology to a new environment (Africa), Smith shows how the myth of the American frontier is an integral piece of African American identity. Further, that the myth is applied to a new environment also serves to impugn America as the place where positive frontier values can be realized.

9. Reed, "An Interview with Ishmael Reed," interview by Ruth Abbott and Ira Simmons, 93.

10. Reed, "My Oakland, There Is a There There," 20.

11. Reed, "Eldridge Cleaver—Writer," 103.

12. Reed, "The Great Tenure Battle of 1977," interview by Jon Ewing, 115.

13. Reed claims in the interview that this was but one reason for having been denied tenure at the University of California at Berkeley. Although such considerations are more often than not determined during closed-door meetings, he claims to have had an inside source confirming his suspicions. Even if this episode was not a factor in the decision, Reed's inference that it was only highlights the aura of distrust and antagonism many African Americans felt toward white authority.

14. Reed, "In Opposition—Which State?," 113.

15. Mary Helen Washington's foreword to Hurston's *Their Eyes Were Watching God* recounts the book's publication history and its impact on many scholars of African American literature.

16. Reed, "In Opposition—Which State?," 113.

17. Ibid., 120.

18. Columbus is a key figure in Gerald Vizenor's own explorations of American multiethnic history, as we will see in chapter 4.

19. Reed, "And That History Is Subject to the Will," 262.

20. Reed, "Ishmael Reed," 18.

21. Reed, "Interview with Ishmael Reed," interview by John O'Brien, 54.

22. Tietchen, "Cowboy Tricksters and Devilish Wangols," 325.

23. For a comprehensive understanding of the multiple aspects of "signifyin(g)," see Henry Louis Gates Jr., *The Signifying Monkey*, 53–88.

24. Ibid., 88.

25. Ibid., 131.

26. I would like to suggest here that the trickster figure can also be read as a figure belonging to the romance tradition, at least as we see it operating in American literature that draws from non-American traditions. It is in the romance that such nonrealistic tropes can appear.

27. Ibid., 217.

28. Ibid., 221.

29. Reed, "Interview with Ishmael Reed," interview by Gaga, [Mark S. Johnson], 54.

30. Gates, *The Signifying Monkey*, 5.

31. Reed, "I Am a Cowboy in the Boat of Ra," 18. See Madge Ambler, "Ishmael Reed: Whose Radio Broke Down?" for an interesting close reading of *Yellow Back Radio Broke-Down* as an expansion of his poem "I am a Cowboy in the Boat of Ra."

32. Wallace, *Constructing the Black Masculine*, 2. Wallace later, in a discussion of Franz Fanon's *Black Skin White Masks*, notes the "emphatically modern character of twentieth-century racial reasoning and its reliance in modernity on stereotype and fetishism" (170–71). The Loop Garoo Kid is certainly constructed as a figure whose presence recalls stereotypes and fetishes in order to counter them; "racial reasoning," Reed here suggests, is not reasoning at all.

33. Reed, *Yellow Back Radio Broke-Down*, 10; hereafter cited parenthetically.

34. Dyer, "The Matter of Whiteness," 10. Dyer also notes that "postmodern multiculturalism may have genuinely opened up a space for the voices of the other, challenging the authority of the white West" (11); although I would be taking him out of context by doing so, this comment could equally apply to the "West," which serves as the frontier.

35. A "yellow back" was an inexpensive edition, bound in yellow cloth or paper. Yellow Back Radio, then, represents the stock image of a frontier town, a stereotype of the typical western frontier town. Radio is a reference to "the dismantling of a genre done in an oral way like Radio," suggesting the interplay of the oral and the written culture that Gates defines as the space for the play of the trickster figure of the signifying monkey ("The Writer as Seer," 63).

36. Reed is obviously trying to emasculate this figure, and does so by alluding to drag, a consciously feminine performance engaged by a male body. Reed has often been charged with misogyny, and so it is not a stretch to see him participating in the portrayal of drag as "nothing but the displacement and appropriation of "women," and hence fundamentally based in a misogyny" (Butler, *Bodies That Matter*, 127).

37. McHale, *Postmodernist Fiction*, 45. McHale notes that "postmodernist fiction draws upon a number of strategies for constructing/deconstructing space" (45) and

also that "borrowed characters abound in postmodernism" (58), which we will see later in this chapter.

38. If we accept that the events of this novel take place after Reconstruction (to which the technological advancements would certainly allude, even if the engagement with stereotypes suggests a more "timeless" setting), we could also read the Loop Garoo Kid as "the black male [who] emerged in popular discourses during Reconstruction as the mythic embodiment of phallic (and hence masculine) potentiality as the black rapist" (Wiegman, *American Anatomies*, 14); Reed alludes to this harmful stereotype with various suggestions of oversexualization, even though Loop himself is one of the sexually tamest characters in the book.

39. Tietchen reads the children as representative of "'60s college students who questioned American institutions," those who rallied behind such chants as "Don't trust anyone over thirty" ("Cowboy Tricksters and Devilish Wangols," 327).

40. Reed proudly states in an interview that white critics were unable to appreciate his participation in the tradition of writing westerns, as none of them understood the reference in his title (see Reed, "Ishmael Reed," interview by O'Brien, 31).

41. The Seven Cities of Cibola were part of the colonial mythology of Mexico, reported to be great cities of gold, and are related to the myth of El Dorado.

42. Butler, *Gender Trouble*, 140.

43. Butler, *Bodies*, 125.

44. Reed, "A Conversation with Ishmael Reed," interview by Judith Moore, 228.

45. Reed, "Race War in America?," 86.

46. The performative nature of masculinity is one of the foundational premises of masculine studies. Todd W. Reeser writes that masculinity "is constantly created and challenged in numerous ways" as a fluid social construct (*Masculinities in Theory*, 18).

47. Halberstam, *Female Masculinity*, 269. Halberstam also notes that "although we seem to have a difficult time defining masculinity, as a society we have little trouble in recognizing it" (1). This is especially the case with stock figures that Reed employs (as does Doctorow, as we saw in chapter 1) in order to provide social critique.

48. By treating Sal as property, Reed here equates the housewife to the slave, a popular analogy evidenced by the work of such feminists as Edith M. Stern who, in 1949, equated the position of women and African Americans in her essay "Women Are Household Slaves," which ends by noting that "it is neither freedom nor democracy when such service is based on color or sex" (qtd. In MacLean, *The American Women's Movement*, 54).

49. M. Johnson, *Black Masculinity and the Frontier Myth*, 101.

50. Schmitz, "Neo-HooDoo," 134. Although these characters are traditionally read as African American because of their speech patterns, Reed does not otherwise mark their race.

51. Turner, "The Significance of the Frontier in American History," 4.

52. Reed, "Neo-HooDoo Manifesto," 21.

53. Ibid., 24.

54. Reed, "Ishmael Reed," interview by O'Brien, 38.

55. It is almost impossible to establish a timeline in Reed's early works, as he appears to maintain no consistency with respect to historical fidelity. As such, it is impossible to pinpoint the frontier chronotope that Reed engages. Bo Shmo can play the music of Hoagy Carmichael, the Field Marshall can speak with Thomas Jefferson,

and the kids of Yellow Back Radio can watch television, with no seeming incongruity to the plot development. What is most important with Reed's early works is that they are symbolic rather than mimetic. For this reason, as much as any other, Reed's works should be read in the tradition of American Romance, as opposed to the American Novel.

56. Reed, "The Traditions of Serious Comedy in Afro-American Literature," 137.

57. Reed has also claimed that he "was delighted when it received a favorable review in a rodeo magazine published in the West, I've never ridden a horse. This book was faithful to the form of the Yellow Backs in another way; they were usually written by dudes from the East, like me" (introduction to *The Reed Reader*, xv–xvi). In other words, the fact that he has never actually been "out West" puts him on the same page as other dime novelists who created tales of frontier heroism, who also never experienced the frontier firsthand.

58. Tietchen, "Cowboy Tricksters and Devilish Wangols," 326.

59. Ibid., 337. One should also remember that stories of actual African American cowboys were often bleached, as with the "Deadwood Dick" dime novels (see note 5 above).

60. Mogen, "The Frontier Archetype and the Myth of America," 18.

61. As Glenda R. Carpio points out, Reed also participates in "a vibrant proliferation since the mid-1960s [of] fictional texts [that] have grappled with the characteristic omissions, gaps, and distortions in the record of New World slavery" ("Conjuring the Mysteries of Slavery," 563). Reed's attacks on the American literary canon and traditional means of representing African Americans are not limited to his "signifyin(g)" on the American frontier mythology. Rather, Reed works to help fill in the gaps of American history in order to present a more multicultural perspective. Carpio implies that Reed was only one of many writers who looked at "the record of New World slavery"; the presence of such a tradition, while not of direct interest to my work here, helps to support my claim that the 1960s provided a unique situation for writers to engage with and critique traditional canons and modes of representation, especially with respect to race.

4 / Speaking for the Mixedblood Other

1. Churchill and Wall, *Agents of Repressions*, 119.

2. Ibid., 141. Sean Kicummah Teuton identifies the Alcatraz occupation as the point of origin for "a decade-long flurry of events [that] would define Red Power" (*Red Land, Red Power*, 6). Although Teuton disagrees with Vizenor's promotion of a trickster politics—particularly Vizenor's "assert[ion] that American Indians are not bound by a fixed cultural category but rather inhabit the interstitial space between the colonies and nations, the white and the Indian, and thus subvert[ing] the demands of each cultural register" (84)—Vizenor's work (particularly *The Heirs of Columbus*) touches upon many of the concerns Teuton notes in his definition of the Red Power novel.

3. Such military actions almost always bring to mind masculine stereotypes, as the competing groups are often characterized in various versions of the "cowboys and Indians" dichotomy. As we will see below, Vizenor attempts to counter this (often unconscious) focus on masculine figures—figures that have been defined by the mythology of the American frontier—through the use of female characters who disrupt traditional associations and frustrate received traditions.

4. Vizenor, *Interior Landscapes*, 236–37.

5. Although not explicitly noted in UPI's rewrite of Vizenor's story, their suggestion alludes to kidnapping, a common motif in captivity narratives, a genre that helped define the role of the "savage Indian" in the developing mythology of the American frontier.

6. Of course, John Barth would remind us not to trust any documentary evidence, particularly when it claims to account for other cultures (see chapter 1).

7. In this novel, members of AIM break into a Bureau of Indian Affairs building and steal the "Bearheart Chronicles," stories written by Bearheart exploring tribal traditions in the contemporary world. Vizenor characterizes the AIM militants as ignorant with respect to tribal traditions as well as tribal language, and employing racist rhetoric against Bearheart for his complicity with BIA, calling him "white" and "whiteindian." Here, AIM is operating under a cultural dichotomy—supported by the myth of the American frontier—that exposes them as militant racists more interested in promoting a political agenda than exploring cross-cultural relations. In addition to his use of AIM in his fiction and his reporting of them in his journalism collected in *Crossbloods: Bone Courts, Bingo, and Other Reports*, Vizenor also discusses the role of AIM in the cultural and political history of the Chippewa in *The People Named the Chippewa: Narrative Histories*, in particular the chapter "Dennis of Wounded Knee," and again in *Everlasting Sky: Voices of the Anishinabe People*.

8. Vizenor, *Interior Landscapes*, 232. Vizenor also recounts an episode of personal intimidation (see 268).

9. I do not have the space here to summarize Bakhtin's theories on dialogism or his impact on the study of the novel, nor could I do a better job than has already been done elsewhere. Instead, I would point the interested reader to several of Bakhtin's relevant writings, as well as some of the more prominent commentaries: Bakhtin, *The Dialogic Imagination* (in particular "Discourse in the Novel"); Bakhtin, *Problems of Dostoyevsky's Poetics* (in particular chapter 1 "Dostoyevsky's Polyphonic Novel and Its Treatment in Critical Literature"); and Pam Morris, ed., *The Bakhtin Reader: Selected Writings of Bakhtin, Medvedev, Voloshinov* (in particular section 1 "Dialogic Discourse"). Further, much work has already been done on employing Bakhtin's theories as a means of understanding contemporary Native American fiction. The reader is directed to the work of Arnold Krupat, particularly "The Dialogic of Silko's *Storyteller*," as a good place to begin.

10. In his essay on border theory and Native American studies, Scott Michaelson notes that "it is 'the Columbus' that enables the discourse of folklore anthropology, that makes it possible in the first place" ("Resketching Anglo-Amerindian Identity Politics," 241). As such, it is not a stretch to consider Vizenor's novel exploring the Columbus legend alongside novels explicitly addressing the Boone mythology, especially given how those traditions overlap, as will be shown below. Further, it is hardly a coincidence that both Boone and Columbus are male figures, and in their own ways have been used as models of masculinity as explorers.

11. Bakhtin, "Discourse in the Novel," 277. In a similar vein, we can understand Vizenor's enterprise to be a Bakhtinian exploration, whereby we broaden Bakhtin's focus to textual traditions as well as languages. Just as Bakhtin claims that "the author utilizes now one language, now another, in order to avoid giving himself wholly to either of them" (314), so too can we read Vizenor utilizing now one textual tradition,

now another (as well as the languages of law, mythology, and the socio-ideological languages of the tribal, nontribal, and mixedblood speakers).

12. D. Moore, "Decolonizing Criticism," 20.

13. Ibid., 8, 1.

14. Ibid., 29.

15. L. Owens, *Mixedblood Messages*, 38.

16. Ibid., 26. See also Pratt, *Imperial Eyes*: "contact zones" are "social spaces where disparate cultures meet, clash, and grapple with each other, often in highly asymmetrical relations of domination and subordination" (4). Further, there is no value judgment to be made with respect to the different cultures; her study in fact demonstrates the meaninglessness of the "savage/civilized" dichotomy, while simultaneously exploring in great detail the intricacies of rhetorical imperialism. More important for understanding Vizenor's *The Heirs of Columbus*, however, are her remarks about "transculturation." Pratt argues that "while subjugated peoples cannot readily control what emanates from the dominant culture, they do determine to varying extents what they absorb into their own, and what they use it for" (6). In other words, we can claim that while Vizenor cannot control the spread of the European concept of the frontier and its development as the national mythology, he is able to engage with it on his own terms, dictating the direction this conversation will take.

17. L. Owens, *Mixedblood*, 52.

18. Ibid., 40–41.

19. Vizenor is certainly not alone in such work, which has also been explored by such writers as Gloria Anzaldúa, in her now-famous work of cultural criticism and personal exploration *Borderlands/La Frontera: The New Mestiza*. Further, Anzaldúa's work on the *mestiza* helps to provide a much-needed feminist perspective on an otherwise masculine approach to border studies and the inheritance of the mythology of the American frontier. In addition to her articulation of the border as "a dividing line, a narrow strip along a steep edge . . . a vague and undetermined place created by the emotional residue of an unnatural boundary" (25), much of her book focuses on the experience of the *mestiza*, a woman of mixed racial ancestry (what Vizenor and Owens would call "mixedblood"); Anzaldúa's explicit focus on women highlights the (perhaps unintentional) focus on men in Owens's study.

20. I have chosen to characterize this relationship as dialogic for two reasons. First, Bakhtin provides a useful model for understanding the relationship between a text and its readers, or in this case, a mythology and its inheritors. Rather than simply accepting the mythology as it has been transmitted, Vizenor demonstrates that one can and should enter into a productive relationship with the mythology. As I will develop later, Vizenor takes great pains to include as many voices as possible in his dialogue with this mythology and its textual tradition. Second, and no less important, is Vizenor's own embracing of Bakhtin as a means of coming to understand what Vizenor calls "Trickster discourse," when he cites *Mikhail Bakhtin: The Dialogical Principle* in his "Postmodern Introduction" to *Narrative Chance*: "There are events that, in principle, cannot unfold on the plan to a single and unified consciousness, but presuppose two consciousnesses that do not fuse; they are events whose essential and constitutive element is the relation of a consciousness to *another* consciousness, precisely because it is *other*. Such are all events that are creatively productive, innovative, unique, and irreversible" (9). Vizenor's own contribution to the Columbus narrative

certainly fulfills the first three of these final criteria; whether it fulfills the fourth can only be known with time.

21. Krupat, "Stories in the Blood," 166.

22. Vizenor, *The Heirs of Columbus*, 14; hereafter cited parenthetically.

23. Including the novels *Bearheart: The Heirship Chronicles* and *Chancers*, as well as his nonfiction collection *Crossbloods: Bone Courts, Bingo, and Other Reports* and his autobiography *Interior Landscapes: Autobiographical Myths and Metaphors*, as well as works of cultural criticism like *Manifest Manners: Narratives on Postindian Survivance*.

24. Vizenor, "On Thin Ice, You Might as Well Dance," 288.

25. Vizenor, "Eternal Havens," 113.

26. Ibid., 107.

27. Ibid., 110.

28. Blaeser, "The New "Frontier" of Native American Literature," 38.

29. Vizenor, "Tricksters of Liberty," 134.

30. Blaeser, *Gerald Vizenor*, 95.

31. However, I do not wish to overstate the case, considering that Vizenor also notes that Samana was "blessed with silence" (4), a "blessing" he would certainly not wish on Native storytellers in the Columbus mythology, and a potential silencing of women that runs counter to the civil rights advancements of the period. If nothing else, Samana serves to both highlight and (somewhat) correct the sexism inherent in the mythology of the American frontier.

32. Krupat, "Stories in the Blood," 168.

33. For Rebecca M. Lush, the "stories in the blood" should be taken almost literally, as "the human body . . . functions as a receptacle for reading practices that engender politically charged questions about tradition and identity" ("Turning Tricks," 3). Nonwhite bodies, as we have seen in the previous chapter, are very much "texts" to be read or, returning to chapter 1, misread as "false documents." Further, although I do not elsewhere make the connection, I want to here note that Lush's discussion of "Columbus's sexual role [which] places him in dialog with the trickster stories" (12) also connects him to Captain John Smith; Columbus's "enormous clubbed penis" (Vizenor, *Heirs*, 112) is as much a marker of frontier masculinity as Smith's efforts at "reliev[ing] Pocahontas of her maidenhead (Barth, *Sot-Weed Factor*, 730).

34. For instance, "Caliban, the great white reservation mongrel and heir to the stone" (16) alludes to Shakespeare's *The Tempest*, whose character Caliban is the indigenous slave of the European Prospero.

35. Blaeser, *Gerald Vizenor*, 96.

36. Qtd. in Vizenor, *Heirs*, 36.

37. For further reading on Vizenor's understanding of "survivance" for mixedbloods in the twentieth century, see "Double Others," in *Shadow Distance: A Gerald Vizenor Reader*, 155–72.

38. Although I recognize Robert Berner's point that "genocide" was "coined in 1944 to describe the Nazi attempt to exterminate the Jews," and that it "refers specifically to the mass killing of the people of a group by a perpetrator who *intends* to destroy the group," I fail to see how "genocide" does not apply to the extermination of Native Americans. That they fought back—that it was "a two-sided war"—does not change the intent of the American army, which worked to slaughter Native Americans. I

disagree with Berner entirely that the application of "genocide" to the massacres of the late nineteenth century on the American frontier in any way works to "trivialize the Jewish Holocaust" ("American Myth," 65–66).

39. Vizenor, "Postindian Warriors," 4.

40. Donnan and Wilson, *Borders*, 3.

41. Monsma, "Liminal Landscapes," 68. In this regard, Point Assinika operates similarly to the "sites of hemispheric pan-Indianism" (72) that Claudia Sadowski-Smith identifies in her chapter on Native American fiction in *Border Fictions: Globalization, Empire, and Writing at the Boundaries of the United States*. However, although Point Assinika is a space for the "pan-tribal impetus of native American civil rights" (75), it is more than that in that it opens its doors to all peoples, regardless of tribal, racial, or national identity.

42. As Sadowski-Smith has noted, this boundary is also known among certain tribal populations as the "*medicine line* [which was coined] in the nineteenth century when differences in U.S. and Canadian policies toward indigenous peoples transformed the shared border into a site of potential refuge" (ibid., 85).

43. Despite writing a narrative that "struggle[s] to better interpret a colonized world . . . to empower the people" (Teuton, *Red Land, Red Power*, 2), Vizenor's work is not considered a Red Power novel by Teuton. This is a result of Vizenor's adoption of a trickster politics (as noted above) as well as Vizenor's clear assessment of the necessity of borders; where Vizenor wishes to tear them down (Point Assinika serving as a site that deconstructs borders), Teuton invests them with cultural authority: "With Indigenous property of all sorts still under siege, however, the actual destruction of cultural and territorial borders is nothing less than disastrous for native people. Borders are absolutely vital for the survival of colonized people" (138). For Teuton, borders help identify and preserve Indigenous space, while for Vizenor, borders inhibit productive cross-cultural experiences.

44. Schöler, "Trickster and Storyteller," 142.

45. L. Owens, *Mixedblood Messages*, 40–41.

46. The Browne family and their exploits are the focus of numerous works of Vizenor's fiction, including *Landfill Meditation: Crossblood Stories*; *Hotline Healers: An Almost Browne Novel*; and *The Trickster of Liberty: Native Heirs to a Wild Baronage*. These collections, along with *The Heirs of Columbus*, show Vizenor's repeated explorations of genealogical and cultural survivance for mixedbloods in a culture that often understands race as inherently dichotomous (self/other, white/black, civilized/savage) and exclusionary of mixed-race or multicultural peoples.

47. Lush, "Turning Tricks," 3–4. Just as it is important that Columbus is male (in that he is the figurehead from whom patrilineal descent follows), it is equally important that Lappet is female. Her testimony is as much a condemnation of traditional masculine approaches to the frontier as it is a defense of Felipa.

48. For a full-length discussion of these issues, see *Crossbloods: Bone Courts, Bingo, and Other Reports*; for a fictional treatment, see *Chancers*.

49. Vizenor, "Gerald Vizenor: The Trickster Heir of Columbus," 104.

50. Vizenor, "On Thin Ice, You Might as Well Dance," 296.

51. A similar "Epilogue" concludes Vizenor's earlier novel *Griever: An American Monkey King in China*.

52. Vizenor, "Trickster Discourse," 189.

53. I don't mean to suggest that all trickster fiction participates in the romance tradition; *The Heirs of Columbus* certainly does, and a more thorough study of Native American fiction would need to take place before any greater generalizations can be made.

54. Vizenor, "Trickster Discourse," 190.

55. Ibid., 194.

56. In this regard, Vizenor is working akin to such historians as Howard Zinn, who similarly refers to a wide range of documentary evidence to reconstruct his history of Columbus as the opening to his magisterial *A People's History of the United States.* Like Zinn, Vizenor is attempting to rewrite history from a viewpoint long ignored by traditional historiography.

57. Osborne, "Legal and Tribal Identity in Gerald Vizenor's *The Heirs of Columbus,*" 116.

58. This definition is taken from the official webpage of the Métis National Council, www.metisnation.ca/who/definition.html.

59. In this regard, my reading of Vizenor's novel does not differ much from Neil Campbell's reading of Vizenor's oeuvre more generally, as "a process of folding, refolding, and unfolding taking place, a complex outflowing of ideas that occurs 'between' claims and points, moving the reader across language in rhizomatic threads and interconnections" (*The Rhizomatic West,* 233–34). Campbell focuses on Vizenor as a paradigmatic example of a Native American theorist whose works push for a breaking of the "ethnic grid" (229) that often imposes a static identity onto Native peoples. Although certainly not alone, the mythology of the American frontier is one of the major discursive factors contributing to the construction and persistence of such a "grid."

60. Ibid., 162.

5 / "The World Which He Inherits Bears Him False Witness"

1. Horrocks, *Male Myths and Icons,* 79.

2. Spurgeon, *Exploding the Western,* 26.

3. Though in a very different manner, Andrew Hoberek has also recently provided a new reading for McCarthy's fiction. Hoberek argues that "McCarthy is one of a number of writers who have recently undermined this structure [established by "program era fiction" as Mark McGurl has defined it in *The Program Era*] by embracing genre models" ("Cormac McCarthy and the Aesthetics of Exhaustion," 485). Hoberek claims that recently "genre fiction resume[d] its status as a respectable terrain for serious writers" (486), though I would like to note that serious writers have long parodied genre fiction, particularly in the romance tradition (Ishmael Reed immediately comes to mind). In this respect, I join Hoberek in the exploration of new contexts within which we can understand McCarthy's (admittedly difficult to classify) work, and my own reading can be said to build off of his in that I hope to explore fully what he only notes in passing, that *Blood Meridian* represents "the program era's suspicion of genre" (496), which I see as part of a larger suspicion of not just the genre of the western, but of the entire mythological inheritance of the American frontier mythology that the western has historically supported. I should also note that I am making no claims regarding McCarthy's own political beliefs or affiliations, for which I have no evidence. Rather, this chapter explores the work done by the texts, and provides a

new reading based on a context in which they should be read. Reading these romances as another manifestation of the American Historical Frontier Romance provides new insights regarding their political work; admittedly, not all readers of McCarthy will agree with my conclusions, and I would like to thank the anonymous readers at the University of Virginia Press for helping me to clarify my position and strengthen my argument.

4. For instance, although set on the Mexican-American border, I do not see *No Country for Old Men* as sufficiently historical. Similarly, while *The Road* is a wonderful romance that also addresses the failure of our national mythology, it is set in the future.

5. Phillips, "History and the Ugly Facts of Cormac McCarthy's *Blood Meridian*," 434.

6. Ibid., 435.

7. I do not mean to suggest, however, that what follows is the only plausible reading of McCarthy's works; in fact, the following reading will go against many of the established readings of McCarthy's fiction. Phillips is correct when he claims of *Blood Meridian* that "its relationship to its context cannot be a simple one" (ibid., 437). However, I disagree with his claim that the novel "does not seem to be very much of its time" (451); I hope to show the ways in which it very much is of its time, as a companion piece to the other postwar critiques of the mythology of the American frontier, particularly given its "implied insistence on the failure in the mid-nineteenth century (and in the mid-1980s, too) of the human desire for utopia" (439), particularly as that utopia was the promised result of the progressive myth of the frontier.

8. These phrases, commonly used by various critics, are provided by Robert L. Jarrett (*Cormac McCarthy*), Neil Campbell ("Beyond Reckoning"), Inger-Anne Softing ("Desert Pandemonium"), and Mark S. Graybill ("'Peeping Toms on History'"), respectively. In many cases, it has also become commonplace to use scare quotation marks when writing of McCarthy's works as "westerns."

9. Though Barclay Owens notes that *Blood Meridian* is a work that "parallels its times," he also argues that "while *Blood Meridian* is indeed part of the continuing reassessment of violence in American culture, it is not a political ally of the revisionist movement" (*Cormac McCarthy's Western Novels*, 20, 10). I disagree with this latter point, and argue that McCarthy's texts (*Blood Meridian* and the Border Trilogy) operate as a sustained effort at revising his readers' understanding of the Mexican-American border, even if not providing revisionist history per se.

10. Anzaldúa, *Borderlands/La Frontera*, 25.

11. As Donnan and Wilson note, "Between 1930 and 1974 historians of this border (US-Mexico) viewed it as a frontier" (*Borders*, 51).

12. McCarthy, *Blood Meridian*, 330; hereafter cited parenthetically.

13. For a detailed discussion of the historical sources of *Blood Meridian*, see John Emil Sepich, "'What Kind of Indians Was Them?': Some Historical Sources in Cormac McCarthy's *Blood Meridian*."

14. Butterfield, introduction to *My Confessions*, by Samuel E. Chamberlain, 4–5.

15. I am indebted to Joshua J. Masters for the phrase "textual enterprise," by which he characterizes "the judge's westward expansion" ("Witness to the Uttermost Edge of the World," 25).

16. Jeffords, *The Remasculinization of America*, 135.

17. "Even in Arcadia, there am I [Death]" (my translation).

18. In many instances, McCarthy provides untranslated Spanish. These instances are more numerous in the Border Trilogy, as well as more important to the Trilogy's central concern.

19. According to John Borneman, "Borders are about security, and external borders are especially about security from violence, the building of barriers, material and immaterial, to arrest the flow of violence" ("Border Regimes, the Circulation of Violence and the Neo-authoritarian Turn," 124).

20. McCarthy does not use the apostrophe in contractions or many possessives, and employs other nonstandard usages.

21. Eaton, "Dis(re)membered Bodies: Cormac McCarthy's Border Fiction," 159.

22. McCarthy, *All the Pretty Horses*, 239; hereafter cited parenthetically.

23. Compare this to Friedan, who writes of the prejudices which "deny [women] full participation in the world" (Friedan, *The Feminine Mystique*, 61).

24. Though any reader familiar with the conventions of the western will have no trouble identifying John Grady Cole as a manifestation of the iconic cowboy figure, for Katherine Sugg, Cole specifically "characterize[s] iconic American masculinity" ("Multicultural Masculinities in John Sayles's *Lone Star* and Cormac McCarthy's Border Trilogy," 128) , and his doomed romance with Alejandra both "acknowledges the links between race, nationality, and gender" while also remains "silen[t] on questions of sexual difference and gender ideologies" (119).

25. Although I will in places suggest that the Border Trilogy presents the reader with a complex understanding of the relationship between Mexico's treatment by the American historical frontier mythology and the reality with which Cole and later Billy Parham are presented, I would also like to point the reader to Daniel Cooper Alarcón's "All the Pretty Mexicos: Cormac McCarthy's Mexican Representations." Alarcón persuasively argues:"Ultimately, McCarthy's Mexican novels fit neatly within the Infernal Paradise tradition, doing little to challenge its assumptions and conventions. Like his storyteller, the fallen priest, he has done a wonderful job of appearing to tell a different Mexican story, when in fact he has retold a very familiar one" (149).

26. Cole's return to "Texas soil" is similarly devoid of ceremony (286). This would seem to run counter to Donnan and Wilson's claim that "when people cross state borders . . . they become part of new systems of value" (107). However, what I am arguing in this chapter is not that there are no differences between such systems of value; rather, McCarthy's work demonstrates that those systems of value are as arbitrary as the borders used to distinguish them. Nor do those systems line up evenly with unmarked territory, even if such territory is clearly marked on a map.

27. Rawlins certainly plays the realist to Cole's idealist, and he continues to accompany Cole throughout the work. Despite his inability to define his life in terms of the American frontier mythology, he similarly seeks to live the life of the cowboy that he and Cole believe no longer exists in America. However, I would suggest that the difference lies in the fact that Rawlins seems concerned primarily with the work itself, while it is Cole who appears to be singled out as the embodiment of heroic frontier virtues (he is the one who wishes to help not only Blevins but also the Mexicans they encounter along the way, is the most skilled horse tamer in the book, and always weighs the moral implications of his actions). It is no surprise, then, that Rawlins is arrested and beaten for something that he not only did not do, but actively advised Cole and Blevins

from doing themselves, stealing back Blevins's horse, which Blevins had stolen in the first place. That Rawlins is more than willing to leave Blevins to his fate at every turn suggests that he is far more self-interested and pragmatic than Cole.

28. Hawkins, "Cold War Cowboys and the Culture of Nostalgia," 95. One should note that many of these also operate as politically sanctioned "colorlines."

29. Reported by Pilkington, "Fate and Free Will on the American Frontier," 312.

30. Anzaldúa, *Borderlands/La Frontera*, 217.

31. Sickles and Oxoby, "In Search of a Further Frontier," 351.

32. McCarthy, *The Crossing*, 130; hereafter cited parenthetically.

33. Billy later suggests that the "papers" of horse ownership can be put to false use, when he suggests to Boyd that the Niño's papers may be used by a thief who can "find a horse to fit them" (265).

34. Following Spurgeon, I see "no practical difference" between the Cole family's employing Mexicans and keeping servants, despite Cole's claims to the contrary in *All the Pretty Horses* (46). Semantic differences aside, both suggest wealth at the expense of Mexican labor.

35. Heyman, "Culture Theory and the US–Mexico Border," 59. Although Heyman is writing specifically about migrant laborers, his characterization is an apt description of Billy Parham, who could be read as a version of a migrant worker, given his various jobs on the frontier zone and his final employment at the end of the Border Trilogy.

36. B. Owens, *Cormac McCarthy's Western Novels*, 64.

37. This attitude can be traced back to James Fenimore Cooper, whose *The Pioneers* can be regarded as the first American Historical Frontier Romance. In *The Pioneers*, Natty Bumppo's young protégé Oliver is distrusted by the cultural elite of Templeton because of his "savage" ways and possible "Indian" heritage (i.e., he is suspected of being a "mixedblood"). However, by the narrative's close, he is revealed to be Oliver Effingham, heir to the Templeton estate and descendant of landed royalty. Though Oliver's bearing and attitude—not to mention his skills and natural grace—remained unchanged throughout the text, his recognition as a "heroic" figure did not come until his true parentage was revealed. I would suggest that the underlying need for frontier heroes to be "purebloods" as opposed to "mixedbloods" has yet to be excised from the critical discussions of the American frontier mythology, as Vizenor clearly demonstrated.

38. Soto, "The Border Paradigm in Cormac McCarthy's *The Crossing*," 61.

39. To return to *The Pioneers*, Natty Bumppo is similarly distrusted by the citizens of Templeton and feels unwelcome, despite Oliver's insistence that he remain. Natty goes west, and we see him again living alone (that is, outside of both white and Native American communities) in *The Prairie*.

40. Cormac McCarthy, *Cities of the Plain* (New York: Vintage International, 1998), 78; hereafter cited parenthetically.

41. McCarthy's next novel, *No Country for Old Men*, employs a narrator who remarks about the war in Vietnam that "*People will tell you it was Vietnam brought this country to its knees. But I never believed that. It was already in bad shape. Vietnam was just the icin on the cake. We didnt have nothing to give em to take over there. If we'd sent em without rifles I dont know as they'd of been all that much worse off. You cant go to war like that. You cant go to war without God. I dont know what is goin to happen when*

the next one comes. I surely dont" (294–95). In the only direct reference to Vietnam in McCarthy's work to date, this passage narrated in the first person may represent McCarthy's own views on the war in Vietnam (though I recognize the same caution here as I did with my reading of Pynchon's politics through his fiction, in chapter 3). McCarthy may here be suggesting that the war in Vietnam, and the sociopolitical war at home that followed it—those "*hippies*" whose "*country . . . was in pieces*" (294) protesting the war—were but one instance of the larger cycle of warfare and protest, and that as bad as Vietnam and its fallout may have been, the next instance of warfare and fallout will surely be worse. This is explored in McCarthy's most recent novel, *The Road*, a description of postapocalyptic America. If war is, as I am suggesting here, connected with the mythology of the American frontier, then perhaps the death of the mythology is necessary for the salvation of American society.

42. It has become common in scholarship on the Border Trilogy to read the various characters as representative of some aspect of the American frontier mythology. For instance, Andrew Blair Spencer (in his analysis of *All the Pretty Horses*) claims that "McCarthy uses Lacey Rawlins and John Grady Cole as vehicles both to mourn the passing of the American frontier, as well as to tell a reality that debunks the popular myths regarding the Old West, namely the myths of the American cowboy" ("A Cowboy Looks at Reality: The Death of the American Frontier and the Illumination of the Cowboy Myth in Cormac McCarthy's *All the Pretty Horses*," 144). Although Spencer later identifies each aspect of the frontier mythology that the trio of Cole, Rawlins, and Blevins represent (respectively, the outdated myth of the American cowboy, the "truth about the west" [155] and return to reality, and the frontier itself), reading McCarthy's critique of the frontier mythology in such allegorical terms runs the risk of simply replacing one symbolic system for another. Similarly, Charles Bailey reads the Border Trilogy as the development of the figure of the hero: "So, *All the Pretty Horses* presents the courtly knight as hero. *The Crossing* presents the tragic man as hero. In sequence, *Cities of the Plain* presents the anti-hero, introduced by Byron and developed in the American novel" ("The Last Stage of the Hero's Evolution," 296). It has become common in scholarship on McCarthy to identify just what his characters represent, symbolize, or invoke. I would like to suggest that such an exercise is due in no small part to McCarthy's self-conscious participation in the development of the American frontier mythology, as both disseminator and reevaluator of the values posited by this mythology.

43. Although Spurgeon does not treat *Cities of the Plain* at length in her study, her discussion of the myth of the "sacred cowboy" is relevant here: "in other words, the myth of the sacred cowboy that demands that a worthy young man should end up with a ranch of his own, a lovely young wife, and 'all the pretty horses' in a gloriously guilt-free Eden simply by virtue of being Anglo, male, and the descendant of colonizers, functions in neither world [Mexico or America], and this is McCarthy's point" (45). The "pale empire" that Cole represents—despite his attempts to cross physical, cultural, and linguistic borders—is carefully taken apart in just these terms that Spurgeon addresses: the ranch that Cole could possibly inherit will soon be taken by the United States government, his "lovely young wife" is murdered, and we have seen throughout the Trilogy the inability of the Anglo characters to keep their horses from being stolen.

44. This is but one possible reading of the significance of Cole's death. Just as critics have provided multiple allegorical readings for the various characters in the Border

Trilogy, multiple readings of the significance of Cole's death have been offered. For Spurgeon, Cole's death is a suicide. He allows himself to be stabbed "in order to deny the truth he sees before him every day on the ranch, that the myth upon which he has structured his life is hollow at its core and shattering to pieces around him" (57). Though I agree with her assessment of the mythology, I do not read Cole's death as a conscious suicide, but rather as the result of the inevitable destruction resulting from the mythology's inherent failures. In a completely different vein, Georg Guillemin has suggested that Cole's death is the result of his being "caught between the idea of Mexico as an ecopastoral utopia and the treacherous reality of the Mexican border town of Juarez," and incapable of separating the two (Guillemin, *The Pastoral Vision of Cormac McCarthy*, 105). However, even this reading—developed out of an ecocritical approach to McCarthy's works—is still dependent upon the frontier mythology and its understanding of separation by means of establishing borders (physical, linguistic, symbolic, etc.). Much as McCarthy critiques the way that borders are employed and the meaning invested in them, it would appear to be impossible to move beyond the rhetoric of borders in approaching his work, an ironic suggestion that perhaps we are incapable of understanding the world in any way other than the flawed frontier rhetoric we have inherited.

45. Luce, "The Vanishing World of Cormac McCarthy's Border Trilogy," 163.

46. Qtd. in Turner, "The Significance of the Frontier in American History," 1.

Coda

1. Qtd. in Turner, "The Significance of the Frontier in American History," 1.

2. Bell, *The Development of the American Romance*, 245.

3. Hawthorne, "The Custom-House," 35.

4. P. Miller, "The Romance and the Novel," 252.

5. L. Owens, *Mixedblood Messages*, 38.

6. Slotkin, *Gunfighter*, 235.

7. Ibid., 231.

8. Ibid. Slotkin argues that "the film was a commercial success on a scale that no single movie had previously achieved."

9. Ibid., 311–12.

10. Based on Annie Proulx's short story of the same name, included in *Close Range: Wyoming Stories*.

11. For an excellent source book of materials on this film—which itself would serve as a fine starting point for further study—please see William W. Handley's wonderful edited collection *The Brokeback Book: From Story to Cultural Phenomenon*.

12. Spurgeon, *Exploding*, 3.

Bibliography

Abbas, Niran, ed. *Thomas Pynchon: Reading from the Margins*. Madison and Teaneck, NJ: Fairleigh Dickinson UP, 2003.

Alarcón, Daniel Cooper. "All the Pretty Mexicos: Cormac McCarthy's Mexican Representations." *Cormac McCarthy: New Directions*. Ed. James D. Lilley. Albuquerque: U of New Mexico P, 2002. 141–52.

Ambler, Madge. "Ishmael Reed: Whose Radio Broke Down?" *Negro American Literature Forum* 6.4 (Winter 1972): 125–31.

Anzaldúa, Gloria. *Borderlands/La Frontera: The New Mestiza*. San Francisco: Aunt Lute: 1987.

Bailey, Charles. "The Last Stage of the Hero's Evolution: Cormac McCarthy's *Cities of the Plain*." *Myth, Legend, Dust: Critical Responses to Cormac McCarthy*. Ed. Rich Wallach. Manchester: Manchester UP, 2000. 293–301.

Baker, Houston A. *Long Black Song: Essays in Black American Literature*. Charlottesville: UP of Virginia, 1972.

Bakhtin, Mikhail. "Discourse in the Novel." *The Dialogic Imagination: Four Essays by M. M. Bakhtin*. Ed. Michael Holquist. Trans. Caryl Emerson and Holquist. Austin: U of Texas P, 1981. 259–422.

———. "Epic and Novel." *The Dialogic Imagination: Four Essays by M. M. Bakhtin*. Ed. Michael Holquist. Trans. Caryl Emerson and Holquist. Austin: U of Texas P, 1981. 3–40.

———. "Form of Time and of the Chronotope in the Novel: Notes toward a Historical Poetics." *The Dialogic Imagination: Four Essays by M. M. Bakhtin*. Ed. Michael Holquist. Trans. Caryl Emerson and Holquist. Austin: U of Texas P, 1981. 84–258.

———. *Problems of Dostoyevsky's Poetics*. Ed. and trans. Caryl Emerson. Minneapolis: U of Minnesota P, 1984.

Barth, John. *The Friday Book: Essays and Other Nonfiction*. Baltimore: Johns Hopkins UP, 1984.

———. "Historical Fiction, Fictitious History, and Chesapeake Bay Blue Crabs, or, About Aboutness." *The Friday Book: Essays and Other Nonfiction*. Baltimore: Johns Hopkins UP, 1984. 180–92.

———. "Intelligent Despisal: An Address to the Graduating Class of Western Maryland College, June 1973." *The Friday Book: Essays and Other Nonfiction*. Baltimore: Johns Hopkins UP, 1984. 110–21.

———. "An Interview with John Barth." Interview by Kevin Bezner. *San Francisco Review of Books* April 1980: 7–8.

———. "The Literature of Exhaustion." *The Friday Book: Essays and Other Nonfiction*. Baltimore: Johns Hopkins UP, 1984. 62–76.

———. "The Literature of Replenishment: Postmodernist Fiction." *The Friday Book: Essays and Other Nonfiction*. Baltimore: Johns Hopkins UP, 1984. 193–206.

———. "A Poet to the Rescue." *The Friday Book: Essays and Other Nonfiction*. Baltimore: Johns Hopkins UP, 1984. 91–96.

———. *The Sot-Weed Factor*. New York: Anchor, 1987.

Baym, Nina. "Concepts of Romance in Hawthorne's America." *Nineteenth-Century Fiction* 38 (1984): 426–43.

Bell, Michael Davitt. *The Development of the American Romance: The Sacrifice of Relation*. Chicago: U of Chicago P: 1980.

Bellis, Peter J. *Writing Revolution: Aesthetics and Politics in Hawthorne, Whitman, and Thoreau*. Athens: U of Georgia P, 2003.

Bergmann, Linda S. "'The Whys and Wherefores of 't'": History and Humor in *The Sot-Weed Factor*." *Markham Review* 12 (Winter 1983): 31–36.

Berner, Robert. "American Myth: Old, New, Yet Untold." *Native American Perspectives on Literature and History*. Ed. Alan R. Velie. Norman: U of Oklahoma P, 1994. 63–75.

Blaeser, Kimberly M. *Gerald Vizenor: Writing in the Oral Tradition*. Norman: U of Oklahoma P, 1996.

———. "The New "Frontier" of Native American Literature: Dis-Arming History with Tribal Humor." *Native American Perspectives on Literature and History*. Ed. Alan R. Velie. Norman: U of Oklahoma P, 1994. 37–50.

Borneman, John. "Border Regimes, the Circulation of Violence and the Neo-authoritarian Turn." *A Companion to Border Studies*. Ed. Thomas W. Wilson and Hastings Donnan. Malden: Wiley-Blackwell, 2012. 119–38.

Borup, Rachel. "Bankers in Buckskins: Caroline Kirkland's Critique of Frontier Masculinity." *ATQ: American Transcendental Quarterly* 18.4 (December 2004): 230–46.

Budick, Emily Miller. *Engendering Romance: Women Writers and the Hawthorne Tradition, 1850–1990*. New Haven: Yale UP, 1994.

———. *Fiction and Historical Consciousness: The American Romance Tradition*. New Haven: Yale UP, 1989.

Butler, Judith. *Bodies That Matter: On the Discursive Limits of "Sex."* New York: Routledge, 1993.

———. *Gender Trouble: Feminism and the Subversion of Identity.* New York: Routledge, 1990.

Cameron, James, dir. *Avatar.* 20th Century Fox, 2009.

Campbell, Neil. "'Beyond Reckoning': Cormac McCarthy's Version of the West in *Blood Meridian, Or The Evening Redness in the West.*" *Literature of Region and Nation.* Ed. Winnifred M. Bogaards. Saint John, New Brunswick, Canada: University of New Brunswick in Saint John, 1998. 32–49.

———. *The Rhizomatic West: Representing the American West in a Transnational, Global, Media Age.* Lincoln: U of Nebraska P, 2007.

Carpio, Glenda R. "Conjuring the Mysteries of Slavery: Voodoo, Fetishism, and Stereotype in Ishmael Reed's *Flight to Canada. American Literature* 77.3 (September 2005): 563–89.

Castronovo, Russ. "Compromised Narratives along the Border: The Mason-Dixon Line, Resistance, and Hegemony." *Border Theory: The Limits of Cultural Politics.* Ed. Scott Michaelson and David E. Johnson. Minneapolis: U of Minnesota P, 1997. 195–220.

Chamberlain, Samuel E. *My Confession.* Introduction and postscript by Roger Butterfield. New York: Harper and Brothers, 1956.

Chase, Richard. *The American Novel and Its Tradition.* Baltimore: Johns Hopkins UP, 1957.

Churchill, Ward, and Jim Vander Wall. *Agents of Repressions: The FBI's Secret Wars Against the Black Panther Party and the American Indian Movement.* Boston: South End, 1988.

Cisneros, Sandra. *Caramelo.* New York: Vintage, 2003.

Clayton, Jay. *The Pleasures of Babel: Contemporary American Literature and Theory.* New York: Oxford UP, 1993.

Cohen, Samuel. "*Mason & Dixon* and the Ampersand." *Twentieth-Century Literature* 48.3 (Fall 2002): 264–91.

Comer, Krista. "Introduction: Assessing the Postwestern." *Western American Literature* 48: 1–2 (Spring–Summer 2013): 3–15.

Connell, R. W. "The History of Masculinity." *The Masculinity Studies Reader.* Ed. Rachel Adams and David Savran. Malden: Blackwell, 2002. 245–61.

Connell, R. W., and James W. Messerschmidt. "Hegemonic Masculinity: Rethinking the Concept." *Gender and Society* 19.6 (December 2005): 829–59.

Cooper, James Fenimore. *The Deerslayer; Or, The First Warpath.* New York: Penguin, 1987.

———. *The Last of the Mohicans.* New York: Signet Classic, 1962.

———. *The Pioneers.* New York: Signet Classic, 1964.

———. *The Prairie.* New York: Penguin, 1987.

———. *Wyandotté, or The Hutted Knoll.* Ed. and with a "Historical Introduction" by Thomas Philbrick and Marianne Philbrick. Albany: State U of New York P, 1982.

Corkin, Stanley. *Cowboys as Cold Warriors: The Western and U.S. History.* Philadelphia: Temple UP, 2004.

Costner, Kevin, dir. *Dances with Wolves.* Orion Pictures, 1990.

Cowart, David. "Pynchon and the Sixties." *Critique* 41.1 (Fall 1999): 3–12.

———. *Thomas Pynchon & the Dark Passages of History.* Athens: U of Georgia P, 2011.

Dalton, Harlon. "Failing to See." *White Privilege: Essential Readings from the Other Side of Racism.* Ed. Paula S. Rothenberg. New York: Worth, 2002. 15–18.

Demetriou, Demetrakis Z. "Connell's Concept of Hegemonic Masculinity: A Critique." *Theory and Society* 30.3 (June 2001): 337–361.

Dick, Bruce, and Amritjit Singh, eds. *Conversations with Ishmael Reed.* Jackson: UP of Mississippi, 1995.

Doctorow, E. L. *Andrew's Brain.* New York: Random House, 2014.

———. "Author, Author: An Interview with Doctorow." Interview by James McInerney. *Conversations with E. L. Doctorow.* Ed. Christopher D. Morris. Jackson: UP of Mississippi, 1999. 88–91.

———. *Big As Life.* New York: Simon and Schuster, 1966.

———. "False Documents." *Jack London, Hemingway, and the Constitution: Selected Essays, 1977–1992.* New York: Random House, 1993. 149–64.

———. "History and the Forms of Fiction: An Interview with E. L. Doctorow." Interview by Jared Lubarsky. *Conversations with E. L. Doctorow.* Ed. Christopher D. Morris. Jackson: UP of Mississippi, 1999. 35–40.

———. "Mr. Ragtime." Interview by Jonathan Yardley. *Conversations with E. L. Doctorow.* Ed. Christopher D. Morris. Jackson: UP of Mississippi, 1999. 7–13.

———. "A Multiplicity of Witnesses: E. L. Doctorow at Heidelberg." Interview by Herwig Friedl and Dieter Schulz. *Conversations with E. L. Doctorow.* Ed. Christopher D. Morris. Jackson: UP of Mississippi, 1999. 112–28.

———. "*Ragtime* Revisited: A Seminar with E. L. Doctorow and Joseph Papaleo." *Nieman Reports. Conversations with E. L. Doctorow.* Ed. Christopher D. Morris. Jackson: UP of Mississippi, 1999. 14–34.

———. "A Spirit of Transgression." Interview by Larry McCaffery. *Conversations with E. L. Doctorow.* Ed. Christopher D. Morris. Jackson: UP of Mississippi, 1999. 72–87.

———. "A Talk with E. L. Doctorow." Interview by Liesl Schillinger. *Conversations with E. L. Doctorow.* Ed. Christopher D. Morris. Jackson: UP of Mississippi, 1999. 107–11.

———. "10 Questions for E. L. Doctorow." Interview by Lev Grossman. *Time* March 6, 2006, 6.

———. *Welcome to Hard Times.* New York: Plume, 1996.

———. "The Writer as Independent Witness." Interview by Paul Levine.

Conversations with E. L. Doctorow. Ed. Christopher D. Morris. Jackson: UP of Mississippi, 1999. 41–52.

Donnan, Hastings, and Thomas M. Wilson. *Borders: Frontiers of Identity, Nation and State.* Berg: Oxford, 1999.

Dyer, Richard. "The Matter of Whiteness." *White Privilege: Essential Readings from the Other Side of Racism.* Ed. Paula S. Rothenberg. New York: Worth, 2002. 9–14.

Eastwood, Clint, dir. *Unforgiven.* Warner Bros., 1992.

Eaton, Mark A. "Dis(re)membered Bodies: Cormac McCarthy's Border Fiction." *Mfs: Modern Fiction Studies* 49.1 (Spring 2003): 155–80.

Elam, Diane. *Romancing the Postmodern.* London: Routledge, 1992.

Elias, Amy J. *Sublime Desire: History and Post-1960s Fiction.* Baltimore: Johns Hopkins UP, 2001.

Engler, Bernd, and Kurt Müller, eds. *Historiographic Metafiction in Modern American and Canadian Literature.* Paderborn: Ferdinand Schöningh, 1994.

Everett, Percival. *God's Country.* Boston: Beacon, 2003.

———. *Walk Me to the Distance.* New York: Ticknor and Fields, 1985.

———. *Watershed.* Boston: Beacon, 2003.

Fanon, Franz. *Black Skin, White Masks.* Trans. Richard Philcox. New York: Grove, 2008.

Farley, Anthony Paul. "The Poetics of Colorlined Space." *Crossroads, Disections, and a New Critical Race Theory.* Ed. Francisco Valdes, Jerome McCristal Culp, and Angela P. Harris. Philadelphia: Temple UP, 2002.

Fludernik, Monika. "History and Metafiction: Experientiality, Causality, and Myth." *Historiographic Metafiction in Modern American and Canadian Literature.* Ed. Bernd Engler and Kurt Müller, Paderborn: Ferdinand Schöningh, 1994. 81–101.

Foucault, Michel. *The Archaeology of Knowledge.* Trans. A. M. Sheridan Smith. New York: Pantheon, 1972.

Friedan, Betty. *The Feminine Mystique: Twentieth Anniversary Edition.* New York: Norton, 1983.

Frye, Northrop. *Anatomy of Criticism: Four Essays.* With a new foreword by Harold Bloom. Princeton: Princeton UP, 1990.

———. "The Four Forms of Fiction." *The Theory of the Novel.* Ed. Philip Stevick. New York: Free Press, 1967. 31–43.

Gado, Frank, ed. *First Person: Conversations on Writers and Writing with Glenway Wescott, John Dos Passos, Robert Penn Warren, John Updike, John Barth, Robert Coover.* Schenectady, NY: Union College Press, 1973.

Gardiner, Judith Kegan. "Theorizing Age with Gender: Bly's Boys, Feminism, and Maturity Masculinity." *Masculinity Studies & Feminist Theory: New Directions.* Ed. Gardiner. New York: Columbia UP, 2002. 90–118.

Gates, Henry Louis, Jr. *The Signifying Monkey: A Theory of African-American Literary Criticism.* New York: Oxford UP, 1988.

Graybill, Mark S. "'Peeping Toms on History': Barry Hannah's *Never Die* as Postmodern Western." *Southern Literary Journal* 33.1 (Fall 2000): 94–110.

Green, Jeremy. *Late Postmodernism: American Fiction at the Millennium.* Hampshire, UK: Palgrave Macmillan, 2005.

Greiner, Donald J. "Thomas Pynchon and the Fault Lines of America." *Pynchon and "Mason & Dixon."* Ed. Brooke and Irving Malin. Newark: U of Delaware P, 2000. 73–83.

Guillemin, Georg. *The Pastoral Vision of Cormac McCarthy.* College Station: Texas A&M UP, 2004.

Halberstam, Judith. *Female Masculinity.* Durham, NC: Duke UP, 1998.

Handley, William W. *The Brokeback Book: From Story to Cultural Phenomenon.* Lincoln: U of Nebraska P, 2011.

Harris, Michael. "Pynchon's Postcoloniality." *Thomas Pynchon: Reading from the Margins.* Ed. Niran Abbas. Madison, NJ: Fairleigh Dickinson UP, 2003. 199–214.

Hawkins, Susan E. "Cold War Cowboys and the Culture of Nostalgia." *Cormac McCarthy: Unchartered Territories/Territoires Inconnus.* Reims, France: Presses Universitaires de Reims, 2003. 95–103.

Hawthorne, Nathaniel. "The Custom-House." *The Scarlet Letter.* New York: Penguin Classics, 1986.

Heyman, Josiah McC. "Culture Theory and the US-Mexico Border." *A Companion to Border Studies.* Ed. Thomas W. Wilson and Hastings Donnan. Malden: Wiley-Blackwell, 2012. 48–65.

Hinds, Elizabeth Jane Wall. "Sari, Sorry, and the Vortex of History: Calendar Reform, Anachronism, and Language Change in *Mason & Dixon.*" *American Literary History* 12.1–2 (Spring–Summer 2000): 187–215.

Hine, Robert V., and John Mack Faragher. *The American West: A New Interpretive History.* New Haven: Yale UP, 2000.

Hipkiss, Robert A. *The American Absurd: Pynchon, Vonnegut, and Barth.* Port Washington, NY: National University Publications Associated Faculty Press, 1984.

Hite, Molly. *Ideas of Order in the Novels of Thomas Pynchon.* Columbus: Ohio State UP, 1983.

Hoberek, Andrew. "Cormac McCarthy and the Aesthetics of Exhaustion." *American Literary History* 23.3 (2011): 483–99.

Holquist, Michael, ed. *The Dialogic Imagination: Four Essays by M. M. Bakhtin.* Trans. Caryl Emerson and Holquist. Austin: U of Texas P, 1981.

Horrocks, Roger. *Male Myths and Icons: Masculinity in Popular Culture.* London: Macmillan, 1995.

Hutcheon, Linda. "Historiographic Metafiction: Parody and the Intertextuality of History." *Intertextuality and Contemporary American Fiction.* Ed. Patrick O'Donnell and Robert Con Davis. Baltimore: Johns Hopkins UP, 1989. 3–32.

———. *A Poetics of Postmodernism: History, Theory, Fiction*. New York: Routledge, 1988.

Irr, Caren. "Postmodernism in Reverse: American National Allegories and the 21st-Century Political Novel." *Twentieth-Century Literature* 57.3–4 (Fall–Winter 2011): 516–38.

James, Henry. *The Art of the Novel*. New York: Scribner's Sons, 1962.

Jameson, Fredric. *Postmodernism, or, The Cultural Logic of Late Capitalism*. Durham: Duke UP, 1991.

Jarrett, Robert L. *Cormac McCarthy*. New York: Twayne, 1997.

Jeffords, Susan. *The Remasculinization of America: Gender and the Vietnam War*. Bloomington: Indiana UP, 1989.

Jeffrey, Julie Roy. *Frontier Women: "Civilizing" the West? 1840–1880*. Rev. ed. New York: Hill and Wang, 1998.

Johnson, David E., and Scott Michaelson, "Border Secrets: An Introduction." *Border Theory: The Limits of Cultural Politics*. Ed. Michaelson and Johnson. Minneapolis: U of Minnesota P, 1997. 1–39.

Johnson, Michael K. *Black Masculinity and the Frontier Myth in American Literature*. Norman: U of Oklahoma P, 2002.

Kennedy, John F. "Address Accepting the Nomination for Presidency of the Unites States of America, July 15, 1960." www.jfklibrary.org/Historical+Resources/Archives/Reference+Desk/Speeches/JFK/JFK+PrePres/1960/Address+of+Senator+John+F.+Kennedy+Accepting+the+Democratic+Party+Nomination+for+the+Presidency+of+t.htm. Accessed December 6, 2008.

Kermode, Frank. *The Sense of an Ending*. New York: Oxford UP, 1967.

King, Thomas. *Green Grass, Running Water*. New York: Bantam, 1994.

Kollin, Susan, ed. *Postwestern Cultures: Literature, Theory, Space*. Lincoln: U of Nebraska P, 2007.

Kolodny, Annette. *The Land Before Her: Fantasy and Experience of the American Frontiers, 1630–1860*. Chapel Hill: U of North Carolina P, 1984.

Krupat, Arnold. "The Dialogic of Silko's *Storyteller*." *Narrative Chance: Postmodern Discourse on Native American Indian Literatures*. Ed. Gerald Vizenor. Norman: U of Oklahoma P, 1989. 55–68.

———. "'Stories in the Blood': *Ratio*- and *Natio*- in Gerald Vizenor's *The Heirs of Columbus*." *Loosening the Seams: Interpretations of Gerald Vizenor*. Ed. A. Robert Lee. Bowling Green: Bowling Green State U Popular P, 2000. 166–77.

Lee, Ang, dir. *Brokeback Mountain*. Focus Features, 2005.

LeMenager, Stephanie. *Manifest and Other Destinies: Territorial Fictions of the Nineteenth-Century United States*. Lincoln: U of Nebraska P, 2004.

Limerick, Patricia Nelson. *The Legacy of Conquest: The Unbroken Path of the American West*. New York: Norton, 1987.

Lincoln, Abraham. "Message to Congress, December 1, 1862." *This Fiery Trial: The Speeches and Writings of Abraham Lincoln*. Ed. William E. Gienapp. New York: Oxford UP, 2002. 143–50.

Lipsitz, George. *The Possessive Investment in Whiteness: How White People Profit from Identity Politics*. Philadelphia: Temple UP, 1998.

Luce, Dianne C. "The Vanishing World of Cormac McCarthy's Border Trilogy." *A Cormac McCarthy Companion: The Border Trilogy*. Ed. Edwin T. Arnold and Luce. Jackson: UP of Mississippi, 2001. 161–97.

Lukács, Georg. *The Historical Novel*. Lincoln: U of Nebraska P, 1983.

Lush, Rebecca M. "Turning Tricks: Sexuality and Trickster Language in Vizenor's *The Heirs of Columbus*. *SAIL: Studies in American Indian Literatures* 24.2 (Summer 2012): 1–16.

MacLean, Nancy. *The American Women's Movement, 1945–2000: A Brief History with Documents*. Boston and New York: Bedford/St. Martin's, 2009.

Masters, Joshua J. "'Witness to the Uttermost Edge of the World': Judge Holden's Textual Enterprise in Cormac McCarthy's *Blood Meridian*." *Critique* 40.1 (Fall 1998): 25–37.

Mattessich, Stefan. *Lines of Flight: Discursive Time and Countercultural Desire in the Work of Thomas Pynchon*. Durham: Duke UP, 2002.

McCarthy, Cormac. *All the Pretty Horses*. New York: Vintage International, 1992.

———. *Blood Meridian, Or the Evening Redness in the West*. New York: Vintage International, 1985.

———. *Cities of the Plain*. New York: Vintage International, 1998.

———. *The Crossing*. New York: Vintage International, 1994.

———. *No Country for Old Men*. New York: Knopf, 2005.

———. *The Road*. New York: Knopf, 2006.

McGurl, Mark. *The Program Era: Postwar Fiction and the Rise of Creative Writing*. Cambridge: Harvard UP, 2009.

McHale, Brian. "Break, Period, Interregnum." *Twentieth-Century Literature* 57.3–4 (Fall-Winter 2011): 328–40.

———. *Postmodernist Fiction*. New York: Methuen, 1987.

Memmi, Albert. *The Colonizer and the Colonized*. New York: Onion, 1965.

Meyer, William. *Native Americans: The New Indian Resistance*. New York: International, 1971.

Michaelson, Scott. "Resketching Anglo-Amerindian Identity Politics." *Border Theory: The Limits of Cultural Politics*. Ed. Michaelson and David E. Johnson. Minneapolis: U of Minnesota P, 1997. 221–52.

Michaelson, Scott, and David E. Johnson, eds. *Border Theory: The Limits of Cultural Politics*. Minneapolis: U of Minnesota P, 1997.

Miller, Keith D., and Kathleen Weinkauf. "Discovering the Erased Feminism of the Civil Rights Movement: Beyond the Media, Male Leaders, and the 1960s Assassinations." *Trauma and the Teaching of Writing*. Ed. Shane Borrowman. Albany: State U of New York P, 2005: 113–25.

Miller, Perry. "The Romance and the Novel." *Nature's Nation*. Cambridge: Belknap Press of Harvard UP, 1967.

Mogen, David. "The Frontier Archetype and the Myth of America: Patterns That Shape the American Dream." *The Frontier Experience and the American Dream: Essays on American Literature*. Ed. Mogen, Mark Busby, and Paul Bryant. College Station: Texas A&M UP, 1989. 15–30.

Monsma, Bradley John. "Liminal Landscapes: Motion, Perspective, and Place in Gerald Vizenor's Fiction." *SAIL: Studies in American Indian Literatures* 9.1 (Spring 1997): 60–72.

Moore, David L. "Decolonizing Criticism: Reading Dialectics and Dialogics in Native American Literatures." *SAIL: Studies in American Indian Literatures* 6:4 (Winter 1994): 7–35.

Moore, Steven. Foreword. *The Letters of Wanda Tinasky*. Ed. TR Factor. Illustrations by Fred Sternkopf. Portland: vers libre press, 1996. ix–xi.

Morgan, Robert. *Boone: A Biography*. Chapel Hill: Algonquin Books of Chapel Hill, 2007.

Morrell, David. *John Barth: An Introduction*. University Park: Pennsylvania State UP, 1976.

Morris, Christopher D., ed. *Conversations with E. L. Doctorow*. Jackson: UP of Mississippi, 1999.

Morris, Pam, ed. *The Bakhtin Reader: Selected Writings of Bakhtin, Medvedev, Voloshinov*. London: Edward Arnold, 1994.

Morrison, Toni. *Paradise*. New York: Plume, 1999.

Müllenbrock, Heinz-Joachim. "John Barth's *The Sot-Weed Factor* as a Prototype of Historiographic Metafiction." *Historiographic Metafiction in Modern American and Canadian Literature*. Ed. Bernd Engler and Kurt Müller. Paderborn: Ferdinand Schöningh, 1994. 163–69.

Müller, Kurt. "The Development toward Historiographic Metafiction in the American Novel." *Historiographic Metafiction in Modern American and Canadian Literature*. Ed. Bernd Engler and Kurt Müller. Paderborn: Ferdinand Schöningh, 1994. 35–51.

Murray, Yxta Maya. *The Conquest*. New York: Harper Perennial, 2003.

———. *The King's Gold*. New York: Harper Paperbacks, 2008.

Olster, Stacey. "A 'Patch of England, as a Three-Thousand-Mile Offset'?" Representing America in *Mason & Dixon*." *MFS: Modern Fiction Studies* 50.2 (Summer 2004): 283–302.

Osborne, Stephen D. "Legal and Tribal Identity in Gerald Vizenor's *The Heirs of Columbus*." *SAIL: Studies in American Indian Literatures* 9.1 (Spring 1997): 115–27.

Owens, Barclay. *Cormac McCarthy's Western Novels*. Tucson: U of Arizona P, 2000.

Owens, Louis. *Mixedblood Messages: Literature, Film, Family, Place*. Norman: U of Oklahoma P, 1998.

Packard, Vance. *The Sexual Wilderness: The Contemporary Upheaval in Male-Female Relationships*. New York: David McKay, 1968.

Patell, Cyrus R. K. *Negative Liberties: Morrison, Pynchon, and the Problem of Liberal Ideology*. Durham, NC: Duke UP, 2001.

Penner, James. *Pinks, Pansies, and Punks: The Rhetoric of Masculinity in American Literary Culture*. Bloomington: Indiana UP, 2011.

Perkins, David. *Is Literary History Possible?* Baltimore: Johns Hopkins UP, 1992.

Phillips, Dana. "History and the Ugly Facts of Cormac McCarthy's *Blood Meridian*." *American Literature* 68.2 (June 1996): 433–60.

Pilkington, Tom. "Fate and Free Will on the American Frontier: Cormac McCarthy's Western Fiction." *Western American Literature* 27.4 (Winter 1993): 311–22.

Porte, Joel. *The Romance in America: Studies in Cooper, Poe, Hawthorne, Melville, and James*. Middletown, CT: Wesleyan UP, 1972.

Pratt, Mary Louise. *Imperial Eyes: Travel Writing and Transculturation*. London: Routledge, 1992.

Proulx, Annie. *Close Range: Wyoming Stories*. New York: Scribner, 2003.

Punday, Daniel. "John Barth's Occasional Writing: The Institutional Construction of Postmodernism in *The Friday Book*." *American Literature* 77.3 (September 2005): 591–619.

Pynchon, Thomas. "Is It O.K. to Be a Luddite?" *New York Times Book Review* 28 October 1984: 1, 40–41.

———. Introduction. *Slow Learner: Early Stories*. Boston: Little, Brown, 1984. 3–23.

———. "A Journey into the Mind of Watts." *New York Times Magazine* 12 June 1966: 34–35, 78, 80–82, 84.

———. *Mason & Dixon*. New York: Henry Holt, 1997.

Reed, Ishmael. "And That History Is Subject to the Will: Ishmael Reed." *Conversations with Ishmael Reed*. Ed. Bruce Dick and Amritjit Singh. Jackson: UP of Mississippi, 1995. 258–70.

———. "A Conversation with Ishmael Reed." Interview by Judith Moore. *Conversations with Ishmael Reed*. Ed. Bruce Dick and Amritjit Singh. Jackson: UP of Mississippi, 1995. 219–34.

———. "Eldridge Cleaver—Writer." *Airing Dirty Laundry*. Reading, MA: Addison-Wesley, 1994. 95–103.

———. *God Made Alaska for the Indians: Selected Essays*. New York: Garland, 1982.

———. "The Great Tenure Battle of 1977." Interview by Jon Ewing. *Conversations with Ishmael Reed*. Ed. Bruce Dick and Amritjit Singh. Jackson: UP of Mississippi, 1995. 111–27.

———. I Am a Cowboy in the Boat of Ra." *New and Collected Poems*. New York: Atheneum, 1988.17–18.

———. "In Opposition—Which State?" *Writin' Is Fightin': Thirty-Seven Years of Boxing on Paper*. New York: Atheneum, 1990. 113–20.

———. "An Interview with Ishmael Reed." Interview by Ruth Abbott and Ira

Simmons. *Conversations with Ishmael Reed*. Ed. Bruce Dick and Amritjit Singh. Jackson: UP of Mississippi, 1995. 74–95.

———. "Interview with Ishmael Reed." Interview by Gaga [Mark S. Johnson]. *Conversations with Ishmael Reed*. Ed. Bruce Dick and Amritjit Singh. Jackson: UP of Mississippi, 1995. 51–58.

———. Introduction. *The Reed Reader*. New York: Basic, 2000. xi–xxx.

———. "Ishmael Reed." Interview by John O'Brien. *Conversations with Ishmael Reed*. Ed. Bruce Dick and Amritjit Singh. Jackson: UP of Mississippi, 1995. 14–24.

———. "My Oakland, There Is a There There." *Writin' Is Fightin': Thirty-Seven Years of Boxing on Paper*. New York: Atheneum, 1990. 11–42.

———. "Neo-HooDoo Manifesto." *New and Collected Poems*. New York: Atheneum, 1988, 20–25.

———. *New and Collected Poems*. New York: Atheneum, 1988.

———. "Race War in America?" *God Made Alaska for the Indians: Selected Essays*. New York: Garland, 1982. 1–34.

———. "The Traditions of Serious Comedy in Afro-American Literature." *Writin' Is Fightin': Thirty-Seven Years of Boxing on Paper*. New York: Atheneum, 1990. 135–41.

———. *Writin' Is Fightin': Thirty-Seven Years of Boxing on Paper*. New York: Atheneum, 1990.

———. "The Writer as Seer: Ishmael Reed on Ishmael Reed." *Conversations with Ishmael Reed*. Ed. Bruce Dick and Amritjit Singh. Jackson: UP of Mississippi, 1995. 59–73.

———. *Yellow Back Radio Broke-Down*. Garden City, NY: Doubleday, 1969.

Reeser, Todd W. *Masculinities in Theory: An Introduction*. Malden: Wiley-Blackwell, 2010.

Robinson, Sally. *Marked Men: White Masculinity in Crisis*. New York: Columbia UP, 2000.

Romine, Scott. "Playing Like a Man: Noncompetitive Manhood and Frontier Humor." *Studies in American Humor* 3.11 (2004): 39–56.

Roosevelt, Theodore. *The Winning of the West; Part 1. The Spread of English-Speaking Peoples*. New York: Current Literature Publishing, 1905.

Rothenberg, Paula S., ed. *White Privilege: Essential Readings from the Other Side of Racism*. New York: Worth, 2002.

Rovit, Earl. "The Novel as Parody: John Barth."*Critical Essays on John Barth*. Ed. Joseph J. Waldmeir. Boston: G. K. Hall, 1980. 116–22.

Sadowski-Smith, Claudia. *Border Fictions: Globalization, Empire, and Writing at the Boundaries of the United States*. Charlottesville: U of Virginia P, 2008.

Safer, Elaine B. *The Contemporary American Comic Epic: The Novels of Barth, Pynchon, Gaddis, and Kesey*. Detroit: Wayne State UP, 1988.

Saltzman, Arthur. "'Cranks of Ev'ry Radius': Romancing the Line in *Mason and Dixon." Pynchon and "Mason & Dixon."* Ed. Brooke Hovarth and Irving Malin. Newark: U of Delaware P, 2000. 63–72.

Schmitz, Neil. "Neo-HooDoo: The Experimental Fiction of Ishmael Reed." *Twentieth Century Literature* 20.2 (April 1974): 126–40.

Schöler, Bo. "Trickster and Storyteller: The Sacred Memories and True Tales of Gerald Vizenor. *Coyote Was Here: Essays on Contemporary Native American Literary and Political Mobilization*." Ed. Schöler. Aarhus, Denmark: SEKLOS, 1984.

Scholes, Robert. *The Fabulators*. New York: Oxford UP, 1967.

Sepich, John Emil. "'What Kind of Indians Was Them?' Some Historical Sources in Cormac McCarthy's *Blood Meridian*." *Perspectives on Cormac McCarthy*. Ed. Edwin T. Arnold and Dianne C. Luce. Jackson: UP of Mississippi, 1999. 123–43.

Sickles, Robert C., and Marc Oxoby. "In Search of a Further Frontier: Cormac McCarthy's Border Trilogy." *Critique* 43.4 (Summer 2002): 347–59.

Silko, Leslie Marmon. *Gardens in the Dunes*. New York: Simon and Schuster, 2000.

Silverman, Kaja. *Male Subjectivity at the Margins*. New York: Routledge, 1992.

Slotkin, Richard. *The Fatal Environment: The Myth of the Frontier in the Age of Industrialization, 1800–1890*. Norman: U of Oklahoma P, 1998.

———. *Gunfighter Nation: The Myth of the Frontier in Twentieth-Century America*. Norman: U of Oklahoma P, 1992.

———. *Regeneration through Violence: The Mythology of the American Frontier; 1600–1860*. Norman: U of Oklahoma P, 1973.

Smith, John. *Captain John Smith's America: Selections from His Writings*. Ed. John Lankford. New York: Harper and Row, 1967.

Smith, Kyle. "'Serving Interests invisible': *Mason & Dixon*, British Spy Fiction, and the Specters of Imperialism." *Thomas Pynchon: Reading from the Margins*. Ed. Niran Abbas. Madison, NJ: Fairleigh Dickinson UP, 2003.183–98.

Softing, Inger-Anne. "Desert Pandemonium: Cormac McCarthy's Apocalyptic "Western" in *Blood Meridian*." *American Studies in Scandinavia* 31.2 (1999): 13–30.

Soto, Isabel. "The Border Paradigm in Cormac McCarthy's *The Crossing*." *Literature and Ethnicity in the Cultural Borderlands*. Ed. Jesus Benito and Ana Maria Manzanas. Amsterdam: Rodopi, 2002. 51–61.

Spencer, Andrew Blair. "A Cowboy Looks at Reality: The Death of the American Frontier and the Illumination of the Cowboy Myth in Cormac McCarthy's *All the Pretty Horses*." *Western Futures: Perspectives on the Humanities at the Millennium*. Reno: Nevada Humanities Committee, 2000. 143–57.

Spurgeon, Sara L. *Exploding the Western: Myths of Empire on the Postmodern Frontier*. College Station: Texas A&M UP, 2005.

Sugg, Katherine. "Multicultural Masculinities and the Border Romance in John Sayles's *Lone Star* and Cormac McCarthy's Border Trilogy." *New Centennial Review* 1.3 (Winter 2001): 117–54.

Teuton, Sean Kicummah. *Red Land, Red Power: Grounding Knowledge in the American Indian Novel.* Durham , NC: Duke UP, 2008.

Thompson, Gary. "Pynchonian Pastiche." *Thomas Pynchon: Reading from the Margins.* Ed. Niran Abbas. Madison, NJ: Fairleigh Dickinson UP, 2003.162–82.

Thompson, G. R., and Eric Carl Link. *Neutral Ground: New Traditionalism and the American Romance Controversy.* Baton Rouge: Louisiana State UP, 1999.

Tietchen, Todd F. "Cowboy Tricksters and Devilish Wangols: Ishmael Reed's HooDoo West." *Western American Literature* 36.4 (Winter 2002): 325–42.

Tilton, Robert. *Pocahontas: The Evolution of an American Narrative.* Cambridge: Cambridge UP, 1994.

Trimble, Alex Young. "Settler Sovereignty and the Rhizomatic West, or, the Significance of the Frontier in Postwestern Studies." *Western American Literature* 48: 1–2 (Spring-Summer 2013): 115–40.

Turner, Frederick Jackson. "The Significance of the Frontier in American History." *The Frontier in American History.* New York: Dover, 1996. 1–38.

Uebel, Michael. "Men in Color: Introducing Race and the Subject of Masculinities." *Race and the Subject of Masculinities.* Ed. Harry Stecopoulos and Michael Uebel. Durham, NC: Duke UP, 1997. 1–16.

van Houtum, Henk. "Remapping Borders. *A Companion to Border Studies.* Ed. Thomas W. Wilson and Hastings Donnan. Malden: Wiley-Blackwell, 2012. 405–18.

Vizenor, Gerald. *Bearheart: The Heirship Chronicles.* Minneapolis: U of Minnesota P, 1990.

———. *Chancers.* Norman: U of Oklahoma P, 2000.

———. *Crossbloods: Bone Courts, Bingo, and Other Reports.* Minneapolis: U of Minnesota P, 1976.

———. "Eternal Havens." *Manifest Manners: Narratives on Postindian Survivance.* Lincoln: U of Nebraska P, 1994. 107–25.

———. *Everlasting Sky: Voices of the Anishinabe People.* St. Paul: Minnesota Historical Society Press, 2001.

———. "Gerald Vizenor: The Trickster Heir of Columbus." Interview by Laura Coltelli. *Native American Literatures: A Forum* 2–3 (1990–91): 101–15.

———. *Griever: An American Monkey King in China.* Minneapolis: U of Minnesota P, 1987.

———. *The Heirs of Columbus.* New York: Fire Keepers/Quality Paperback Book Club, 1996.

———. *Hotline Healers.* Hanover: Wesleyan UP, 1997.

———. *Interior Landscapes: Autobiographical Myths and Metaphors.* Minneapolis: U of Minnesota P, 1990.

———. *Landfill Meditation: Crossblood Stories.* Hanover: Wesleyan UP, 1991.

———. *Manifest Manners: Narratives on Postindian Survivance.* Lincoln: U of Nebraska P, 1994.

———, ed. *Narrative Chance: Postmodern Discourse on Native American Indian Literatures.* Norman: U of Oklahoma P, 1993.

———. "On Thin Ice, You Might as Well Dance: An Interview with Gerald Vizenor." Interview by Larry McCaffery and Tom Marshall. *Some Other Frequency: Interviews with Innovative American Authors.* Ed. Larry McCaffery. Philadelphia: U of Pennsylvania P, 1996. 287–309.

———. *The People Named the Chippewa: Narrative Histories.* Minneapolis: U of Minnesota P, 1984.

———. "Postindian Warriors." *Manifest Manners: Narratives on Postindian Survivance.* Lincoln: U of Nebraska P, 1994. 1–44.

———. "A Postmodern Introduction." *Narrative Chance: Postmodern Discourse on Native American Indian Literatures.* Norman: U of Oklahoma P, 1993. 3–16.

———. *Shadow Distance: A Gerald Vizenor Reader.* Hanover: Wesleyan UP: 1994.

———. "Trickster Discourse: Comic Holotropes and Language Games." *Narrative Chance Postmodern Discourse on Native American Indian Literatures.* Norman: U of Oklahoma P, 1993. 187–211.

———. *The Trickster of Liberty: Native Heirs to a Wild Baronage.* Norman: U of Oklahoma P, 2005.

———. "Tricksters of Liberty." Interview by A. Robert Lee. *Postindian Conversations.* Ed. A. Robert Lee and Vizenor. Lincoln: U of Nebraska P, 1999. 127–35.

Wallace, Maurice O. *Constructing the Black Masculine: Identity and Ideality in African American Men's Literature and Culture: 1775–1995.* Durham: Duke UP, 2002.

Washington, Mary Helen. Foreword. *Their Eyes Were Watching God.* By Zora Neale Hurston. New York: Harper and Row, 1990.

Watkins, Elizabeth Siegel. *On the Pill: A Social History of Oral Contraceptives, 1950–1970.* Baltimore: Johns Hopkins UP, 1998.

Weixlmann, Joseph. "The Use and Abuse of Smith's *Generall Historie* in John Barth's *The Sot-Weed Factor.*" *Studies in American Humor* 2 (1975): 105–15.

Welch, James. *Killing Custer: The Battle of the Little Big Horn and the Fate of the Plains Indians.* With Paul Stekler. New York: Penguin, 1995.

White, Hayden. *The Content of the Form: Narrative Discourse and Historical Representation.* Baltimore: Johns Hopkins UP, 1987.

———. "Droysen's *Historik*: Historical Writing as a Bourgeois Science." *The Content of the Form: Narrative Discourse and Historical Representation.* Baltimore: Johns Hopkins UP, 1987. 83–103.

———. "The Question of Narrative in Contemporary Historical Theory." *The Content of the Form: Narrative Discourse and Historical Representation.* Baltimore: Johns Hopkins UP, 1987. 26–57.

White, Richard. *Railroaded: The Transcontinentals and the Making of Modern America.* New York: Norton, 2012.

Wiegman, Robyn. *American Anatomies: Theorizing Race and Gender.* Durham: Duke UP, 1995.

Wilson, Michael T. "'Saturnalia of the Blood': Masculine Self-Control and American Indians in the Frontier Novel." *Studies in American Fiction* 33.2 (Autumn 2005): 131–46.

Wilson, Thomas W., and Hastings Donnan, eds. *A Companion to Border Studies.* Malden: Wiley-Blackwell, 2012.

Worden, Daniel. *Masculine Style: The American West and Literary Modernism.* New York: Palgrave Macmillan, 2011.

Yamashita, Karen Tei. *I Hotel.* Minneapolis: Coffee House Press, 2010.

Zaplana, Esther. "Breaking the Mold: Male Rock Performance, Glam, and the (Re-)Imagination of the Male Body in the 1960s and 1970s." *Embodying Masculinities: Towards a History of the Male Body in U.S. Culture and Literature.* Ed. Josep M. Armengol. New York: Peter Lang, 2013. 63–82.

Ziegler, Heide. *John Barth.* London: Methuen, 1987.

Zinn, Howard. *A People's History of the United States.* New York: Harper Colophon, 1980.

Zwick, Edward, dir. *The Last Samurai.* Warner Bros. Pictures, 2003.

Index

Cultural Frames, Framing Culture

Books in this series examine both the way our culture frames our narratives and the way our narratives produce the culture that frames them. Attempting to bridge the gap between previously disparate disciplines, and combining theoretical issues with practical applications, this series invites a broad audience to read contemporary culture in a fresh and provocative way.

Nancy Martha West
Kodak and the Lens of Nostalgia

Raphael Sassower and Louis Cicotello
The Golden Avant-Garde: Idolatry, Commercialism, and Art

Margot Norris
Writing War in the Twentieth Century

Robin Blaetz
Visions of the Maid: Joan of Arc in American Film and Culture

Ellen Tremper
I'm No Angel: The Blonde in Fiction and Film

Naomi Mandel
Against the Unspeakable: Complicity, the Holocaust, and Slavery in America

Debra Walker King
African Americans and the Culture of Pain

Jon Robert Adams
Male Armor: The Soldier-Hero in Contemporary American Culture

Rachel Hall
Wanted: The Outlaw in American Visual Culture

Stephanie L. Hawkins
American Iconographic: "National Geographic," Global Culture, and the Visual Imagination

Stephanie Harzewski
Chick Lit and Postfeminism

Samuel Chase Coale
Quirks of the Quantum: Postmodernism and Contemporary American Fiction

Eric Aronoff
Composing Cultures: Modernism, American Literary Studies, and the Problem of Culture

James J. Donahue
Failed Frontiersmen: White Men and Myth in the Post-Sixties American Historical Romance